ADVANCES IN ACCOUNTING

ADVANCES IN ACCOUNTING

Series Editor: Philip M. J. Reckers

Recent Volumes:

Volumes 13–21:   Edited by Philip M. J. Reckers

ADVANCES IN ACCOUNTING

EDITED BY

PHILIP M. J. RECKERS

Arizona State University, Tempe, USA

ASSOCIATE EDITORS

SALVADOR CARMONA

Instituto de Empresa, Universidad Carlos III de Madrid, Spain

GOVIND IYER

Arizona State University, USA

ERIC JOHNSON

Indiana University, USA

LOREN MARGHEIM

University of San Diego, USA

RICHARD MORTON

Florida State University, USA

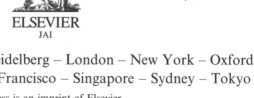

ELSEVIER
JAI

Amsterdam – Boston – Heidelberg – London – New York – Oxford
Paris – San Diego – San Francisco – Singapore – Sydney – Tokyo

JAI Press is an imprint of Elsevier

JAI Press is an imprint of Elsevier
The Boulevard, Langford Lane, Kidlington, Oxford OX5 1GB, UK
Radarweg 29, PO Box 211, 1000 AE Amsterdam, The Netherlands
525 B Street, Suite 1900, San Diego, CA 92101-4495, USA

First edition 2006

British Library Cataloguing in Publication Data
A catalogue record for this book is available from the British Library

ISBN-13: 978-0-7623-1360-0
ISBN-10: 0-7623-1360-9
ISSN: 0882-6110 (Series)

For information on all JAI Press publications
visit our website at books.elsevier.com

Printed and bound in The Netherlands

06 07 08 09 10 10 9 8 7 6 5 4 3 2 1

Working together to grow
libraries in developing countries

www.elsevier.com | www.bookaid.org | www.sabre.org

ELSEVIER   BOOK AID
International   Sabre Foundation

CONTENTS

PERSPECTIVES ON GLOBAL RESEARCH

LIST OF CONTRIBUTORS

Barbara Arel	W. P. Carey School of Business, School of Accountancy, Arizona State University, Tempe, AZ, USA
Allen W. Bathke, Jr.	College of Business, Florida State University, Tallahassee, FL, USA
Duane M. Brandon	School of Accountancy, Auburn University, Auburn, AL, USA
Richard Brody	College of Business, University of South Florida – St. Petersburg, St. Petersburg, FL, USA
Steve Buchheit	Area of Accounting, Texas Tech University, Lubbock, TX, USA
Salvador Carmona	Instituto de Empresa Business School, Madrid, Spain
Vincent K. Chong	Accounting and Finance, UWA Business School, University of Western Australia, WA, Australia
Aaron D. Crabtree	School of Accountancy, University of Nebraska – Lincoln, NE, USA
Carol Callaway Dee	Department of Accounting, College of Business, Florida State University, Tallahassee, FL, USA
Ian R. C. Eggleton	Waikato Management School, University of Waikato, Hamilton, New Zealand
Michael Favere-Marchesi	Simon Fraser University, Burnaby, BC, Canada

Timothy J. Fogarty   Department of Accountancy, Weatherhead
                              School of Management, Case Western
                              Reserve University, Cleveland, OH, USA

Maretno A. Harjoto   Accounting & Finance Department, College
                              of Business, San Jose State University,
                              San Jose, CA, USA

Sabam Hutajulu   SAP Project Implementation, Comptroller
                              Division of PERTAMINA Finance
                              Directorate, Jakarta, Republic of Indonesia

Michele K. C. Leong   Accounting and Finance (M250), UWA
                              Business School, University of Western
                              Australia, WA, Australia

Kenneth S. Lorek   College of Business Administration, Northern
                              Arizona University, AZ, USA

Ayalew Lulseged   Department of Accounting, College of
                              Business, Florida State University,
                              Tallahassee, FL, USA

Martti Luoma   Department of Mathematics and Statistics,
                              University of Vaasa, Vaasa, Finland

John J. Maher   Department of Accounting and Information
                              Systems, Pamplin College of Business,
                              Virginia Tech, VA, USA

Tanya S. Nowlin   University of Louisiana, Lafayette, LA, USA

Kurt Pany   W. P. Carey School of Business, School of
                              Accountancy, Arizona State University,
                              Tempe, AZ, USA

William R. Pasewark   Area of Accounting, Texas Tech University,
                              Lubbock, TX, USA

Reijo Ruuhela   Department of Accounting and Finance,
                              University of Vaasa, Vaasa, Finland

Petri Sahlström   Department of Accounting and Finance,
                              University of Oulu, Oulu, Finland

Jerry R. Strawser	Texas A&M University, College Station, TX, USA
Howard F. Turetsky	Accounting & Finance Department, College of Business, San Jose State University, CA, USA
G. Lee Willinger	School of Accounting, Price College of Business, University of Oklahoma, OK, USA

EDITORIAL BOARD

xi

STATEMENT OF PURPOSE AND REVIEW PROCEDURES

Advances in Accounting (AIA) is a research series publication providing academics and practitioners a forum to address current and emerging issues in accounting. Manuscripts may embrace any research methodology and examine any accounting-related subject. Manuscripts may range from empirical to analytical; timely replications will be considered. Manuscripts must be readable, relevant, and reliable. To be readable, manuscripts must be understandable and concise. To be relevant, manuscripts must be related to problems facing the accounting and business community. To be reliable, conclusions must follow logically from the evidence and arguments presented. For empirical reports, sound research design and execution are critical. For theoretical treatises, reasonable assumptions and logical developments are essential.

REVIEW PROCEDURES

AIA intends to provide authors with timely reviews clearly indicating the acceptance status of their manuscripts. The results of initial reviews normally will be reported to authors within 90 days from the date the manuscript is received. All manuscripts are blind reviewed by two members of the editorial board and an associate editor. Editorial correspondence pertaining to manuscripts should be sent to the editor. A $50 submission fee is required.

Editorial correspondence pertaining to manuscripts should be sent to:
Philip M.J. Reckers
School of Accountancy & Information Management
W. P. Carey School of Business
Arizona State University
Tempe, AZ, USA

EDITORIAL POLICY AND MANUSCRIPT FORM GUIDELINES

1. Manuscripts should be typewritten and double-spaced on $8^1/_2$ "by 11" white paper. Only one side of a page should be used. Margins should be set to facilitate editing and duplication except as noted:
   a. Tables, figures, and exhibits should appear on a separate page. Each should be numbered and have a title.
   b. Footnote should be presented by citing the author's name and the year of publication in the body of the text; for example, Schwartz, 1989; Lowe, Reckers, and Whitecotton (2002).
2. Manuscripts should include a cover page, which indicates the author's name and affiliation.
3. Manuscripts should include on a separate lead page an abstract not exceeding 200 words. The author's name and affiliation should not appear on the abstract.
4. Topical headings and subheadings should be used. Main headings in the manuscript should be centered and secondary headings should be flushed with the left-hand margin. (As a guide to usage and style, refer to William Strunk, Jr., and E. B. White, *The Elements of Style*.)
5. Manuscripts must include a list of references, which contains only those works actually cited. (As a helpful guide in preparing a list of references, refer to Kate L. Turabian, *A Manual for Writers of Term Papers, Theses, and Dissertations*.)
6. In order to be assured of an anonymous review, authors should not identify themselves directly or indirectly. Reference to unpublished working papers and dissertations should be avoided. If necessary, authors may indicate that the reference is being withheld for the reasons cited above.
7. Accepted manuscripts ultimately must be submitted on disk.
8. Manuscripts currently under review by other publications should not be submitted. Complete reports of research presented at a national or regional conference of a professional association and "State of the Art" papers are acceptable.

9. Four copies of each manuscript should be submitted to the Editor-In-Chief. Copies of any and all research instruments should also be included.
10. The author should send a check for $50.00 made payable to *Advances in Accounting* as a submission fee.

FINDINGS ON THE EFFECTS OF AUDIT FIRM ROTATION ON THE AUDIT PROCESS UNDER VARYING STRENGTHS OF CORPORATE GOVERNANCE

Barbara Arel, Richard Brody and Kurt Pany

ABSTRACT

While performing an annual audit of a client's financial statements, an audit firm's staff identified what seems to be a material misstatement. Two discussions with the client have led to an impasse in that the client refuses to record what the auditor regards as a necessary adjustment. Our experimental study analyzes whether the likelihood of public accountants modifying their audit report for this departure from generally accepted accounting principles is affected by whether audit firm rotation is about to occur (no rotation v. rotation) under each of the two levels of corporate governance (weak v. strong). Our subjects include 105 CPA firm employees and partners who have an average experience level slightly less than 14 years. Results suggest that auditors in the rotation condition are more likely to modify their audit report as contrasted to those in a situation in which a continuing relationship is expected.

Advances in Accounting, Volume 22, 1–27
ISSN: 0882-6110/doi:10.1016/S0882-6110(06)22001-7

1. INTRODUCTION

This study provides evidence about the effects of audit firm rotation on the resolution of a difference of opinion between external auditors and management as to proper financial accounting. The evidence is from 105 CPA firm partners and employees who replied to an experimental instrument that systematically manipulates audit firm rotation (no rotation v. rotation) under two forms of corporate governance (weak v. strong).

Our research instrument first presents subjects with information indicating that the CPA firm's audit team has discovered a situation in which it believes that a journal entry that will decrease income needs to be recorded by the client. The instrument describes two meetings with the client, after each of which subjects are asked about the likelihood that they believe the client will record the entry. The purpose of obtaining these responses is to increase the tension in the situation relating to the experimental task, to increase realism, to involve the subjects and to obtain subjects' impressions on the likely effects of varying corporate governance on the client's decision to record the entry. Ultimately, management refuses to record the entry.[1] The instrument then requires subjects to estimate the likelihood with which their firm would modify the audit opinion.

Our findings indicate statistically significant differences in means for the likelihood of the firm appropriately modifying the audit opinion for the departure from generally accepted accounting principles, with a higher likelihood of audit report modification when there is audit firm rotation. More precisely, accountants in the rotation condition are more likely to issue a report modified for the departure from generally accepted accounting principles than accountants who believe that a possibility of retaining the client exists. The effect is largest for the situation in which corporate governance is weak.

The remainder of the paper is organized as follows. Section 2 presents background information on the area of audit firm rotation. Sections 3 and 4 develop our hypotheses and approach and Section 5 provides our research results. Finally, Section 6 presents a discussion of our results.

2. BACKGROUND

The study is motivated by the recent accounting problems and instances of alleged corporate fraud at many high-profile companies such as Enron,

WorldCom, Tyco and HealthSouth that have led regulators to re-examine the relationships between management and audit firms in an attempt to strengthen the corporate governance process and thereby better protect shareholders' interests. This re-examination culminated in passage of the Sarbanes-Oxley Act of 2002 (Public Law 107–204, 2002) with its numerous modifications to corporate governance and requirements relating to external auditors. The changes relating to external audits seem to have in common a goal of increasing the quality of financial information, audit quality and the likelihood of auditor independence. The business press and regulators suggest that there is a link between auditor tenure and fraudulent financial reporting as long-term relationships between companies and their auditors create a troublesome degree of closeness between the auditor and management that adversely affects auditor independence, thereby reducing audit quality. When a contentious issue arises during the audit, auditors may experience a conflict of interest over identifying with the impact of the issue on the client and management and maintaining professional skepticism in accordance with the auditing standards.

Mandatory audit firm rotation has been suggested as a potential solution to help break the link and increase audit quality (e.g., Winters, 1976; Kemp, Reckers, & Arrington, 1983; Wolf, Tackett, & Claypool, 1999).[2] Indeed, Section 207 of the Sarbanes-Oxley Act of 2002 required the Comptroller General of the United States to conduct a study and review the potential effects of requiring the mandatory rotation of registered public accounting firms. In November 2003, the General Accounting Office (GAO) issued its report on auditor rotation and concluded that various provisions of the Sarbanes-Oxley Act were directed at enhancing auditor independence (especially provisions related to corporate audit committees) and that

> ... more experience needs to be gained with the act's (other) requirements. Therefore, the most prudent course at this time is for the SEC and the PCAOB to monitor and evaluate the effectiveness of the act's (current) requirements to determine whether further revisions, including mandatory audit firm rotation, may be needed (GAO, 2003, p. 5).

In addition, the GAO recommended additional research to help better predict the benefits and future need for mandatory audit firm rotation (GAO, 2003, p. 47).

In the business press, *The Wall Street Journal* questioned the long-term relationship between Enron Corporation and Arthur Andersen, its auditor since its inception in the early 1980s

> Andersen auditors and consultants were given permanent office space at Enron headquarters here and dressed business-casual like their Enron colleagues. They shared in

office birthdays, frequented lunchtime parties in a nearby park and weekend fund-raisers
for charities. They even went on Enron employees' ski trips to Beaver Creek, Colo.
"People just thought they were Enron employees," says Kevin Jolly, a former Enron
employee who worked in the accounting department. "They walked and talked the same
way .... It was like Arthur Andersen had people on the inside, ... the lines become very
fuzzy." (Herrick & Barrionuevo, 2002).

The article also points out the significant number of ex-Andersen employees
who had accepted subsequent employment with Enron. Questions as to
the propriety of these relationships which develop due to long-term relationships are not new. For example, in 1985 Congressman Shelby asked
"How can an auditing firm remain independent ... when it has established
long-term personal and professional relationships with a company by auditing the same company for many years, some 10, 20 or 30 years?" (Shelby,
1985).

The impact of long-term relationships between auditors and clients on the
audit process is not known. However, results of a GAO survey of CPA firms
and Fortune 1000 public companies reveal that approximately 69% of the
Tier 1 CPA firms (audit firms defined as having 10 or more public clients)
and 73% of the Fortune 1000 public company respondents surveyed did not
believe that long-term auditor relationships increase the risk of audit failures. Yet, 38% of those CPAs and 65% of the Fortune 1000 company
respondents acknowledged that investor perceptions of auditor independence would increase under mandatory audit firm rotation. The report has
been attacked, as it includes no survey results of investors or "the public"
relating to rotation.[3]

In essence, the question we are asking is whether auditors will "stand up"
to their clients in a situation in which the result may be loss of that client.
This conflict of interest may impact the audit independence during the audit
process and may be driven by the business goals of audit firms to maintain clients as sources of revenue. The PCAOB Chief Auditor Douglas
Carmichael recently noted the importance of auditors following professional
standards and not their own business goals

Auditors should have the support of professional standards as well as their firms
when they challenge clients on accounting issues. Too often, in the past, the challenges
did not occur, because the auditor or the firm feared losing the client's business. (Colson,
2004).

Although mandatory rotation at some level would seem a "zero sum game"
for auditing firms in that each rotation involves a successor firm replacing a

predecessor firm, auditors find it a disagreeable proposition. Accountancy Age (2003) surveyed the top 30 British CPA firms (including the Big 4) and received the following results relating to a question as to whether audit firms should be subject to compulsory rotation:

No	20 firms (including all Big 4)
Yes	1 firm
No reply	9 firms

Consistently, the AICPA (1992, 2003) historically and currently opposes mandatory rotation, arguing that rotation will increase rather than decrease the number of audit failures. These arguments generally cite statistics indicating higher than average "audit failure" rates the first several years of an audit relationship with a client[4] and expected increases in audit costs.

Recognizing that corporate governance procedures may also be responsible for a number of the auditing and accounting problems, both the Sarbanes-Oxley Act and the major United States stock exchanges adopted stricter requirements for audit committee membership in the areas of independence, expertise and number of members while granting more authority to the audit committees in the audit process.[5] This enhanced audit committee authority includes the hiring and firing of the company's audit firm. These corporate governance procedures and requirements interact with the professional auditing standards in both the general areas of internal control (SAS No. 78 and 94, AICPA, 2004) and fraud (SAS No. 99, AICPA, 2004) and on communications between CPAs and the audit committee (SAS Nos. 60, 61, 78, 87, 89 and 90, AICPA, 2004). While the changes implement minimum levels of independent directors and financial expertise, some companies choose to strengthen their corporate governance structure beyond the minimum requirements by increasing the number of independent directors or the level of financial expertise on the audit committee (Shearman & Sterling, 2004). In particular, we believe that a strong audit committee's ability to make an independent decision on retaining the current audit firm is likely to lead to enhanced auditor independence. It is for this reason that we test audit firm rotation under both relatively weak and strong corporate governance environments. Both of the levels tested are currently acceptable under the Sarbanes-Oxley Act and requirements of the stock exchanges.

3. HYPOTHESES DEVELOPMENT

3.1. Audit Firm Rotation

Both prior analytical discussions and empirical research results are relevant to audit firm rotation. Analytical research suggests that auditors provide value to the capital market by serving an information role as well as providing compensation when they "fail" in providing that role.[6] Wallace (1981) discusses the manner in which the audit process may serve as a monitoring device that will reduce managers' incentives to manipulate reported earnings. DeAngelo (1981) and Watts and Zimmerman (1983) show that through verification of financial statement information, auditors may both discover and report breaches from proper accounting disclosure.

But the discovery of a misstatement measures quality in terms of an auditor's knowledge and ability; the reporting of the misstatement is dependent upon the auditor's incentives to disclose the breach. Watts and Zimmerman (1983) emphasize the need for auditor independence, and suggest that a reasonable measure of independence is the likelihood that an auditor will report any breach of the contract between the principal and agent involved in the financial reporting process. It is this measure that we use in our experiment. While we consider it a measure of independence, it is more directly a measure of subjects' beliefs as to the expected nature of the basic product of the audit, the audit report. The auditor has discovered a misstatement, and we solicit a reply as to the likelihood that the subject's firm would disclose this misstatement ("breach") in its audit report. This measure is also consistent with recent discussions of auditor reliability and independence presented by Taylor, DeZoort, Munn, and Thomas (2003) and Johnstone, Sutton, and Warfield (2001).

DeAngelo's (1981) analytical analysis suggests that incumbent auditors can earn quasi-rents (economic rents) from maintaining existing clients due to high initial start-up costs for audits of new clients and due to significant transaction costs incurred by the client when a change in auditors occurs. Consistent with this, Palmrose (1989) determined that audit hours decline as audit firm tenure increases.

To motivate a company to make an auditor change, a potential successor auditor may "low-ball" first-year audit fees, that is bid fees lower than the expected marginal costs for initial engagements with clients (e.g., Dye, 1991; Dopuch, King, & Schwartz, 2001). Studies by Simon and Francis (1988) and Ettredge and Greenberg (1990) suggest that auditors have "low-balled" the first-year bid to obtain the client, and therefore hope to retain the client so as to recover those costs and to subsequently earn the quasi-rents discussed by DeAngelo.

The combination of potentially earning long-term quasi-rents and acquiring a client through low-balling may result in a situation in which auditor independence may be impaired due to a financial need to retain the client. Thus, a client that wishes to misstate reported financial statements might attempt to prevent an auditor from reporting such a misstatement by threatening to replace the auditors, and thereby eliminate the annuity-like stream of quasi-rents.[7] Indeed, Casterella, Knechel, and Walker (2001) examined a sample of firms that were subject to SEC enforcement actions in the period 1980–1991 and found that audit quality as measured by fraudulent financial reporting is lower as auditor tenure increases. Consistently, Dopuch et al. (2001), using a laboratory markets approach, find that a rotation requirement decreased auditor subjects' willingness to issue-biased reports.

The arguments in favor of audit firm rotation generally suggest that with rotation auditors will both appear more independent, and be more independent (Brody & Moscove, 1998; Wolf et al., 1999). This argument is not new in that more than 40 years ago Mautz and Sharaf (1961) warned auditors that

> The greatest threat to his independence is a slow, gradual, almost casual erosion of this honest disinterestedness .... the auditor in charge must constantly remind his assistants of the importance and operational meaning of independence. (p. 208)

Similarly, Bazerman, Loewenstein, and Moore (2002) more than 40 years later argue that auditor independence is impaired by an unconscious self-serving bias in auditor judgments driven by the auditors' incentive to satisfy clients – see Nelson (2003) and Moore, Loewenstein, Tanlu, and Bazerman (2003) for reviews of conflicts of interest research in auditing and in general. Mandatory audit firm rotation can help eliminate the unconscious self-serving bias in auditors to agree with the client by removing the incentive, quasi-rents, that cause the auditor's interest to align with the clients.

Those arguing against rotation have questioned whether the likely benefits of rotating audit firms outweigh the increased costs for the audit firm, client and public. Potential legal liability and a desire to maintain reputation with other clients help the auditor to remain independent. Also, high "start-up costs" relating to the audit lead to a situation in which audit firm rotation may be both costly and risky in that errors may not be detected. Consistently, the Cohen Commission Report (AICPA, 1978) asserts that the benefits did not outweigh the costs and recommended no mandatory audit firm rotation. The GAO study (GAO, 2003) asserts that further analysis is needed to determine the benefits of mandatory rotation because the benefits are harder to predict and quantify than the additional costs. The combination of no regulatory requirement of audit firm rotation and few companies voluntarily establishing such a policy has made research directly addressing the issue of audit firm rotation difficult.[8] But, a number of studies report higher than normal early-year "audit failure rates" (e.g., Geiger & Raghunandan, 2002; St. Pierre & Anderson, 1984; Palmrose, 1986; Stice, 1991) and Carcello and Nagy (2004), using a sample of firms cited for fraudulent reporting from 1990 to 2001, found that fraudulent financial reporting is more likely to occur in the first three years of the auditor–client relationship and with no evidence that it is more likely given longer auditor tenure. Mansi et al. (2004) find that on an overall basis, investors in debt securities require somewhat lower rates of return as the length of tenure increases. Consistently, Myers, Myers, and Omer (2003a) and Myers, Myers, Palmrose, and Scholz (2003b) find higher earnings quality (as measured by accruals) in longer auditor tenure situations and that auditor tenure was not associated with an increase in subsequent restatements. Yet, despite these findings, one observes that the many corporate failures cited earlier in this paper in general have a pattern of long-term auditor tenure, generally accompanied by what in hindsight seems to be dramatically overstated earnings.

In summary, analytical analysis and arguments relevant to audit firm rotation have been presented and to a limited extent tested empirically. Counteracting forces exist in that long relationships fostering quasi-rents may adversely affect auditor independence, while limited knowledge obtained during first-year audits may result in higher rates of "audit failure" during the first year of an audit relationship. In this paper, we attempt to address the "independence" portion of the question by presenting a situation in which the auditors have identified a potential misstatement and reply as to the likely type of audit report their firm would issue.

3.2. Corporate Governance

Although the Sarbanes-Oxley Act and resulting changes in stock-exchange listing requirements include increased corporate governance standards for all registrants, a significant level of flexibility still exist in the manner in which such reforms are implemented. To illustrate, differences in the following areas are allowable:

• Leadership of the board and the proportion of independent directors on the Board.

- Level of financial expertise of members of the audit committee.
- Audit committee diligence.

Importantly, research such as that summarized below has shown that such differences are likely to affect the effectiveness of the corporate governance process.

3.2.1. Board Leadership and Proportion of Independent Directors

Prior research suggests that boards structured to be independent of the CEO are more effective in monitoring the corporate financial accounting process. Firms investigated for financial statement fraud have been found to be more likely to have a CEO that also serves as the chairman of the board of directors (Dechow, Sloan, & Sweeney, 1996) and a board composed of non-independent directors (Beasley, 1996; Dechow et al., 1996). Also, prior research has found a negative relationship between independent audit committee members and abnormal accruals, an indicator of earnings management (Klein, 2002; Bedard, Chtourou, & Courteau, 2004) and the occurrence of restatements (Abbott, Parker, & Peters, 2004). Using an experimental approach, Cohen and Hanno (2000) found that auditors' client-acceptance judgments and substantive testing judgments were more favorable when the board and audit committee were described as strong and independent of management than when they were described as weak and heavily reliant on management. For firms experiencing financial distress, Carcello and Neal (2000) found that the likelihood of an auditor issuing a going-concern report is inversely related to the percentage of affiliated directors on the audit committee. Recognizing that creditors rely on the integrity of financial reports, Andersen, Mansi, and Reeb (2004) found that the cost of debt is inversely related to board and audit committee independence.

3.2.2. Audit Committee Financial Expertise

Prior research has found a negative association between the financial expertise of audit committee members and aggressive earnings management practices (Bedard et al., 2004) and the occurrence of restatements (Abbott et al., 2004). Audit committee member's financial expertise (DeZoort, Hermanson, & Houston, 2003) and audit knowledge (DeZoort & Salterio, 2001) also increase the likelihood that the audit committee will support the auditor in a financial reporting dispute between the auditor and management. Related to this research, Ng and Tan (2003) provide evidence that the existence of either a strong audit committee to support the auditor's position or authoritative guidance for a conservative position decreases the likelihood that an auditor will allow aggressive financial reporting.

3.2.3. Audit Committee Diligence

While the requirements regarding audit committee members' independence and financial expertise are important in improving the capability of members to monitor the financial reporting process, the committee must also be diligent in performing its responsibilities to improve effectiveness. One proxy for audit committee diligence that prior research has examined is meeting frequency (DeZoort, Hermanson, Archambeault, & Reed, 2002). Using this proxy, Abbott et al. (2004) found a significant negative association between the activity level of audit committees and the occurrence of restatements. Utilizing market-based evidence, Andersen et al. (2004) found a negative relation between yield spreads and audit committee meeting frequency. Audit committee size has also been used in prior research as a proxy for audit committee diligence. Based on the belief that an audit committee should not be so large as to become unwieldy, but large enough to ensure effective monitoring (Bedard et al., 2004), the general recommendation is to limit the size of the committee to five (Andersen, 1998). Andersen et al. (2004) again provide market-based evidence that yield spreads are negatively related to audit committee size although no significant association was found between size and the occurrence of restatements (Abbott et al., 2004) or earnings management (Bedard et al., 2004). The results suggest that audit committees which meet more frequently and are more appropriate in size are more likely to be diligent in performing their duties as monitors of the financial reporting process.

In summary, research conducted on the changing requirements of corporate governance indicates that the new requirements for board and audit committee membership do have an impact on the financial reporting process. Prior research has shown a significant association between board and audit committee independence, financial expertise, audit committee diligence and financial reporting quality. In our study, we investigate the impact of these corporate governance items on audit quality as measured by the auditor judgments of the need for their audit firm to modify audit reports for an apparent departure from generally accepted accounting principles. For both practical reasons (e.g., the need to have a manageable number of forms of the questionnaire) and because our emphasis is on auditor rotation, as is discussed later in the paper, we consider only a relatively "weak" and a relatively "strong" level of corporate governance. We do not attempt to isolate the effects of financial board leadership, proportion of independent directors and audit committee expertise and diligence.

3.2.4. Hypotheses

This study addresses the effects of audit firm rotation and corporate governance on auditing quality. Our measure of audit quality is whether subjects believe their firm will modify the audit opinion if management does not record what the subject believes to be a necessary adjusting journal entry. Although not necessary for interpretation of the results consistent with the prior noted research, we consider our measure of audit quality to be a measure of audit firm independence. Fig. 1 illustrates the stages and the situation. This study emphasizes the bold sections of that figure. The italicized portion relates to communications with the audit committee. Although the timing on this communication is flexible in that SAS No. 90 (AICPA, 2004) suggests that it is not required prior to the issuance of the audit report, in a matter as significant as the one discussed in this case one might expect the audit committee to become involved after the CPA firm has decided that the matter is so important as to merit audit report modification. Our study addresses the auditors' judgments prior to this point in that subjects are asked for their reactions after management has decided not to record the entry. Related, SAS No. 90 requires presentation of information on the adjustment by the auditors to the audit committee regardless of whether the entry is recorded by the management.

If management does not record the adjustment, the situation described in our research instrument, the CPA firm is in a position in which issuance of a qualified or adverse audit opinion is ordinarily appropriate – regardless of

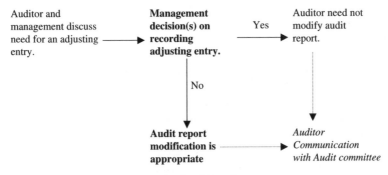

Fig. 1. Decision Steps.

audit firm rotation policy or level of corporate governance. The discovery of a misstatement measures quality in terms of the auditor's knowledge and ability; the reporting of the misstatement is dependent upon the auditor's incentives to disclose. In our study, the misstatement has been identified and correcting it or modifying the audit report for that misstatement is the issue.

We deal directly with the auditor's ordinary role in that the questions address whether the subject believes the audit firm will modify the audit report when such circumstances are encountered in his or her firm. Our measure of audit quality, report modification, addresses the fundamental notion of whether a proper audit report will be issued by the firm. As indicated earlier, although not entirely necessary, we interpret this concept as a measure of auditor independence consistent with previous research (e.g., DeAngelo, 1981; Watts & Zimmerman, 1983). Neither the corporate governance structure nor the rotation policy should affect overall responses to the need for report modification when auditors are independent. However, auditor independence may be impaired when an auditor faces a conflict between their professional responsibilities and their audit firm's business goals (i.e., to maintain the client's business in the following year).

Without a strong corporate governance structure or client audit firm rotation policy, this conflict may influence the auditor's report. The existence of a client audit firm rotation policy may reduce the quasi-rents related to the conflict of interest for the auditor, as the auditor's firm will not audit the client in the following year regardless of the outcome of the audit. This reduction in incentive to agree with the client will allow the auditor to report independently. It is the reporting in the audit report of a known departure from acceptable accounting principles, which our first hypothesis addresses

H1. Auditor beliefs as to whether the audit firm will modify the audit report to reflect an apparent departure from generally accepted accounting principles will be higher (lower) when the client has an audit firm rotation policy (no policy).

While our primary goal is to address auditor rotation, because we address it under two levels of corporate governance, our design allows us to measure whether auditor responses differ under these levels. Under the Sarbanes-Oxley Act, audit committees have the authority to hire and dismiss auditors. Yet, their decision will be made at least in part based on input from management. Also, if an auditor believes that the audit committee does not possess the knowledge necessary to understand and provide effective oversight of financial reporting matters, the auditor may not depend on support from the audit committee in the resolution of a financial reporting matter. Accordingly, we hypothesize

H2. Auditor beliefs as to whether the audit firm will modify the audit report to reflect an apparent departure from generally accepted accounting principles will be higher (lower) when the client has strong (weak) corporate governance.

4. RESEARCH APPROACH

4.1. Subjects

Subjects were public accountants from a variety of accounting firms in the northeast section of the United States. Firms were contacted, and an administrator for each firm distributed and collected the research instruments.

Table 1 provides demographic information on the respondents. The auditors have on average 13.9 years of public accounting experience (standard

Table 1. Profile of Subjects ($n = 105$).

	Mean (Standard Deviation)
Age	39.3 (10.9)
Years of public accounting experience (total)	13.9 (10.4)
Percentage female	35.8
Percentage CPA	74.3
Position in firm (%)	
Staff	14.1
Senior	22.6
Supervisor	3.8
Manager	20.7
Partner	27.4
Owner	3.8
Other	7.6
Type of firm (%)	
One office	54.3
Multiple office	7.6
Regional	21.9
National	14.3
Big 4	1.9

deviation of 10.4 years). Also, approximately 74% of the subjects are certified public accountants. Approximately, 86% of the subjects report a
position above staff level.

4.2. Research Task

Subjects were provided with experimental materials that depicted a hypothetical audit client. It included background information on the audit client
such as a general description of the client's business and industry (audio
systems manufacturer) and a statement that the company tended to follow
"aggressive" accounting procedures that recognize income as early as possible. It also included background information detailing the relationship
between the audit firm and the audit client. The subjects were told the CPA
firm had audited the client for the last three years with "clean" opinions
issued each year. Each subject was asked to assume the role of an audit team
member. The materials describe the audit client as the largest client for this
individual, although the fees represent only 2% of the total fees for the firm.
The background information also included the primary manipulated independent variables – the level of corporate governance and audit firm rotation policy – in place at the audit client. Also included in the instrument
was operating income information for the prior four years (audited) and the
current year (unaudited), and a description of the problem-facing management in the current year.

The point of conflict in the case is related to the inventory valuation of
certain audio equipment. The subjects were told that the impact of recording
the write down of these items to market values below cost in the current year
would reduce net income below that of any of the four preceding years
and were asked whether they believed that the management would record
the journal entry. This sort of entry was selected because there is some
subjectivity here, although the auditor has a belief as to the least amount
necessary as an adjustment, and because research indicates that attempts
at earnings management often involve such subjective transactions (e.g.,
Nelson, Elliott, & Tarpley, 2002). Subjects were informed that management
did not initially record or disclose the situation prior to the audit and is in
disagreement with the audit team over the proper accounting procedure
during audit fieldwork.

The portion of the case analyzed in detail in this paper[9] addresses subject
responses to whether they believed that their firm would modify the audit
opinion to reflect a departure from generally accepted accounting principles.

4.3. Independent Variables

Two variables in the case were manipulated to address the hypotheses: the level of audit firm rotation policy and corporate governance.

4.3.1. Audit Firm Rotation

This variable has two levels – no rotation v. rotation of the client next year to another audit firm according to company policy. Rotation in this study involves change to another CPA firm after a set period (four years),[10] as contrasted to a more limited form of rotation in which a continuing audit firm rotates top personnel on the engagement (the current requirement in the United States).

A firm rotation level requires consideration of both the fact that the company has such a policy, and the current year in the rotation cycle. For example, if a company rotates auditors every four years, the CPA firm involved could be in any one of the first through the fourth years of the relationship. One way of viewing this is that any year might be selected, as auditors must maintain independence for all years. Yet, to provide the strongest possible test, we tested the fourth year. That represents a situation in which the CPA firm will lose the client within the next year regardless of how the accounting matter is handled. Thus, the CPA firm has the least to lose as compared to the loss of the client in a preceding year. Following DeAngelo's analysis, no future quasi-rents remain. Also, the CPA firm personnel is well aware that the manner in which the accounting issue in this case is resolved will be obvious to the successor auditors who will be expected to review this year's audit documentation. This is all in contrast to the company with no rotation policy in which the CPA firm stands to lose an annuity for an indefinite time period into the future.

4.3.2. Corporate Governance

The other manipulated variable was the audit client's corporate governance level. While any number of variables within corporate governance might be manipulated, we selected combinations that comply with current corporate governance requirements (Securities and Exchange Commission, 2003), are realistic[11] and have been found to have an effect on the financial reporting process by prior research. The objective here was to enrich the study of audit firm rotation by considering two different, yet possible levels of corporate governance – one weak and one strong.

Consistent with the previously cited research, we manipulated the leadership of the board and the proportion of independent directors on the

	Strong	**Weak**
Board of Directors		
Size	15	15
Number Independent of Management	12	8
Chairman	Independent	Company Founder
Audit Committee		
Size	5	3
Members all independent?	Yes	Yes
Summary Description	Strong	Relatively weak,
Relationship to NASDAQ Stds.	More than meets	Technically meets
Meetings in 2002	6	2

Fig. 2.   Details of Corporate Governance Manipulation.

Board, the level of financial expertise of members of the audit committee and audit committee diligence. Fig. 2 provides details of the corporate governance manipulation, which we summarize in this paper as strong v. weak corporate governance.

4.3.3. Manipulation Checks
Manipulation checks on both manipulated variables were included at the end of the task. The percentage of subjects that responded correctly to the question asking participants to identify the description of the type of audit committee present at the audit client was 91.1%. In response to the question of whether the audit firm anticipated a long relationship with the client or whether the client rotates its auditors, 97% of subjects responded correctly. Although results do not differ significantly with or without those who missed a manipulation check, we only included respondents who replied accurately to both manipulation checks. We also deleted 13 subjects that did not have any audit experience.

4.4. Dependent Variable

The dependent variable in the study is the response from the subjects as to the likelihood that their firm would modify the audit opinion to reflect a departure from GAAP (or resign from the engagement if such a report modification is not acceptable to the company) as a result of the situation in the case. A response scale with endpoints labeled "not at all likely" (0) and "extremely likely" (10) was used for this question. This variable directly mirrors the ultimate audit reporting decision made and as indicated earlier, we interpret this variable as a measure of auditor independence.

One may ask why subjects would not at all reply "10" or the likelihood the audit firm would modify the audit report is extremely likely. We have argued that fear of loss of the client is a major risk to the CPA firm and may result in a decrease in replies. A less sinister motivation might be to recognize that the adjustment is an "estimation transaction" that involves judgments and assumptions on which individuals may arrive at differing conclusions. Specifically, the background information states that

> ... based on your work, you know that the items involved have been extremely slow moving, and that the $700,000 decrease in net income is a good guess of the minimum needed writedown.

Another reason that replies may be less than the maximum is that others in the firm who may become involved with the audit may consider the entry as unnecessary or overstated. Accordingly, our emphasis is on differences among the replies as opposed to the average response levels themselves.

4.5. Experimental Design and Data Analysis

Panel A of Fig. 3 summarizes the experimental design. Subjects were randomly assigned to one of the four forms of the questionnaire. A 2×2 between subjects design was used to test level of corporate governance (strong v. weak) and audit firm rotation (no rotation v. rotation).[12]

We used a between subjects design so as to make it impossible for subjects to identify the exact nature of the variables being manipulated (see Pany & Reckers, 1987 for more on this topic). Panel B of Fig. 3 summarizes the levels of the variables included in each of the forms of the questionnaire.

Analysis of variance (ANOVA) was used to assess the overall relationship between audit firm, corporate governance and the dependent variable, the likelihood of report modification.

5. RESULTS

The ANOVA results and group means relating to the likelihood of audit report modification are reported in Table 2. The means, reported in Panel B, show that the subjects were relatively confident in the likelihood that their firm would modify the report for the departure from generally accepted accounting principles. The existence of an audit firm rotation policy had a significant impact on the subject's assessment of the likelihood of an audit

Panel A
2 x 2 Anova

Independent Variables	Levels Tested	Type of Variable
Audit Firm Rotation	No v. Yes	Between subjects
Corporate Governance	Weak v. Strong	Between subjects

Panel B
Questionnaire Forms

Group Number		Audit Firm Rotation		Corporate Governance
1		No		Weak
2		Yes		Weak
3		No		Strong
4		Yes		Strong

Fig. 3.   Experimental Design.

report modification by the firm. Subjects in the rotation condition reported a significantly higher likelihood of a report modification (mean of 7.39) than subjects in the no rotation condition (mean of 6.29). The results suggest that in a situation in which audit firm rotation is imminent, it is significantly more likely that a report modification will occur reporting a client's departure from generally accepted accounting principles.

While all means for auditor rotation are in the expected direction (that is rotation leads to higher replies), the difference in means for rotation under strong corporate governance is lower than what we had expected. Thus, in our study, the effect of rotation is strongest under weak corporate governance. Yet, the overall governance and governance/rotation interaction effects are insignificant. But, the results do not indicate a significant increase in the likelihood of reporting under strong corporate governance.

5.1. Ancillary Analysis

Our sample includes a diverse group of auditors that come from all levels of a CPA firm. Although we asked respondents to reply as to how likely it was

Table 2. Likelihood of Audit Report Modification.

	D.F.	Sums of Squares	Mean Square	F Value
Panel A: Analysis of Variance[a]				
Source				
Rotation[b]	1	25.63	25.63	4.30*
Corporate governance[c]	1	7.71	7.71	1.29
Rotation* corporate governance	1	13.18	13.18	2.21
Error	101	602.52	5.97	

Rotation	Corporate Governance		
	Weak	Strong	Mean
Panel B: Rotation and Corporate Governance Treatment Means (Standard Deviations)			
No rotation	6.22	6.38	6.29
	(2.85)	(2.48)	(2.66)
	$n = 30$	$n = 26$	$n = 56$
Rotation	7.93	6.67	7.39
	(1.92)	(2.37)	(2.20)
	$n = 28$	$n = 21$	$n = 49$
Mean	7.04	6.51	
	(2.58)	(2.41)	
	$n = 58$	$n = 47$	

*Significant at 0.02, one-tailed.

[a]Table presents statistical conclusions on subjects' views of the likelihood their audit firm would modify the audit report to reflect departure from GAAP. The response scale indicated "not at all likely" (0) to "extremely likely" (10).

[b]Client has an audit firm rotation policy or not.

[c]Corporate governance structure at the client is strong or weak.

that they believed that their firm would modify their audit report for the unresolved exception, the diversity of the subjects is potentially problematical since one would ordinarily expect decisions to be made by high-level employees and partners. Thus, approximately 1/2 of our subjects are replying as to how they believe these top-level personnel would resolve the issue. One may question whether lower-level employees have a valid basis for making such a judgment. We further analyzed our data to address this issue.

Our ancillary analysis on the audit quality results include considering the following measures of experience:

• Years experience (split at median of approximately 11 years);

- Level within the firm (managers, partners and owners v. others); and
- CPA (no v. yes).

We included an independent measure for each of the above variables in our analysis. In all cases, neither the main effect nor any of its interactions with the other independent measures (rotation and corporate governance) were significant. Thus, our significant results relating to auditor rotation remain when these variables are addressed as mentioned above.

Finally, we considered the effect of CPA firm size – that is, the respondents from the smallest firms might be expected to have few, if any, publicly traded clients. We compared (1) subjects in one office firms with those in the other firms and (2) subjects in one office firms plus firms with multiple offices within one state with subjects in the other firms. No significant differences in replies were identified, thus suggesting that CPA firm size did not systematically affect the results.

6. DISCUSSION

Before discussing any possible implications of our study, we acknowledge several of its primary limitations. First, our subjects are all from the northeastern part of the United States and may not be representative of CPAs throughout the country. Yet, we have no reason to believe that they systematically differ on the issues addressed in the study from other CPAs. A second limitation is that limited subject availability made it necessary that we were only able to test limited levels for both corporate governance and audit firm rotation; as such, our findings are restricted to these levels. Third, related to the second limitation, our auditor rotation manipulation only addressed the situation in which rotation was scheduled to occur in the following year; accordingly, the study does not directly address situations in which there is a rotation policy but rotation is not imminent. Indeed, several years prior to the scheduled rotation date, a client's threat to replace the auditor may be a very viable threat to auditor independence. Just as the "quasi-rents" described by DeAngelo (1981) occur with long auditor/client relationships of unspecified duration, some level of them would be expected to exist in the years prior to the final year of a required rotation relationship. But, extremely different audit pricing would be necessary in the rotation circumstance – periods from three to nine years have been recommended – to involve the level of quasi-rents that would be expected to exist in the current situation with its relatively low level of auditor change.[13]

Subject to the above limitations, our study's basic finding relating to auditor rotation is that subjects placed in an experimental situation with auditor rotation replied differently than those with a firm that hoped to continue the relationship. More specifically, when audit firm rotation was imminent, the mean likelihood of reporting the departure from generally accepted accounting principles exceeded that of subjects whose firm hoped to continue the relationship. If the likelihood of reporting a known departure from generally accepted accounting principles is accepted as a measure of auditor independence (e.g., DeAngelo, 1981; Dopuch et al., 2001; Watts & Zimmerman, 1983), our study finds a more independent audit firm, on average, when a required rotation will occur within the next year. Thus, in such a rotation circumstance, auditors may be freer of incentives to retain the client, and are therefore more independent in their assessments of the fairness of the financial statements. But, regardless of whether one accepts our dependent measure as a measure of independence, the statistically difference in replies between the rotation and non-rotation conditions remains.

May we generalize our findings further to address mandatory auditor rotation on a broader basis? This is a difficult question to answer since a widespread requirement of audit firm rotation is likely to lead to a variety of other changes. For example, the effects on the auditors of a much larger annual "supply" of possible new audit clients for the various CPA firms are not obvious. Would such an increase in potential clients lead to "marketing ability" becoming an even more important skill to CPAs, possibly at the cost of technical competence? Also, perhaps CPA firms would staff their audits differently toward the end of the rotation period in an effort to keep other audit clients early in the rotation cycle from "prematurely" rotating audit firms.

An argument against rotation has been what seem to be high early-year audit failure rates. If one accepts this premise, it would seem that a cost of audit firm rotation to investors would include a higher level of audit failures. However, an alternative possibility is that the increased number of first- and second-year audits resulting from audit firm rotation will lead to higher auditor skill level in these situations and a lower level of audit failure during early years. Also, a closer working relationship with the predecessor auditor than is now the case might be possible that would limit early-year audit failures. Uncertainties such as these make it seem that research will never fully answer the rotation question.

Despite the above uncertainties, we believe that our study's finding that auditor reporting behavior in today's environment was affected by a policy of required firm rotation should not be discounted. The General Accounting

Office (2003) suggested that further analysis is needed to consider possible benefits of mandatory rotation. That conclusion was based in part on their survey indicating that the great majority of CPA firm and Fortune 1000 respondents did not believe that long-term auditor relationships increase the risk of audit failures. In a sense, our findings are the opposite – in the situation in which a long-term relationship could be maintained (no rotation), our subjects in the aggregate reported that their firms would be less likely to modify their audit reports for a departure from generally accepted accounting principles as compared to the subjects in our rotation condition. Related, our findings using real-world accountants are consistent with those of the laboratory markets approach used by Dopuch et al. (2001). Thus, at least two studies, using different approaches and subjects, have now found that a rotation policy increases the likelihood of accurate reporting – at least as rotation becomes imminent. While the findings of the two studies certainly do not justify a decision on its own to require rotation, they do not lead to a conclusion that rotation is unnecessary.

NOTES

1. Data on replies to whether the subjects believed that management would record the journal entry is available from the authors. In brief, subjects believed it more likely that the entry was recorded under conditions of strong corporate governance. The existence of audit firm rotation did not affect replies.

2. We do not review the mass of independence research that is available in this paper. See the Ramsey Report (2001) for independence research. Although written for Australian governmental use, the Report provides an outstanding presentation of United States (and other) research.

3. Questions have been asked about the fairness of the GAO's study. Perhaps most extreme are comments of the Fulcrum Financial Group (2003, p. 3) who suggest that

> Not one scrap of new research or analysis of the pro-rotation position was included in the GAO's report .... With the extremely low turnover of audit relationships, no wonder the public accounting firms are slow to upset their relationship with management. This is especially true since the vast majority of audit partners serving the largest clients have only one client. If that one client is lost, the individual audit partner face likely employment termination because there is little chance of obtaining sufficient new work to replace the lost client. This places intense pressure on an individual audit partner whose entire livelihood depends on serving his only client.

Consistent with the above concerns, Jennings, Pany, and Reckers (2004) report that their sample of judges perceive that when audit firm rotation occurs (1) auditors are more likely to be independent; (2) financial statements more reliable; and (3) auditors should be less liable to plaintiffs when firm rotation is to occur, particularly in circumstances of strong corporate governance.

4. The AICPA (1992) cites such data. Consistently, the South African Institute of Chartered Accountants suggests that it normally takes between two and three years to fully understand the nuances of a complex audit (Report of the Joint Disciplinary Task Team, 2002, pp. 6–7).

5. Krishnamoorthy, Wright, and Cohen (2002) Krishnamoorthy et al. (2002) provide a discussion of the process involved, including the formation of the Blue Ribbon Committee on Improving the Effectiveness of Corporate Audit Committees. That committee's recommendations have subsequently been adopted by the major stock exchanges.

6. Dye (1993) and Mansi, Maxwell, and Miller (2004) present this as two separate roles, as it may indeed be seen. The later present both an analysis that attempts to separate the roles and an excellent review of related literature and difficulties with respect to such separation. Our analysis emphasizes the information role in that the CPA firm itself is held constant across the various cases.

7. Using an experimental economic design, Mayhew and Pike (2004) found that transferring the power to hire and fire the auditor from managers to investors significantly decreases the proportion of auditor independence violations.

8. Speaking as a corporate monitor in the WorldCom Case, Richard C. Breeden (2003) has proposed that the company, now known as MCI Inc., should regularly rotate its external auditors. Audit firm rotation is required to varying extents in Italy, Brazil, Bolivia, Ecuador and Paraguay, although only very limited information on its effectiveness is available – see Elorietta (2002) and Zea (2002).

9. See note 1 for other information obtained.

10. We selected the four-year period based on the recommended period by Ellen Seidman (2001), Director of the Office of Thrift Supervision, who suggested in her testimony before U.S. Senate Committee on Banking, Housing and Urban Affairs that audit firm rotation every three to four years was desirable in that it would allow a "fresh look" at the organization. Other periods (presumably longer) are certainly possible.

11. See Taub (2004) for a discussion of continuing differences in strength of corporate governance and audit committees.

12. The correlation analysis revealed potential covariates. ANCOVAs performed on the data including both the manipulated variables and potential covariates are similar to the ANOVA results. The results related to the hypotheses do not change with the inclusion of covariates.

13. The Fulcrum Financial Group (2003) observes that the current tenure of auditors among Fortune 1000 companies averages 22 years and would be much higher except for the demise of Andersen; the top 10% of these companies have had the same auditor for 50 years, with the average tenure of this group being 75 years.

ACKNOWLEDGEMENTS

We acknowledge helpful comments from Phil Reckers, Steve Kaplan, anonymous reviewers and seminar participants at the 2004 AAA Audit meeting and the 2003 AAA Northeast Region meeting.

REFERENCES

Abbott, L. J., Parker, S., & Peters, G. F. (2004). Audit committee characteristics and restatements. *Auditing: A Journal of Practice & Theory, 23*, 69–87.

Accountancy Age. (2003). Thumbs down for audit firm rotation, *Accounting Age*, September 1, pp. 1–5.

American Institute of Certified Public Accountants (AICPA). (1978). *The commission on auditor's responsibilities: Report, conclusions and recommendations (Cohen Commission)*. New York: AICPA.

American Institute of Certified Public Accountants (AICPA). (1992). *SEC practice section. Statement of position regarding mandatory rotation of audit firms of publicly held companies*. New York: AICPA.

American Institute of Certified Public Accountants (AICPA). (2003). *How the Sarbanes-Oxley Act of 2002 impacts the accounting profession*. New York: AICPA.

American Institute of Certified Public Accountants (AICPA). (2004). *Professional standards*. New York: AICPA.

Andersen, A. (1998). *Global best practices for audit committees*. Chicago, IL: Arthur Andersen.

Andersen, R. C., Mansi, S. A., & Reeb, D. M. (2004). Board characteristics, accounting reporting integrity and the cost of debt. *Journal of Accounting and Economics, 37*, 315–342.

Bazerman, M. H., Loewenstein, G., & Moore, D. A. (2002). Why good accountants do bad audits. *Harvard Business Review, 80*, 97–102.

Beasley, M. S. (1996). An empirical analysis of the relation between the board of director composition and financial statement fraud. *The Accounting Review, 71*, 443–466.

Bedard, J., Chtourou, S. M., & Courteau, L. (2004). The effect of audit committee expertise, independence, and activity on aggressive earnings management. *Auditing: A Journal of Practice & Theory, 23*, 13–35.

Breeden, R. C. (2003). *Restoring trust*. Report to the Honorable Jed S. Rakoff. The United States District Court, for the Southern District of New York on Corporate Governance for the Future of MCI, Inc., August, p. 117.

Brody, R. G., & Moscove, S. A. (1998). Mandatory audit firm rotation. *National Public Accountant, 43.2*, 32–35.

Carcello, J. V., & Nagy, A. L. (2004). Audit firm tenure and fraudulent financial reporting. *Auditing: A Journal of Practice & Theory, 23*, 55–69.

Carcello, J. V., & Neal, T. L. (2000). Audit committee composition and auditor reporting. *The Accounting Review, 75*, 453–467.

Casterella, J., Knechel, W. R., & Walker, P. L. (2001). *The relationship of audit failures and mandatory audit firm rotation: Explanatory models and empirical evidence*. Working Paper. University of Florida.

Cohen, J., & Hanno, D. (2000). Auditor's consideration of corporate governance and management control philosophy in preplanning and planning judgments. *Auditing: A Journal of Practice & Theory, 19*, 133–146.

Colson, R. H. (2004). Audit standards in transition: An interview with PCAOB Chief Auditor Douglas R. Carmichael. *The CPA Journal, 74.9*, 20–26.

DeAngelo, L. (1981). Auditor size and audit quality. *Journal of Accounting and Economics, 3*, 183–199.

Dechow, P. M., Sloan, R. G., & Sweeney, A. P. (1996). Causes and consequences of earnings manipulation: An analysis of firms subject to enforcement actions by the SEC. *Contemporary Accounting Research, 13*, 1–36.

DeZoort, F. T., Hermanson, D. R., Archambeault, D. S., & Reed, S. A. (2002). Audit committee effectiveness: A synthesis of the empirical audit committee literature. *Journal of Accounting Literature, 21*, 38–75.

DeZoort, F. T., Hermanson, D. R., & Houston, R. W. (2003). Audit committee support for auditors: The effects of materiality justification and accounting precision. *Journal of Accounting and Public Policy, 22*, 175–199.

DeZoort, F. T., & Salterio, S. E. (2001). The effects of corporate governance experience and financial-reporting and audit knowledge on audit committee member's judgments. *Auditing: A Journal of Practice & Theory, 20*, 31–47.

Dopuch, N., King, R. R., & Schwartz, R. (2001). An experimental investigation of retention and rotation requirements. *Journal of Accounting Research, 39*, 93–117.

Dye, R. (1991). Informationally motivated auditor replacement. *Journal of Accounting and Economics, 14*, 347–374.

Dye, R. (1993). Auditing standards, legal liability and auditor wealth. *Journal of Political Economy, 101*, 877–914.

Elorietta, A. M. (2002). Disclosure and transparence accounting and auditing. Organization for Economic Co-operation and Development Third meeting of the Latin American Corporate Governance Roundtable, April 8–10, pp. 1–6.

Ettredge, M., & Greenberg, R. (1990). Determinants of fee cutting on initial audit engagements. *Journal of Accounting Research, 28*, 198–210.

Fulcrum Financial Inquiry. (2003). GAO kills mandatory auditor rotation. http://www.fulcruminquiry.com/article68.htm

Geiger, M. A., & Raghunandan, K. (2002). Auditor tenure and audit reporting failures. *Auditing: A Journal of Practice & Theory, 21*, 67–78.

General Accounting Office (GAO). (2003). Public accounting firms: Required study on the potential effects of mandatory audit firm rotation (GAO-04-216).

Herrick, T., & Barrionuevo, A. (2002). Were Enron and Andersen too close to allow the auditor to do its job? *Wall Street Journal*, January 21, pp.C1, C4.

Jennings, M. M., Pany, K., & Reckers, P. M. J. (2004). *Legislating auditor independence through corporate governance and audit firm rotation: Views of U.S. judges.* Working Paper. Arizona State University.

Johnstone, K. M., Sutton, M. H., & Warfield, T. D. (2001). Antecedents and consequences of independence risk: Framework for analysis. *Accounting Horizons, 15*, 1–18.

Kemp, R. S., Jr., Reckers, P. M. J., & Arrington, C. E. (1983). Bank credibility: The need to rotate auditors. *Journal of Retail Banking, 5*, 38–44.

Klein, A. (2002). Audit committee, board of director characteristics, and earnings management. *Journal of Accounting and Economics, 33*, 375–400.

Krishnamoorthy, G., Wright, A. M., & Cohen, J. (2002). Auditors' views on audit committees and financial reporting quality. *The CPA Journal, 72*, 56–66.

Mansi, S. A., Maxwell, W. F., & Miller, D. P. (2004). Does auditor quality and tenure matter to investors? Evidence from the bond market. *Journal of Accounting Research, 42*, 755–793.

Mautz, R. K., & Sharaf, H. A. (1961). *The philosophy of auditing.* American Accounting Association Monograph No. 6. Sarasota, FL: American Accounting Association.

Mayhew, B. W., & Pike, J. E. (2004). Does investor selection of auditors enhance auditor independence? *The Accounting Review, 79*, 797–822.

Moore, D. A., Loewenstein, G., Tanlu, L., & Bazerman, M. H. (2003). *Conflict of interest and the unconscious intrusion of bias.* Unpublished Working Paper.

Myers, J. N., Myers, L. A., & Omer, T. C. (2003a). Exploring the term of the auditor–client relationship and the quality of earnings: A case for mandatory audit firm rotation? *The Accounting Review, 78*, 779–800.

Myers, J. N., Myers, L. A., Palmrose, Z. V., & Scholz, S. (2003b). *Mandatory auditor rotation: Evidence from restatements.* Working Paper. University of Illinois at Urbana-Champaign.

Nelson, M. W. (2003). *A review of empirical conflicts-of-interest research in auditing.* Working Paper written for NSF/CBI Conference on Conflicts of Interest.

Nelson, M. W., Elliott, J. A., & Tarpley, R. L. (2002). Evidence from auditors about managers' and auditors' earnings management decisions. *The Accounting Review, 77*, 175–203.

Ng, T. B., & Tan, H. (2003). Effects of authoritative guidance availability and audit committee effectiveness on auditor's judgments in auditor–client negotiation context. *The Accounting Review, 78*, 801–818.

Palmrose, Z.-V. (1986). Litigation and independent auditors: The role of business failures and management fraud. *Auditing: A Journal of Practice & Theory, 6*, 90–103.

Palmrose, Z.-V. (1989). The relation of audit contract type to audit fees and hours. *The Accounting Review, 64*, 488–499.

Pany, K., & Reckers, P. M. J. (1987). Within- vs. between-subjects experimental designs: A study of demand effects. *Auditing: A Journal of Practice & Theory, 7*, 60–74.

Public Law 107-204. (2002). Public company accounting reform and investor protection act (Sarbanes-Oxley Act), , July 30, H.R. 3763.

Ramsey, I. (2001). Independence of Australian company auditors (Ramsey Report). Review of Current Australian Requirements and Proposals for reform to the Minister for Financial Services and Regulation, October.

Report of the Joint Disciplinary Task Team. (2002). The South African Institute of Chartered Accountants, May 8, pp. 16–17.

Securities and Exchange Commission. (2003, February 18). Standards Relating to Listed Company Audit Committees. 17 CFR Parts 228, 229, 240, 249, and 274. Release Nos. 33-8173; 34-47137; IC-25885; File No. S7-02-03.

Seidman, E. (2001, February 26). Prepared testimony for the U.S. Senate Committee on Banking, Housing, and Urban Affairs hearing on the failure of Superior Bank, FSB, Hinsdale, Illinois.

Shearman & Sterling. (2004). Corporate governance practices of the 1000 largest U.S. public companies. Found at http://www.shearman.com/cg_survey05/.

Shelby, R. (1985). *Hearings before the subcommittee on oversight and investigations and the committee on energy and commerce, 99th Congress.* First Session, February 20 and March 6. Untied States House of Representatives, Government Printing Office.

Simon, D. T., & Francis, J. R. (1988). The effects of auditor change on audit fees: Tests of price cutting and price recovery. *The Accounting Review, 63*, 255–269.

St. Pierre, K., & Anderson, J. A. (1984). An analysis of the factors associated with lawsuits against public accountants. *The Accounting Review, 59*, 242–263.

Stice, J. D. (1991). Using financial and market information to identify pre-engagement factors associated with lawsuits against auditors. *The Accounting Review, 66*, 516–533.

Taub, S. (2004). Best practices elude most audit committees: The corporate accounting watch-dogs still wrangle with how best to install confidence. CEO.com, April 2, p. 1.

Taylor, M. H., DeZoort, F. T., Munn, E., & Thomas, M. W. (2003). A proposed framework emphasizing auditor reliability over auditor independence. *Accounting Horizons, 17,* 257–266.

Wallace, W. A. (1981). The role of the audit in free and regulated markets. American Accounting Association. http://raw.rutgers.edu/raw/wallace/homepage.html

Watts, R. L., & Zimmerman, J. L. (1983). Agency problems, auditing and the theory of the firm: Some evidence. *Journal of Law and Economics, 26,* 613–633.

Winters, A. J. (1976). Looking at the audit firm rotation issue. *Management Accounting, 58,* 29–30.

Wolf, F. R., Tackett, J. A., & Claypool, G. A. (1999). Audit disaster futures: Antidotes for the expectations gap? *Managerial Auditing Journal, 14,* 468–478.

Zea, A. (2002). Study backs fears over audit firm rotation. Accountancy Age.com, August 6, pp. 1–2.

THE SECURITY MARKET'S REACTION TO FIRMS' QUARTERLY EARNINGS EVIDENCING VARYING DEGREES OF AUTOCORRELATION

Allen W. Bathke Jr., Kenneth S. Lorek and G. Lee Willinger

ABSTRACT

On a full sample basis, our results are consistent with a security market that significantly underestimates the magnitude of autocorrelation at the 1st and 4th lags where autocorrelation is high but estimates autocorrelation unbiasedly at lags 2 and 3 where autocorrelation is low. Reinforcing the full sample results, when we partition the sample firms into subsamples based upon the magnitude of first lag autocorrelation, we find results consistent with the security market significantly underestimating the level of autocorrelation at the 1st lag for the high autocorrelation subsample of firms, but not for the moderate and low autocorrelation subsamples.

Advances in Accounting, Volume 22, 29–43
Copyright © 2006 by Elsevier Ltd.
All rights of reproduction in any form reserved
ISSN: 0882-6110/doi:10.1016/S0882-6110(06)22002-9

1. INTRODUCTION

The stock market under-reaction to quarterly earnings documented by Bernard and Thomas (1990) (hereafter BT) and Ball and Bartov (1996) (hereafter BB), among others, is a topic that has fueled considerable research efforts aimed at examining the causes of the so-called, post-earnings announcement drift. We extend this research stream by examining whether the security market reacts differentially to varying levels of first lag autocorrelation in the seasonally differenced quarterly earnings series. Our objective is to determine whether the security market's reaction is related to the *magnitude* of the aforementioned autocorrelation.

We corroborate the findings of BB that the security market acts as if it recognizes the correct sign of autocorrelation in seasonally differenced quarterly earnings across lags 1 through 4 but underestimates its magnitude overall. Our findings on a full sample basis are consistent with a security market that acts as if it: (1) significantly underestimates the autocorrelation in seasonally differenced quarterly earnings at the 1st and 4th (seasonal) lags (where the level of autocorrelation is substantially higher than at lags 2 and 3), and (2) estimates the level of autocorrelation unbiasedly at lags 2 and 3 (where the level of autocorrelation is relatively lower). By partitioning our sample into low, moderate, and high autocorrelation subsets, we are able to assess more precisely whether the security market processes varying levels of autocorrelation differentially.[1] The security market significantly underestimates autocorrelation at the 1st lag only for the high autocorrelation subset. This finding suggests that the extent of security market underestimation is linked to the *magnitude* of 1st lag autocorrelation in the seasonally differenced quarterly earnings series. Our results are generally consistent with findings in the psychology literature (see e.g., Beach & Scopp, 1966; Jennings, Amabile, & Ross, 1982) since there was greater underweighting when autocorrelation was strongly present than when it was weakly present. It appears that the behavioral biases in information processing reported in laboratory studies at the individual level in the accounting literature (see Maines & Hand, 1996) do not perfectly manifest themselves in the aggregate in capital market settings.

The remainder of this paper is organized as follows. In the next section, we provide background information that contains a literature review of works most salient to the present study. We discuss research design issues in Section 3 and provide our empirical findings in Section 4. Finally, in the final section of the paper, we discuss the limitations and conclusions of our findings as well as suggesting some avenues for future research.

2. BACKGROUND

The accounting literature is replete with evidence consistent with the notion that the security market processes complex information in a timely fashion. The security market's reaction to information pertaining to earnings is evidenced by the work of Ball and Brown (1968), Foster (1977), BT (1990), BB (1996), Soffer and Lys (1999), and Brown and Han (2000), among others.[2] BT find, however, that the security market reacts to changes in quarterly earnings that should *not* have conveyed new information to the market. BT's results are indicative of stock prices that: (1) do not fully reflect all implications of current earnings for future earnings, and (2) ignore some value-relevant information at the time that it becomes publicly available.

BT examined the ability to predict abnormal returns conditional upon values of the autoregressive (φ) and moving-average (θ) parameters of the Brown and Rozeff (1979) ARIMA model which is of particular importance to our current study. In customary (pdq) × (PDQ) notation, the Brown and Rozeff model is a $(100) \times (011)$ ARIMA process, where p, P represent the regular and seasonal autoregressive parameters; d, D represent regular and seasonal differencing; and q, Q represent the regular and seasonal moving average parameters, respectively (BT, 1990, pp. 329–331). For each parameter, they stratified their sample into quartiles based on the magnitude of that parameter. While differences in abnormal returns were observed, they were not statistically significant. We also stratify our sample firms, not on the basis of parameter values, but on first lag autocorrelation of the seasonally differenced quarterly earnings series. BT's approach is subject to measurement error in the estimation of the parameters in that cross-sectional differences in time-series model parameters are typically not predictable out of sample.[3] Our tests on the first lag autocorrelation of the seasonally differenced quarterly earnings series, however, serve to mitigate measurement error since we do not require model identification or the estimation of parameters.

BB extend the work of BT by analyzing the extent to which the security market uses information related to past quarterly earnings in forming expectations of future quarterly earnings. BB find that the security market acts as if it: (1) recognizes that the seasonal random walk model is not the appropriate earnings expectation model; (2) is aware of the autocorrelation in seasonally differenced quarterly earnings across lags 1 through 4; (3) recognizes the correct sign of the autocorrelation across lags 1 through 4; but (4) underestimates the magnitude of the autocorrelation overall.

Maines and Hand (1996) (hereafter, MH), motivated by the aforementioned findings from capital market research as well as research in cognitive psychology, employed MBA students as subjects in a laboratory study. Specifically, they investigated whether investors underestimate the degree of autocorrelation in some instances but overestimate it in others, a so-called contextual interpretation. Interestingly, research in cognitive psychology indicates that individuals underestimate the level of correlation in data (see e.g., Beach & Scopp, 1966; Jennings et al., 1982). Consistent with such underestimation, research also shows that individuals are unable to detect low levels of correlation in data. In contrast to the aforementioned findings in the psychology literature as well as MH's priors (see MH's stated hypothesis (h2a, p. 322)), MH find that, on average, subjects overweighted autocorrelation when it was low or nonexistent, appropriately weighted it when it was moderate, and underweighted it when it was high. We assess whether the findings of MH, obtained at the individual level in a laboratory setting, can be generalized to the aggregate level in a security-market setting. Our analysis provides an important triangulation of the laboratory findings of MH by introducing capital-market evidence on the robustness of the contextual interpretation of the market's under-reaction to quarterly earnings.

Brown and Han (2000) identified a number of firms whose quarterly earnings time-series properties differ systematically from the seasonal behavior exemplified by the seasonal random walk model. They found that 16% and 18% of their sample firms exhibited nonseasonal quarterly earnings patterns using a 1961–1983 and 1961–1988 estimation period, respectively. They adopted a first-order autoregressive structure [i.e., AR(1)] for these firms and examined whether stock prices fully reflect the implications of current quarterly earnings for future quarterly earnings for firms whose quarterly earnings are nonseasonal. Rather than identifying nonseasonal firms, however, we partition sample firms on the basis of the magnitude of the first lag autocorrelation of seasonally differenced quarterly earnings. Once again, our approach is not dependent upon the descriptive validity of a particular ARIMA model nor is it subject to measurement error in the estimation of any parameters.

3. RESEARCH DESIGN ISSUES

We construct two estimates of the magnitude of autocorrelation in seasonally differenced quarterly earnings for the full sample at each of the first four lags. Specifically, we compare the implied security market estimate of the level of autocorrelation in seasonally differenced quarterly earnings to the observed level of autocorrelation (i.e., time-series estimate) at various lags. This allows us to assess whether the market appears to underestimate (overestimate or estimate unbiasedly) the level of autocorrelation at a particular lag. Since the magnitude of correlation should differ across lags (i.e., the correlation should be higher at lags 1 and 4 relative to lags 2 and 3), it also allows us to assess whether the magnitude of autocorrelation affects the implied security market estimate.

We adopt similar notation and features of the methodology of BB for comparative purposes (see the Appendix). Unlike BB we control for the differential 1st lag autocorrelation in seasonally differenced quarterly earnings by partitioning sample firms with respect to the 1st lag autocorrelation's magnitude (i.e., low, moderate, and high). This enables us to test the extent to which the security market underestimates autocorrelation in seasonally differenced quarterly earnings across sample firms whose 1st lag autocorrelation patterns vary.

The appendix includes discussion of: (1) the seasonal random walk with drift model (SRWD) that we employ (see Eq. (A1)); (2) the earnings upon earnings regression model that provides the time-series estimates of β at lags 1 through 4 (see Eq. (A3)); and (3) the security return upon earnings regression model that enables us to calculate the implied security market estimates of the aforementioned time-series β (see Eq. (A4)). We are particularly interested in the time-series versus implied market estimates of the first (adjacent) lag β given evidence from the time-series literature that this lag exhibits autocorrelation significantly different from zero (e.g., as opposed to the second lag whose β is typically insignificantly different from zero).

Our tests assess whether BB's finding that the market systematically underestimates autocorrelation in seasonally differenced quarterly earnings is affected by the magnitude of first lag autocorrelation. For example, is BB's underestimation finding sufficiently robust to be operative across low, moderate, and high levels of autocorrelation? Or is underestimation confined to firms that exhibit particular autocorrelation patterns? We also contrast our security market results with the laboratory findings obtained using MBA subjects in the MH study.

4. EMPIRICAL RESULTS

Sampling Procedures

We selected a sample of calendar year-end, New York and American Stock Exchange firms from the Quarterly *COMPUSTAT* tapes. Our proxy for earnings was quarterly net income before extraordinary items, consistent with BT. We required each sample firm to have a complete quarterly earnings history from the first quarter of 1978 through the fourth quarter of 1997 (i.e., 20 years = 80 quarters). These filters resulted in a test sample of 536 firms for the 20-year period, or 42,880 firm/quarter observations (i.e., 536 firms × 80 quarters).

Variability in Autocorrelation

We estimated Eq. (A3) in the appendix on a time-series basis individually for each sample firm, regressing current period *SUE* on lagged *SUEs*. Similar to both BT (1990, p. 322) and BB (1996, p. 327) all regressions were run using SUE deciles for both dependent and independent variables. The most recent 66 observations (i.e., $66 = 80-10-4$) for each firm were employed since 10 quarters were used to estimate a drift term and standard deviation and 4 quarters were used to determine the independent variables (i.e., forecast errors for lags $1-4$). This resulted in the utilization of 35,376 firm/quarter observations (i.e., 536 firms × 66 observations) in the estimation of the time-series regressions.

Table 1 provides descriptive information on the variability of the standardized value of the b_1 coefficient in Eq. (A3). We focus on the b_1 coefficient, as opposed to the b_2-b_4 coefficients, because its forecast errors have the greatest impact on one-quarter-ahead earnings forecasts (see Soffer & Lys,

Table 1. Descriptive Evidence on Standardized b_1 Coefficient in Eq. (A3)[a] ($n = 536$).

$$SUE_{i,t} = b_0 + b_1 SUE_{i,t-1} + b_2 SUE_{i,t-2} + b_3 SUE_{i,t-3} + b_4 SUE_{i,t-4} + e_{i,t}$$

b_1 *Values*
Mean = 2.799
Median = 2.775
Minimum = −0.847
Maximum = 7.463
First Quartile (25%) = 1.745
Third Quartile (75%) = 3.765

[a]Variables are defined as in Ball and Bartov (1996). $SUE_{i,t}$ is the forecast error based on a seasonal random walk with drift model for firm i in quarter t. For each quarter the forecast error for each firm is scaled by the standard deviation of earnings from the estimation period. Forecast errors for all firms for a given quarter are ranked from highest to lowest and then partitioned into deciles. The deciles are then assigned values between 0 and 1, with 1 representing the highest decile. All regressions use the decile values as the dependent and independent variables.

1999). Moreover, there is considerable evidence in the time-series literature (see Brown, 1993, among others) documenting the pervasiveness of quarter-to-quarter or adjacent autocorrelation in the quarterly earnings series that is captured by the b_1 coefficient. We observe considerable variability in the b_1 coefficient, which captures the autocorrelation in the seasonally differenced quarterly earnings series. Specifically, b_1 coefficient values range from 0.847 to 7.463 with mean (median) values of 2.799 (2.775).[4]

We partitioned test sample firms on the basis of the magnitude of the b_1 coefficient to obtain three subsets of firms: those with low, moderate and high levels of autocorrelation in the quarterly earnings series. Specifically, sample firms that exhibited values of $b_1 < 2$ were classified as low ($n = 150$), those that exhibited b_1 values between 2–3 were classified as moderate ($n = 143$), and those that exhibited values of $b_1 > 3$ were classified as high ($n = 243$).[5]

Time-Series Estimates

Consistent with BT and BB, we ranked *SUEs* for all sample firms in a given quarter from highest to lowest and partitioned them into deciles. The deciles were then assigned values between 0 and 1, with 1 representing the highest decile. Decile rankings of *SUEs* (for both the dependent variable and the independent variables) were used to estimate Eq. (A3) in the Appendix.

Eq. (A3) was estimated initially on a pooled, cross-sectional, time-series basis for the entire sample of 536 firms then separately for the subgroups evidencing low, moderate and high levels of autocorrelation to obtain the time-series estimates of the magnitude of the autocorrelation in seasonally differenced quarterly earnings. The results for the full sample are provided first in Panel A of Table 2. The signs and magnitudes of the coefficients are similar to those reported in extant work.[6] As expected, we observe positive correlation at each of the first three lags and negative correlation at the fourth lag (i.e., 0.3574, 0.1389, 0.0833, −0.2631). There is a monotonic decline in the level of correlation from the 1st to the 3rd lag and a sharply negative correlation at lag 4, consistent with expectations. These results indicate that there is a positive, diminishing relation between the current period's forecast error from the SRWD model and each of the three previous forecast errors. In contrast, there is a negative relation between the current period forecast error and the forecast error from the corresponding quarter of the prior fiscal year. We also note that the impact of the first-order correlation is substantially greater than lags 2–3 as well as the seasonal lag of 4 which serves to reinforce our strategy of partitioning the sample on the basis of the b_1 coefficient.

Table 2.   Relation of Current Period to Lagged $SUEs$[a].

$SUE_{i,t} = b_0 + b_1 SUE_{i,t-1} + b_2 SUE_{i,t-2} + b_3 SUE_{i,t-3} + b_4 SUE_{i,t-4} + e_{i,t}$

	No. of Observations	b_0	b_1	b_2	b_3	b_4	Adjusted R^2
Panel A: Full Sample							
	35,376	0.3755	0.3574	0.1389	0.0833	−0.2631	22.82%
Panel B: By Level of Autocorrelation							
Low	9,900	0.4977	0.1543	0.1199	0.1030	−0.2822	11.55%
Moderate	9,438	0.4067	0.3222	0.1318	0.0640	−0.2616	19.78%
High	16,038	0.3098	0.5176	0.0923	0.0529	−0.2280	34.44%

Note: All coefficients are significant at the 0.01 level.
[a]Variables are defined as in Ball and Bartov (1996). $SUE_{i,t}$ is the forecast error based on a seasonal random walk with drift model for firm i in quarter t. For each quarter the forecast error for each firm is scaled by the standard deviation of earnings from the estimation period. Forecast errors for all firms for a given quarter are ranked from highest to lowest and then partitioned into deciles. The deciles are then assigned values between 0 and 1, with 1 representing the highest decile. All regressions use the decile values as the dependent and independent variables.

Panel B provides similar analyses after the sample has been partitioned into subsamples of firms that exhibit low, moderate or high levels of 1st lag autocorrelation. The partitioning scheme that we employed successfully induced the expected monotonic increase in the magnitude of the b_1 coefficient across subsamples (i.e., 0.1543, 0.3222, and 0.5176). We observe that the forecast error from the SRWD model at lag 1 has the greatest impact on forecasts of future quarterly earnings (relative to lags 2–3) consistent with the results of Soffer and Lys (1999).

Implied Security Market Estimates

We next considered the impact of these differential levels of autocorrelation upon the security market's ability to form such estimates. (See the Appendix for a detailed explanation of precisely how these estimates are derived.) Specifically, we analyze whether the magnitude of the autocorrelation in quarterly earnings affects the security market's estimate of such correlation. We estimated Eq. (A4), in the Appendix on a pooled, cross-sectional, time-series basis for the entire sample of 536 firms as well as for each of the three subsamples. These results are reported in Table 3.

Table 3 reports the relation between lagged earnings and returns at the current earnings announcement, controlling for current earnings. Panel A

Table 3. Relation Between Current Period *CAR* and Current and Past *SUEs*[a].

$$CAR_{i,t} = k + a_0 SUE_{i,t} + a_1 SUE_{i,t-1} + a_2 SUE_{i,t-2} + a_3 SUE_{i,t-3} + a_4 SUE_{i,t-4} + e_{i,t}$$

	k	a_0	a_1	a_2	a_3	a_4	Adjusted R^2
Panel A: Full Sample							
$n = 35{,}376$	−1.053**	3.322**	−0.571**	−0.510**	−0.389**	0.449**	3.77%
Panel B: By Level of Autocorrelation							
Low $n = 9{,}900$	−1.068**	2.406**	−0.171	−0.199	−0.344*	0.466**	3.20%
Moderate $n = 9{,}438$	−0.871**	3.254**	−0.807**	−0.561**	−0.377*	0.600**	3.25%
High $n = 16{,}038$	−1.149**	4.002**	−0.820**	−0.734**	−0.197	0.251	4.44%

[a]Variables are defined as in Ball and Bartov (1996). $CAR_{i,t}$ is sum of the daily abnormal returns for days −2,−1 and 0 for firm i in quarter t. Daily abnormal returns represent the difference between the actual return for that firm and the returns of the NYSE-AMEX firms of the same size decile, based on January 1, market values of equity. $CAR_{i,t}$ is regressed on the current quarter forecast error and the forecast errors from the preceding 4 quarters, i.e., the regression INCLUDES the forecast error for the current quarter. Consistent with Ball and Bartov all coefficients are multiplied by 100. Please see Table 2 for a description of the *SUEs*.
n = number of observations.
*Significant at the 0.05 level.
**Significant at the 0.01 level.

results on the full sample are consistent with lagged *SUEs* (a_1–a_4) contributing significantly to the explanatory power of the regression of returns on current *SUE*. Similar to BB, the coefficients of the four lagged *SUEs* all have the predicted reversed signs (−, −, −, +) relative to Table 2 and are significant at the 1% level. When the sample is stratified by level of first lag autocorrelation in Panel B, all 12 signs (i.e., four lags for each of the three subsamples) are consistent with investors recognizing the signs of autocorrelation in seasonally differenced quarterly earnings. We note that the moderate and high autocorrelation subsamples exhibit a_1 coefficients that are significant at the 1% level whereas the a_1 coefficient for the low autocorrelation subset is insignificant. These results are consistent with a security market that reacts differentially to firms that exhibit varying levels of autocorrelation in their quarterly earnings.

Time-Series versus Security-Market Estimates

Table 4 compares the time-series estimate of autocorrelation in seasonally differenced quarterly earnings to the implied security market estimate. For

Table 4.   Time-Series Estimates and Implied Security Market Estimates of Autocorrelation in the Seasonally Differenced Quarterly Earnings Series.

	Time Series Estimate	Implied Security Market Estimate	Under-or Overestimation	t-Statistic p-Values
Panel A: Full Sample				
Lag 1	0.3574	0.1719	0.1855 Underestimation	0.0001
2	0.1389	0.1535	0.0146 Overestimation	0.5679
3	0.0833	0.1171	0.0338 Overestimation	0.3199
4	−0.2631	−0.1352	0.1279 Underestimation	0.0010
Panel B: By Level of Autocorrelation				
Low				
Lag 1	0.1543	0.0711	0.0832 Underestimation	0.6272
2	0.1199	0.0827	0.0372 Underestimation	0.6330
3	0.1030	0.1430	0.0400 Overestimation	0.1728
4	−0.2822	−0.1937	0.0885 Underestimation	0.6449
Moderate				
Lag 1	0.3222	0.2480	0.0742 Underestimation	0.6471
2	0.1318	0.1724	0.0406 Overestimation	0.2201
3	0.0640	0.1159	0.0519 Overestimation	0.9790
4	−0.2616	−0.1844	0.0772 Underestimation	0.1163
High				
Lag 1	0.5176	0.2049	0.3127 Underestimation	0.1071
2	0.0923	0.1834	0.0911 Overestimation	0.2153
3	0.0529	0.0492	0.0037 Underestimation	0.4107
4	−0.2280	−0.0627	0.1653 Underestimation	0.0444

Note: Time-series estimates are based on Eq. (A3) as reported in Table 2. Implied security market estimates are based on the ratio of the coefficient for the lagged *SUE* to the negative coefficient of the current period *SUE* from Eq. (A4) as reported in Table 3, i.e., $a_1/−a_0$, $a_2/−a_0$, $a_3/−a_0$ and $a_4/−a_0$.

the full sample in Panel A, the market acts as if it uses coefficients of 0.1719, 0.1535, 0.1171 and −0.1352 compared to the respective time-series estimates of 0.3574, 0.1389, 0.0833 and −0.2631. These results suggest that while the market is aware of the existence and sign pattern of autocorrelation, it significantly underestimates its magnitude at lag 1 ($p = 0.0001$) and lag 4 ($p = 0.0010$) while estimating unbiasedly its magnitude at lag 2 ($p = 0.5679$) and lag 3 ($p = 0.3199$).[7]

Panel B of Table 4 compares the time-series and implied security market estimates of autocorrelation for the subsamples partitioned on the basis of the magnitude of the autocorrelation at the first lag. At the first lag, the time-series estimates of the autocorrelation are 0.1543, 0.3222 and 0.5176, for the low, moderate and high autocorrelation subsamples, respectively. The implied security market estimates of the autocorrelation are 0.0711, 0.2480 and 0.2049, for the low, moderate and high autocorrelation subsamples, respectively. At lag one, only for the high autocorrelation subsample are the results consistent with the security market significantly underestimating the magnitude of correlation (albeit marginally, p value of 0.1071). Our results suggest that security market reaction is sensitive to the *magnitude* of the autocorrelation in seasonally differenced quarterly earnings. Finally, as expected, the results at the other lags (e.g., at the second lag) are mixed.[8]

Panel B's results, unlike those of MH, are consistent with findings in the psychology literature (e.g., Beach & Scopp, 1966; Jennings et al., 1982) since the security market consistently underestimates autocorrelation at the 1st lag regardless of the level of autocorrelation. Consistent with MH, the high autocorrelation subset exhibits the greatest degree of underestimation at the 1st lag (0.3127) and the underestimation is significant (albeit marginally, $p = 0.1071$). However, MH found overestimation when the level of autocorrelation was low, unlike our findings. Further research is necessary to explore precisely why information processing findings reported in laboratory studies at the individual level like MH do not perfectly manifest themselves in the aggregate in capital market settings.

5. CONCLUDING REMARKS

Any empirical financial-based work like ours that invokes sampling filters spanning two decades is subject to a potential survivorship bias that limits the external validity of its findings. While our results pertain to a large number of surviving firms, newly formed firms and failed firms are not represented in our sample.[9] With these caveats in mind, our findings shed light on whether the security market's reaction is related to the *magnitude* of the first lag autocorrelation in the seasonally differenced quarterly earnings series of our sample firms.

We provide new evidence with regard to the underestimation phenomenon documented by BB. Our empirical results on a full sample basis are consistent with a security market that acts as if it (1) significantly underestimates the autocorrelation at the 1st and 4th (seasonal) lags (where the level of autocorrelation is substantially higher than at lags 2 and 3), and (2) estimates autocorrelation at lags 2 and 3 (where the level of autocorrelation is extremely low) in an unbiased fashion. We partition our sample into three subsets (i.e., low, moderate and high) based upon the magnitude of the 1st lag autocorrelation in seasonally differenced quarterly earnings. By doing so, we are able to determine that the security market significantly underestimates the level of autocorrelation at the 1st lag for the *high* autocorrelation subset of firms, but not the low and moderate autocorrelation subsets.

Our security market results reported in Table 4 also provide new evidence consistent with greater underweighting of the autocorrelation in seasonal differences when autocorrelation is strongly present (0.3127 for firms with a high level of autocorrelation at lag 1) than when it is weakly present (0.0832 for firms with a low level of autocorrelation at lag 1). Our security market results are consistent with the psychology literature referenced in MH, MH's stated hypothesis (H2a, p. 322), as well as the security market results pertaining to underweighting of autocorrelation reported by BB, among others. Yet, our findings are inconsistent with MH who report that human subjects overestimate autocorrelation when it is weak or nonexistent.

What might explain the differences in our security market results and the laboratory findings of MH? Such differences may be simply attributable to the so-called fallacy of composition. That is, behavioral biases in information processing detected in individuals in laboratory studies may not perfectly manifest themselves in the aggregate in capital market settings. Alternatively, our partitioning of firms in the low autocorrelation subsample assures that such firms exhibit relatively lower levels of 1st lag autocorrelation than firms in the moderate or high subsamples. However, this does not assure that such low autocorrelation firms exhibit low levels of autocorrelation on an absolute basis. For example, the level of autocorrelation at lag 1 for firms in the low subset (0.1543) exceeds the level of autocorrelation for lags 2 and 3 for the full sample (0.1389 and 0.0833) reported in Table 4. Such differences are unavoidable given our employment of archival data versus the laboratory study of MH where they manipulate the level of autocorrelation via simulation and/or the selection of an individual firm that exhibits low autocorrelation. Further research is necessary to assess the impact of such different research methods.

Similar to BB and BT, our findings raise more questions for future research. For example, it might be interesting to assess whether the security market consistently under-or overestimates the parameters in ARIMA-based quarterly earnings expectation models such as those attributed to Brown and Rozeff (1979) or Foster (1977). Further research directed at isolating behavioral biases in information processing that appear to manifest themselves in aggregate security-market behavior (i.e., underestimation of high levels of autocorrelation at lag 1) versus those that do not carry over to aggregate security-market behavior (i. e., overestimation of low levels of autocorrelation at lag 1) may also prove informative.

NOTES

1. The partitioning scheme we employed relied solely on autocorrelation at the first lag. Therefore, our lag 4 (as well as lag 2 or lag 3) comparisons across subgroups are conditional upon the first lag partitions.

2. While the literature addressing the post-earnings announcement drift is voluminous, we limit our discussion to a smaller subset of studies that are most relevant to the present study. See Kothari (2001) for a review of this literature.

3. See Albrecht, Lookabill, and McKeown (1977), Foster (1977), and Watts and Leftwich (1977) for empirical evidence on this issue.

4. We computed another proxy to capture the variability in autocorrelation of seasonally differenced quarterly earnings, namely the first lag of the sample autocorrelation function of seasonally differenced quarterly earnings. It also evidenced considerable variability across sample firms with a range of −0.299 to 0.885.

5. Alternate partitioning schemes resulted in findings qualitatively similar to those that we report in Table 1.

6. The level of explained variation is slightly less than that of earlier research (i.e., 22.82% in the current study versus 28.57% in BB).

7. We ran cross-sectional regressions for each quarter in the holdout period for the models depicted in Tables 2 and 3 to derive β coefficients for the time-series estimates and the implied security market estimates of autocorrelation in seasonally differenced quarterly earnings. The t-statistic p-values, which are used to assess whether the aforementioned estimates differ are presented in the last column of Table 4.

8. Recall that the partitioning scheme we employed relied solely on autocorrelation at the first lag. Therefore, our comparisons across subgroups at other lags (e.g., second lag) are conditional upon the first lag partitions.

9. Other possible reasons for our security market results include: (1) measurement error induced by over-differencing of a stationary time series (see Jacob, Lys, & Sabino, 2000) and, (2) measurement error induced by our partitioning of sample firms into low, medium and high autocorrelation subsets.

REFERENCES

Albrecht, S. L., Lookabill, L., & McKeown, J. (1977). The time series properties of annual earnings. *Journal of Accounting Research, 15*, 226–244.

Ball, R., & Bartov, E. (1996). How naïve is the stock market's use of earnings information? *Journal of Accounting and Economics, 21*, 319–337.

Ball, R., & Brown, P. (1968). An empirical evaluation of accounting income numbers. *Journal of Accounting Research, 6*, 159–178.

Beach, L. R., & Scopp, T. S. (1966). Inferences about correlations. *Psychonomic Science, 6*, 253–254.

Bernard, V. L., & Thomas, J. (1990). Evidence that stock prices do not fully reflect the implications of current earnings for future earnings. *Journal of Accounting and Economics, 13*, 305–340.

Brown, L. D., & Rozeff, M. (1979). Univariate time-series models of quarterly accounting earnings per share: A proposed model. *Journal of Accounting Research, 17*(Spring), 179–189.

Brown, L. D. (1993). Earnings forecasting research: Its implications for capital markets research. *International Journal of Forecasting, 9*, 295–320.

Brown, L., & Han, J. (2000). Do stock prices fully reflect the implications of current earnings for future earnings for AR1 firms? *Journal of Accounting Research, 38*, 149–164.

Foster, G. (1977). Quarterly accounting data: Time-series properties and predictive-ability results. *The Accounting Review, 52*, 1–21.

Jacob, J., Lys, T., & Sabino, J. (2000). Autocorrelation structure of forecast errors from time-series models: Alternative assessments of the causes of post-earnings announcement drift. *Journal of Accounting and Economics, 28*, 329–358.

Jennings, D. L., Amabile, T., & Ross, L. (1982). Informal covariation assessment: data-based versus theory-based judgments. In: D. Kahneman, P. Slovic & A. Tversky (Eds), *Judgment under uncertainty: Heuristics and biases* (pp. 211–230). New York, NY: Cambridge University Press.

Kothari, S. P. (2001). Capital markets research in accounting. *Journal of Accounting and Economics, 31*(September), 105–231.

Maines, L. A., & Hand, J. R. M. (1996). Individuals' perceptions and misperceptions of time-series properties of quarterly earnings. *The Accounting Review, 71*, 317–336.

Soffer, L. C., & Lys, T. (1999). Post-earnings announcement drift and the dissemination of predictable information. *Contemporary Accounting Research, 16*, 305–331.

Watts, R., & Leftwich, R. W. (1977). The time series of annual accounting earnings. *Journal of Accounting Research, 15*, 253–271.

APPENDIX

We explain two approaches to estimating the magnitude of the level of autocorrelation in seasonally differenced quarterly earnings in this appendix. Since the correlations in the forecast errors from the SRWD model provide estimates of the autocorrelation in seasonally differenced quarterly earnings (i.e., the time-series estimates), we start with a description of this model. The SRWD model forecasts quarterly earnings for firm i and quarter t as follows:

$$F(EARN_{i,t}) = EARN_{i,t-4} + d_i \qquad (A1)$$

where

$F(EARN_{i,t})$ = forecast of quarterly earnings for firm i and quarter t
$EARN_{i,t-4}$ = quarterly earnings for firm i for quarter $t-4$
d_i = drift (trend) for firm i

Based on the SRWD model, the unexpected earnings for firm i in quarter t, $UE_{i,t}$, is the forecast error for firm i and quarter t, i.e., actual quarterly earnings, $EARN_{i,t}$, less forecasted quarterly earnings as shown below:

$$UE_{i,t} = EARN_{i,t} - F(EARN_{i,t}) \tag{A2}$$

Consistent with BB and BT, $UE_{i,t}$ is then scaled by the standard deviation of earnings for firm i to produce a standardized measure of unexpected earnings, $SUE_{i,t}$. These firm-specific measures are then partitioned into deciles. BB indicate that the decile rankings of the current period standardized unexpected earnings, $SUE_{i,t}$, can be viewed as a function of past SUEs as follows:

$$SUE_{i,t} = b_0 + b_1 SUE_{i,t-1} + b_2 SUE_{i,t-2} + b_3 SUE_{i,t-3} + b_4 SUE_{i,t-4} + e_{i,t} \tag{A3}$$

where $SUE_{i,t}$ is the forecast error (i.e., decile ranking) based on a SRWD model for firm i in quarter t.

The regression coefficients from Eq. (A3) provide convenient estimates of the correlation between the current period forecast error from the SRWD model and prior period forecast errors. These regression estimates from Eq. (A3) provide the time-series estimates of autocorrelation in seasonally differenced quarterly earnings. These time-series estimates are compared to the implied security market estimates of this correlation.

Per BB, the expectation model implicit in the security market price reaction to current earnings can be examined by estimating the following model:

$$CAR_{i,t} = k + a_0 SUE_{i,t} + a_1 SUE_{i,t-1} + a_2 SUE_{i,t-2}$$
$$+ a_3 SUE_{i,t-3} + a_4 SUE_{i,t-4} + e_{i,t} \tag{A4}$$

where $CAR_{i,t}$ is the sum of the daily abnormal security returns for days -2, -1 and 0 for firm i and quarter t.

Based on Eq. (A4), we can develop proxies for the implied security market estimates of the autocorrelation in seasonally differenced quarterly earnings. The latter were derived by dividing the respective β coefficients for lagged SUEs in Eq. (A4) (i.e., a_1, a_2, a_3, and a_4) by the negative coefficient of the current period SUE from Eq. (A4) (i.e., $-a_0$). Consistent with BB (see p. 329), we compared the time-series estimates of β in Eq. (A3) with the implied security market estimates of beta.

EVIDENCE FROM AUDITORS ABOUT THE CAUSES OF INACCURATE BUDGETS: DO CLIENTS CAUSE BUDGET OVERRUNS?

Steve Buchheit, William R. Pasewark and Jerry R. Strawser

SUMMARY

The goal of this study is to identify primary drivers of audit budget inaccuracy. Our results show a positive association between using the budget for evaluative purposes and favorable (or less unfavorable) budget variances. In addition, despite the fact that our sample is comprised of continuing audit engagements, weak client controls and relatively uncooperative clients have the greatest impact on unfavorable budget variances. Our results suggest audit budgets insufficiently accommodate client-controlled factors.

INTRODUCTION

Labor costs are the largest single cost incurred by international accounting firms (O'Keefe, King, & Gaver, 1994), making the audit time budget a

Advances in Accounting, Volume 22, 45–66
ISSN: 0882-6110/doi:10.1016/S0882-6110(06)22003-0

critical planning tool. When audit budgets are inaccurate, accounting firms can experience an excess or shortage of required personnel on individual audit jobs resulting in an opportunity cost to the firm. Further, if audit budgets are used to establish audit fees (in a fixed fee engagement) or to provide fee estimates (in a variable fee engagement), then inaccurate budgets may affect planned profitability or may result in client dissatisfaction.

Audit budget accuracy has related implications for audit quality. Specifically, audit staff may feel pressure to complete an audit quickly in order to "meet the budget." The Commission on Auditors' Responsibilities (1978) and the Panel on Audit Effectiveness (POB, 2000) both express concern that the pressure to complete an audit quickly potentially results in substandard audits and academic research suggests these concerns are potentially well-founded (Coram, Ng, & Woodliff, 2004). Further, budget-related pressures may affect job satisfaction and turnover of audit staff (POB, 2000). Although numerous dimensions of audit budgets have been investigated, little research sheds light on the relative importance of factors that influence audit budget accuracy.

This study is an exploratory analysis of data obtained using a questionnaire in which 57 senior auditors from two international accounting firms answered questions related to budget accuracy. Given the documented misfit between research and practice in certain general budgeting areas (Selto & Widener, 2004), the goal of this study is to identify the major determinants of inaccurate audit budgets. By identifying significant determinants of inaccurate audit budgets, future audit budget research can better focus on issues relevant to practitioners.

We gathered information about a wide range of potential budget influencing variables identified in (1) specific audit budget literature, (2) general budget literature (i.e., areas outside of auditing), and (3) discussions with audit managers and partners. From these sources, we created a survey instrument designed to measure 13 separate factors that potentially influence audit budget accuracy. We find only three factors that exhibit a strong relationship with audit budget accuracy.

First, although respondents, on average, believed that budget outcomes did not factor into remuneration at their firms, we find that using the budget for performance evaluation is significantly related to favorable (or less unfavorable) budget variances.[1] Extensive prior research (Kelley & Margheim, 1990; McNair, 1991; Ponemon, 1992), industry discussion,[2] and firm policies point out the potential dangers of emphasizing budget outcomes to performance evaluation. However, the results of this study point out a continued need to monitor potential dysfunctional audit behavior related to budget outcomes.

In addition, we find that relatively weak client internal controls and a relative lack of client cooperation are related to unfavorable budget variances. Interestingly, these factors were identified through discussions with audit partners and managers and, to our knowledge, have not been addressed in previous audit budget accuracy literature.[3] Given that our data come from continuing audit engagements, our results suggest that audit budgets are, on average, insufficient to accommodate these client-controlled drivers of audit effort in spite of past experience with the client that potentially should have enabled the firm to identify and prepare for these drivers.

The remainder of the paper is organized as follows. The next section discusses how we identified factors that potentially influence budget accuracy. The third section describes our data collection process and results are presented in the fourth section. The final section summarizes our findings, discusses limitations of our results, and suggests directions for future research.

DETERMINING THE CAUSE OF AUDIT BUDGET VARIANCES

Previous research shows the audit profession typically experiences budget variances of relatively high magnitudes, suggesting relatively inaccurate audit budgets. In addition, these variances are typically budget overruns (i.e., instances in which actual audit hours exceed budgeted audit hours). For example, Gist and Davidson (1999) report results from 62 audits where budget overruns averaged 11.5% with individual budget variances ranging from 18% under budget to 226% over budget. Pasewark and Strawser (1994) report results from 60 audits where budget overruns averaged 12.3% with individual budget variances ranging from 10% under budget to 30% over budget. More recently, Ettredge, Bedard, and Johnstone (2004) report results from 53 audits where budget overruns averaged only 7.95% with individual budget variances ranging from 31.92% under budget to 71.48% over budget. In addition, past research suggests that auditors sometimes feel pressure to underreport actual hours worked (Margheim & Pany, 1986; Kelley & Margheim, 1990; McNair, 1991; Ponemon, 1992; Houston, 1999). As such, the budget overruns reported in these studies may be understated.

The quality of budget-based decisions depends on the accuracy and reliability of ex-ante budget figures. In other words, if relatively large budget variances are the norm rather than the exception, then budget information may not be useful in evaluating staff performance or planning subsequent operations. As previously discussed, the tendency toward budget overruns may also result in client dissatisfaction (e.g., higher than expected fees) or opportunity costs for the firm (e.g., unbilled fees or excess audit staff).

Past research suggests that client characteristics such as client size and number of subsidiaries are associated with budget accuracy (Gist & Davidson, 1999); however, Ettredge et al. (2004) note that such client characteristics are relatively ineffective in explaining audit budget variances. In an attempt to better understand the causes of inaccurate budgets, we followed a two-step process.

First, we reviewed over 45 articles that investigated budgeting in an audit context or a general context. We used survey questions from these articles to identify and assess nine separate factors that potentially influence audit budget accuracy in large firms. In several cases, wording was modified to accommodate an audit budgeting scenario. For example, prior studies have examined managers' self-rated, subjective, budget performance (e.g., Govindarajan, 1986; Kenis, 1979). In audit scenarios, "budget performance" is largely an objective measure (budgeted audit hours minus actual audit hours), which necessitated minor wording changes relative to the original survey questions. These nine factors are discussed in Appendix A.

Next, we conducted semi-structured interviews with 11 audit partners and managers.[4] During each interview (approximately 15 min each), we asked why budget variances typically occur. Our intent was to identify factors that potentially affect audit budget accuracy that had not been identified during our literature review. These interviews led to questions aimed at capturing the four factors discussed in Appendix B.

DATA COLLECTION

We limited survey participation to audit seniors because they typically create the detailed time budgets for each stage in the audit process (McNair, 1991). The surveys were conducted in two south-central US cities with two national CPA firms participating. A contact person at each office randomly distributed our survey packet and responses were directly returned to the authors in order to preserve participant anonymity and to encourage honest participant responses. During 2000, a total of 180 survey packets were given to firm contacts and we received 57 usable responses (25 males and 32 females) for a 32% response rate.[5]

Survey Instrument

Our survey packet contained a (1) cover letter from the authors explaining the purpose of the study, (2) a stamped envelope addressed to one of the authors, and (3) the survey instrument. The survey cover letter indicated that (1) research results would only be reported in the aggregate and (2) individual responses would remain completely anonymous. Given potentially sensitive questions in the survey (for example, the existence of budget slack) respondents did not identify themselves (other than through the demographic responses they provided) anywhere on the research survey. The survey instrument instructed participants to consider the most recent audit in which (1) the participant had primary budgeting responsibility, and (2) the participant's firm had audited the client for at least two years. Ettredge et al. (2004) suggest that subsequent year budgets are increased in response to significant prior year budget overruns, resulting in greater budget accuracy over time. Our sample of continuing audit clients was designed to mitigate dramatic differences between budgeted and actual audit hours attributable to "first-year" effects. Participants provided demographic information (e.g., type of fee structure, client industry) and numeric data (e.g., total budgeted audit hours, total actual audit hours) for the client they considered (see Table 1 for descriptive data).

The survey next asked 60 questions about audit tasks and audit budgets. Table 2 lists these questions, grouped by the 13 factors listed in Appendices A and B. Each question required a response to a 5-point scale where 1 represents *strongly agree*, 3 *neutral or no opinion*, and 5 *strongly disagree*.

RESULTS

Descriptive Data about Budget Accuracy and Survey Responses

Table 1 presents descriptive information about the budget variances in our sample. We observe average budget overruns of 7.4% – an average lower than older studies (Gist & Davidson, 1999; Pasewark & Strawser, 1994), but on par with more recent evidence (Ettredge et al., 2004). Regarding descriptive information associated with our survey questions, Table 2 presents the mean and standard deviation of survey responses as well as the Pearson correlation between each survey question and the audit budget variance. As discussed below, these simple statistics provide insights into factors that affect budget accuracy.

Table 1.   Descriptive Data.

Budget Variance[a]	Frequency	Percent
Panel A: Distribution of budget variances		
Under 10%	4	7
0–10%	12	21
Under budget	16	28
Met budget	8	14
0–10%	17	30
10–20%	9	16
Over 20%	7	12
Over budget	33	58
Total	57	100

	Mean	Standard Deviation
Panel B: Budgeted and actual hours		
Budget variance	−7.43%[b]	16.9%
Budgeted audit hours	2,123	2,570
Actual audit hours	2,340	3,129

	Frequency
Panel C: Fee structure	
Fixed fee	52
Variable fee	5
	57
Panel D: Industry	
Manufacturer	29
Service	9
Other	19
	57
Panel E: Experience in audit budgeting	
Over 20 engagements	2
10–20 engagements	17
3–10 engagements	24
Less than 3 engagements	14
	57

[a](Budgeted audit hours−actual audit hours)/budgeted audit hours.
[b]Median budget variance: −4.03%.

Of the 60 questions, nine exhibited high correlation ($p < 0.05$) with the audit budget variance. Four of the questions related to the *weakness of client controls* and four related to *client cooperation*. The final correlated question related to *subordinate participation* and stated, "If my

Table 2. Descriptive Information: Survey Questions (All Questions are on a 1–5 Scale, where 1 = "Strongly Agree" and 5 = "Strongly Disagree").

		Mean Response	Standard Deviation	Correlation with Budget Variance
Subordinate participation (SUBPART)				
1.1	If my staff had complete autonomy, they would have requested increased budget hours for this engagement	2.91	0.87	0.42**
1.2	When setting my budget, I used my staff's experience with this client in order to set a more accurate budget	2.61*	0.94	−0.06
1.3	My audit staff members were made aware of the budget status periodically throughout the audit	2.19*	0.83	−0.06
1.4	My audit staff believe they had ample opportunities to participate in setting the budget for this engagement	3.49*	0.86	0.07
Control over budget formation (BUDFORM)				
2.1	I have a high degree of flexibility when determining budget goals	3.03	0.90	0.18
2.2	I have little voice in the formulation of my budget goals	3.50*	0.84	−0.01
2.3	The setting of my budget goals is pretty much under my control	3.00	0.90	0.01
2.4	My superior usually asks for my feedback before determining my final audit budget	2.21*	0.79	−0.07
2.5	My audit budget is not finalized until I am completely satisfied with it	3.21	0.95	−0.04
Influence of superior (INFSUP)				
3.1	My supervisor significantly changed my original estimate of required audit hours for this engagement	3.36*	1.07	0.21
3.2	The budgeted hours for this audit reflect my supervisor's expectations more than my own	2.73	1.06	0.19
3.3	My supervisor gave me a specific number of hours to complete this audit	2.77	1.08	0.07
Usefulness of budget in personal development (PERSDEV)				
4.1	Audit hour budgets enable me to be a more innovative leader	3.12	0.92	0.16
4.2	Audit hour budgets enable me to be a better business manager	2.43*	0.80	0.10
4.3	Audit hour budgets enable me to track my success as a leader in this firm	3.19	0.83	0.05
4.4	Audit hour budgets enable me to better plan audit activities	1.89*	0.45	0.20

Table 2. (*Continued*)

		Mean Response	Standard Deviation	Correlation with Budget Variance
Role of budget in personal motivation (PERSMOT)				
5.1	Performing well relative to budget gives me a feeling of accomplishment	2.05*	0.69	0.11
5.2	Attaining budgeted goals contributes to my personal growth within the firm	2.36*	0.72	0.09
5.3	I get a great sense of personal satisfaction when my actual performance compares favorably with the budget	2.12*	0.65	0.04
Clarity of budget goals (BUDGOAL)				
6.1	My budget goals are very clear and specific. I know exactly how many hours I have been allocated	2.38*	0.77	−0.06
6.2	Sometimes my budget goals are ambiguous and unclear	3.03	1.03	0.11
6.3	I fully understand which of my budget goals are more important than others and I have a clear sense of priorities on these goals	2.14*	0.58	0.00
Use of budgets for evaluation (BUDEVAL)				
7.1	During this engagement, I inspired my staff by encouraging them to achieve budgeted hours	2.92	0.86	0.05
7.2	The audit hours budget for this client was instrumental to motivate staff performance	3.35*	0.93	−0.08
7.3	My superior has mentioned budgets while talking to me about my efficiency as an in-charge	2.49*	0.96	−0.21
7.4	My superior on this engagement would have held me (did hold me) personally accountable for audit hour budget variances	2.98	0.99	−0.03
7.5	For this engagement, budget variances factored into the way I evaluated my staff	3.21	1.01	−0.11
7.6	My superiors discuss budget variances during my performance evaluation interviews	2.71*	0.90	−0.08
7.7	Audit hour budget variances factor into my pay raises	3.47*	0.75	0.08
Budget importance (BUDIMP)				
8.1	If given a choice, I prefer working with budgets rather than working without budgets	2.52*	1.05	−0.13
8.2	If budgets were discarded, audit efficiency would increase	3.87*	0.75	−0.03
8.3	I can work effectively and efficiently without budgets	2.54*	0.88	0.16

Table 2. (*Continued*)

		Mean Response	Standard Deviation	Correlation with Budget Variance
Budget slack (BUDSLACK)				
9.1	Audit hour budgets are rarely set at achievable levels in my firm	3.26*	0.89	0.16
9.2	In order to protect themselves, accountable auditors should submit budgets that can safely be attained	2.94	0.97	0.22
9.3	In-charges auditors set two standards: one between themselves and their staff, and another between themselves and their supervisor to be safe	3.08	0.91	−0.01
9.4	Building slack into the budget allows some flexibility to perform activities that are unexpected	2.28*	0.75	0.10
9.5	Building slack into the budget allows me to provide value-added service to my clients	2.59*	0.92	0.22
9.6	With some skill, I can make my budget look better	2.78*	0.72	−0.17
9.7	I can accommodate problems with staff performance by altering (i.e., increasing) their budget	3.40*	0.86	0.01
Weakness of client controls (CLICONT)				
10.1	The client lacked adequate internal controls in certain areas	3.42*	1.30	0.44**
10.2	During the most recent year, the client had audit exceptions requiring non-budgeted investigation	2.87	1.25	0.29**
10.3	Our ability to rely on the client's internal control was much more limited than we had anticipated when establishing the budget	3.71*	1.09	0.34**
10.4	Client evidence was not adequately documented	3.42*	1.21	0.35**
Client cooperation(CLICOOP)				
11.1	This client made an effort to minimize conventional audit work	2.87*	0.94	−0.37**
11.2	During this engagement, my audit staff had difficulty obtaining access to necessary audit evidence	3.14	1.18	0.10
11.3	Throughout this engagement, my staff had easy access to corporate officers who promptly provided necessary audit information	3.03	1.01	−0.44**
11.4	My staff had little difficulty obtaining client assistance in a timely manner	3.15	1.09	−0.30**

Table 2. (*Continued*)

	Mean Response	Standard Deviation	Correlation with Budget Variance
11.5 The client's staff were genuinely concerned with cooperating with our requests to minimize downtime	2.78	0.99	−0.32**
Staff effectiveness (STAFFEFF)			
12.1 Some staff members on this engagement lacked the work ethic to complete their tasks effectively	3.68*	1.28	−0.04
12.2 I found it difficult to motivate certain staff members during this audit	3.63*	1.09	0.04
12.3 During this engagement, I could rely on my staff to work in an efficient manner	2.36*	0.89	−0.06
12.4 Staff members on this engagement had adequate experience to complete their tasks efficiently	2.43*	0.90	−0.15
12.5 This engagement would have been completed faster had I been provided with more experienced staff	2.94	1.05	−0.02
12.6 During this audit, certain staff members required on-site training because they lacked the necessary experience to complete the task	2.57*	0.94	0.14
12.7 The staff assigned to this engagement had the necessary competence to complete their tasks	2.14*	0.66	−0.15
Budget training (BUDTRAIN)			
13.1 I have attended firm-sponsored training that specifically addressed how to prepare audit hour budgets	3.59*	1.17	−0.03
13.2 My firm provides literature that is helpful when formulating audit hour budgets	3.45*	1.00	−0.03
13.3 Preparing audit hour budgets is a common subject of informal discussion within the firm	2.49*	0.94	0.06
13.4 I have discussed how to budget audit hours with other colleagues at my level in the firm	2.29*	0.92	−0.00
13.5 In my firm, supervisors educate subordinates regarding how to budget audit hours	2.43*	0.88	−0.07

*Non-neutral mean response (i.e., a mean response of 3 signifies "neutral" or "no opinion") based on a two-tailed *t*-test ($p < 0.05$).

**Significant correlation ($p < 0.05$) with budget variance ([budgeted. hours−actual hours] ÷ budgeted hours).

staff had complete autonomy, they would have requested increased budget hours for this engagement." The high correlation for this question may reflect a cynical belief that audit staff might act in self-interest given the chance.

Questions related to certain previously explored factors such as *the role of budgets in personal motivation* and *clarity of budget goals* elicit strong responses from auditors (i.e., there is significant agreement that the budget is "motivating" and that budget goals are "clear"); however, these questions lack a significant association with budget accuracy (reflected by the weak correlations between individual questionnaire items and budget variance). In contrast, questionnaire items related to *client cooperation* generally do not elicit strong responses (respondents are mainly neutral and/or have no opinion about individual questionnaire items); however, there is a clear negative correlation between most client cooperation items and the budget variance.

For each *client cooperation* question, higher scores (less agreement or more disagreement) imply a less cooperative client. Relatively uncooperative clients are associated with negative (or less positive) budget variances. Taken at face value, this result is not surprising; however, we emphasize two points. First, *client cooperation* questionnaire items are based on discussions with partners and managers and, to our knowledge, this factor has not been previously investigated as a reason for audit budget variances. Second, *client cooperation* stands out among other items, which have been investigated previously. The relative strength of each factor is formally analyzed in the next section of the paper.

Similarly, questions relating to *client control* are based on discussions with partners and managers rather than previous literature. The high mean responses to questionnaire items relating to client controls suggest that, in general, respondents believe their clients have fairly strong controls. In addition, questions relating to client control consistently exhibit a significant positive relationship with budget variances. Again, at face value, an association between 'relatively bad client controls' and 'negative budget variances' is not surprising. However, our sample is comprised of continuing clients at large accounting firms. If these firms increased audit budgets in response to relatively weak client controls (cf. Bedard & Johnstone, 2004), our results suggest that such increases were, on average, insufficient. Similarly, Ettredge et al., 2004 find that while larger budget variances stimulate firms to increase the subsequent year budget, these budget increases are typically not sufficient.

Factor Analysis

While the simple statistics presented in Table 2 illustrate certain potentially useful results, additional insights come from more rigorous analysis. Specifically, we perform confirmatory factor analysis to determine which constructs have been reliably measured, then we include these constructs into a single analysis in order to more clearly assess the relative importance of each factor with regard to budget variance.

Factor analysis using structural equation modeling (SEM) was employed to confirm satisfactory loading of questionnaire items onto their respective factors.[6] Nine of the 60 questionnaire items were eliminated due to non-loading questions. Referring to Table 2, all seven budget slack items, item 1.3, and item 6.3 did not load on their respective factors and were excluded from further analysis.

Next, the measurement of each factor was assessed for reliability by calculating the construct composite reliability index (Hair, Anderson, Tatham, & Black, 1998). Two factors did not exceed the recommend index level of 0.70. Specifically, subordinate participation had an index level under 0.15 and budget training had an index level of 0.65.[7] These factors are not included in further analysis. With *subordinate participation*, *budget training*, and *budget slack* excluded (see above), estimates of covariance among the 10 remaining factors were calculated via confirmatory factor analysis in SEM. All 10 factors have composite reliability indices above 0.70 (Hair, Anderson, Tatham, & Black 1998).

Regression Results

The factor scores from the SEM analysis were utilized in ordinary least-squares regression to determine their relationship to the audit budget variance.[8] The dependent variable was defined as the logarithm of the percentage budget variance.[9] The respondent's budgeting experience was included as a control variable (see Table 1, Panel E). Other control variables were analyzed, but excluded from our final analysis due to a lack of statistical significance (see Table 3).[10]

The regression reveals three significant factors: *client controls*, *client cooperation*, and the *use of budgets in evaluation*. One factor, *use of budgets in evaluation*, exhibits a somewhat lower degree of significance ($p = 0.058$) compared to the client-related factors. As noted in Table 2, no individual component question for this factor exhibits a significant correlation with the budget variance. However, when taken collectively, the significance of this

Table 3. Regression Model for Audit Budget Variance.

Variable	Standardized Coefficient	t-Statistic	p-Value
Intercept		−0.275	0.785
BUDEVAL	−0.290	−1.952	0.058*
BUDFORM	−0.237	−1.506	0.140
BUDGOAL	0.098	0.737	0.465
BUDIMP	−0.137	−0.950	0.347
CLICONT	0.372	2.607	0.013**
CLICOOP	−0.346	−2.198	0.034**
PERSDEV	0.240	1.646	0.107
PERSMOT	−0.047	−0.327	0.745
STAFFEFF	0.075	0.535	0.595
Control variable[a]			
BUDEXP	0.509	3.444	0.001**
$F = 2.56$	$p < 0.009$		
$R^2 = 0.484$	Adjusted $R^2 = 0.295$		
$n = 57$			

Note: Model: $\ln(\text{BUDVAR}) = \beta_0 + \beta_1 \text{ BUDEVAL} + \beta_2 \text{ BUDFORM} + \beta_3 \text{ BUDGOAL} + \beta_4 \text{ BUDIMP} + \beta_5 \text{ CLICONT} + \beta_6 \text{ CLICOOP} + \beta_7 \text{ PERSDEV} + \beta_8 \text{ PERSMOT} + \beta_9 \text{ STFFEFF} + \beta_{10} \text{ BUDEXP} + \varepsilon$. Variable descriptions: ln (BUDVAR), natural log of [(Audit hours budgeted−actual audit hours)/audit hours budgeted]; BUDEVAL, use of budgets for evaluation; BUDFORM, control over budget formation; BUDGOAL, clarity of budget goals; BUDIMP, budget importance; CLICONT, weakness of client controls; CLICOOP, client co-operation; PERSDEV, usefulness of budget in personal development; PERSMOT, role of budget in personal motivation; STAFFEFF, staff effectiveness; BUDEXP, the respondent's budgeting experience (number of engagements).
[a]The following control variables are statistically insignificant and have been excluded from the above analysis: (1) audit firm experience with the client (number of years), (2) budget prep-aration time (number of hours spent preparing the budget), (3) fee type (fixed fee or variable fee), (4) CPA firm, and (5) industry (dummy variables indicating whether the client was a manufacturing or service company).
**$p < 0.05$.
*$p < 0.10$.

factor gives some credence to the notion that using budgets in employee evaluations provides motivation for reducing budget overruns. While over-all results indicate that audit efficiency was a factor in performance eval-uations, respondents tended to disagree with the notion of causality between budget variances and pay raises. The mean response to a question relating to the use of budget variances in determining pay raises indicate that most respondents do not feel their pay is related to budget variances (see Question 7.7, $\mu = 3.47$ out of 5.00, $\sigma = 0.75$).

Of all considered control variables, only budgeting experience significantly affects budget variance. Respondents reported the number of times they had primary responsibility for budgeting an audit engagement (within the four categories shown in Table 1, Panel E). Consistent with Ettredge et al., 2004, our results show that more budgeting experience is associated with more favorable (or less unfavorable) budget variances. Presumably, this phenomenon is due to the incorporation of knowledge gained in past budget experiences; however, it is possible that more experienced audit budgeters had greater comfort in asking for more budgeted hours.

SUMMARY, LIMITATIONS, AND DIRECTIONS FOR FUTURE RESEARCH

In this study, we analyzed survey evidence provided by senior auditors in large accounting firms in an effort to learn what factors cause budget variances for continuing audit clients. Our primary research goal is to identify significant determinants of accurate budgets to better focus future audit budget research on topics relevant to practitioners. Of the 13 factors examined, we find that favorable (or less unfavorable) budget variances are significantly related to (1) the use of budgets in the performance evaluation process, (2) relatively strong client internal controls, and (3) relatively co-operative clients.[11]

In our opinion, the client-related factors represent open avenues for future research because, as far as we know, *client controls* and *client cooperation* have not been previously examined as potential causes of audit budget variance. For example, recent research finds that audit effort (in the form of additional budgeted hours) increases when weak client controls are present (Bedard & Johnstone, 2004). Our results indicate that accounting firms establish insufficient budgets for clients with weak controls even though they recognize the need to allocate additional hours. In conjunction with our results, the recent study by Ettredge et al. (2004) suggests that failure to adequately budget for known client budget difficulties may be a general phenomenon. Future research could directly address why firms with on-going client relationships systematically fail to adequately budget for negative client factors.

Additionally, future research might directly examine how audit budgets differ between clients known to be relatively cooperative vs. uncooperative. Certainly, rating clients on a 'cooperative/uncooperative' scale would be subjective and potentially sensitive; however, some form of improved documentation might improve audit budget accuracy.[12] Finally, to the extent that our results capture client-driven audit resource consumption that firms cannot ex-ante anticipate, future research might employ a sociological perspective (see Covaleski, Evans, Luft, & Shields, 2003) to explore how relations between audit firms and clients might be altered in an effort to create more accurate audit budgets.

From a practical aspect, this research highlights the limited control that audit firms have over budget outcomes. This study indicates that the lack of budget success is more likely to be explained by problems outside of the firm, or more specifically, with the client. Previous research both inside (McNair, 1991) and outside (Brown & Solomon, 1993) an auditing context highlight potential dangers of evaluating performance using budgets that are not directly within the control of the person being evaluated. While the importance of audit budgets in staff allocation and performance evaluation is not disputed, this study does recognize that these aspects of the budget are less practical under conditions in which internal control structures have been jeopardized or the flow of information from the client has been hindered.

The results of this study are particularly interesting in light of Section 404 of the Sarbanes-Oxley Act of 2002, which requires auditor attestation of the management assessment of internal controls. This survey was conducted prior to the enactment of Sarbanes-Oxley and found weakness of client internal controls to be a primary source of budget variances. With increased emphasis of client internal controls under the Sarbanes-Oxley Act, firms may be faced with a likelihood of uncertainties in forming and meeting the audit budget.

Our study is subject to limitations. First, we attempted to analyze a large number of potentially important factors. Given that we examine many factors with a relatively small database, it is likely premature to label any factor that we find to be statistically insignificant as 'unimportant'.

In addition, the validity of our results depends on the accuracy and completeness of our survey data. While certain variables are highly significant, the correlation coefficient of the model (R^2) indicates that we have not exhausted the potential variables affecting budget variance. For example, when considering the effect of budget outcomes on employee performance, our survey focused on the effects on remuneration. We did not consider the potential effect of budget outcomes on other variables such as the attractiveness of the employee for other or future audit jobs, the likelihood of promotion, or reputation as an effective employee. That being said, we believe our results offer some relatively 'low hanging fruit' vis-à-vis previously unexamined client-related factors that are significantly associated with budget variances even in our relatively small sample.

Another potential limitation of our study relates to survey responses. To the extent that participant anonymity failed to eliminate attribution bias in our participants (i.e., auditors wrongly blaming clients for budget overage), then the influence of client-controlled factors could be overstated in our results. While we cannot rule out the possibility that auditors are eager to "pass the blame" by attributing budget overruns to clients, mean survey responses (Questions 10.1 and 10.4 in Table 2) indicate auditors were generally satisfied with the adequacy of client controls. Similarly, auditors had neutral (rather than negative) feelings concerning the degree of client cooperation (Questions 11.1 through 11.5 in Table 2).

To further investigate this possibility, we created an additional model eliminating observations in which the actual audit hours exceeded budgeted hours by 10% ($n = 41$). Based on historical averages, this model presumably only includes budgets likely to be considered "successful" and therefore the inclination to blame the client would be decreased. In this model, both *budget experience* ($p < 0.047$) and *weakness of client controls* ($p < 0.014$) remain significant. Client cooperation, which was significant in the primary model, was not significant in the reduced model. Clearly, the cooperation of the client is regarded by auditors as particularly significant when actual audit hours exceed the budget by greater than 10%. Whether this accusation is justified or not remains a topic for future study.

Finally, our survey was of audit seniors with budget formation responsibilities. While we believe this individual to be the most informed concerning budget outcomes, we acknowledge that responses may have differed if we surveyed other related parties such as the partner, other members of the audit team, or even the client.

NOTES

1. The terms "favorable" and "unfavorable" are phrased from the perspective of the accounting firm. That is, a favorable budget variance represents a situation in which actual audit hours are less than budgeted audit hours. An unfavorable budget variance represents a situation in which actual audit hours exceed budgeted audit hours.

2. For example, the report of the Panel on Audit Effectiveness (POB, 2000, §4.26) expresses such concern by recommending that "Performance measures need to be balanced and clearly and carefully communicated to all professionals to ensure that all personnel understand that quality work, not meeting time deadlines and budget estimates, is the ultimate priority."

3. Although prior research shows that auditors increase engagement effort for clients with internal control weaknesses (e.g., Kaplan & Reckers, 1985; Kruetzfeldt & Wallace, 1986), these studies do not investigate budget accuracy.

4. Both empirical (McNair, 1991) and anecdotal evidence suggest that senior accountants have the greatest responsibility concerning detailed budget formation. However, we utilized partners and managers at this stage because we wanted to gain insight from those who have a broad variety of budgeting experience. Seniors were the subjects of this study when we sought evidence concerning specific audit budgets.

5. We were unable to use 10 responses because participants failed to provide budgeted and actual audit hours for their engagement (i.e., we had no dependent variable for these participants).

6. In order to maintain directional consistency within each factor, the following questionnaire items were reverse scored in the factor analysis: 2.2, 6.2, 8.1, 11.2, 12.3, 12.4, and 12.7.

7. In some cases, composite reliability of 0.65 is considered acceptable (e.g., Viator & Pasewark, 2005); however, we elected to eliminate the budget training factor because (1) it was not based on prior research, (2) individual budget training questionnaire items are not strongly correlated with budget variance (see Table 2), and (3) our sample size is likely too small for tangential investigation.

8. We also conducted SEM regression that modeled all significant covariances and used percentage of budget variance as the dependent variable ([budgeted audit hours−actual audit hours] ÷ budgeted audit hours). Results from this regression are nearly identical to the OLS regression results presented in the following section. We report standard OLS regression results rather than SEM-based results for five reasons. First, our dependent variable (budget variance) is observable, not latent (making SEM potentially inappropriate). Second, our SEM-based results show a negative variance calling the validity of this model into question. Third, the SEM-based model is more data intensive than standard OLS regression and, given our relatively small sample size, a less data-intensive model is preferred. Fourth, results from the SEM and OLS regressions are nearly identical. Finally, for most readers, the OLS regression output is easier to interpret.

9. The logarithm of the percentage budget variance was used to minimize the effects of three audits whose variances exceeded |50.0%|. The same analysis without a logarithmic transformation of the dependent variable yielded similar results except that the factor *Use of Budgets for Evaluation* (BUDEVAL) becomes slightly more significant.

10. Tests for multicollinearity among independent variables were conducted using variance inflation factors (VIF). VIFs ranged from 1.30 to 1.97 indicating no significant degree of multicollinearity (Meyers, 1986). Also, given the large number of independent variables, we were concerned whether the order of entry into the model affected results. Forward stepwise regression yielded similar results for the independent variables found to be statistically significant.

11. We discussed these results with a partner from a firm in the study who was not surprised by these results. Specifically, the partner noted the difficulty of dealing with uncooperative clients by saying, "Sometimes I don't know why we have audit planning meetings with the client. They make promises and don't fulfill them. That's what causes a budget variance." The following section discusses each factor contained in our analysis.

12. Analogously, many case studies in the activity-based costing literature involve known cost distortions that are not quantified. Although decision makers mentally

adjustments for these distortions, improved decisions are made after the magnitude of the cost distortion is documented and quantified (typically with ABC information). In other words, auditors may be aware that client-related factors inhibit accurate budgeting; however, auditors appear to systematically underestimate the negative effect these factors have on audit resource needs.

ACKNOWLEDGEMENTS

We appreciate the helpful comments of Rich Houston, Karla Johnstone, Jim Lampe, and Ralph Viator.

REFERENCES

Bedard, J. C., & Johnstone, K. M. (2004). Earnings manipulation risk, corporate governance risk, and auditors' planning and pricing decisions. *The Accounting Review, 79*, 277–304.

Brown, C., & Solomon, I. (1993). An experimental investigation of explanations for outcome effects on appraisals of capital-budgeting decisions. *Contemporary Accounting Research, 10*, 83–111.

Bruns, W. J., & Waterhouse, J. H. (1975). Budgetary control and organization structure. *Journal of Accounting Research, 13*, 177–203.

Commission on Auditors' Responsibilities. (1978). *Report, Conclusions, and Recommendations.*

Coram, P., Ng, J., & Woodliff, D. R. (2004). The effect of risk misstatement on the propensity to commit reduced audit quality under time budget pressure. *Auditing: A Journal of Practice & Theory, 23*(2), 159–168.

Covaleski, M. A., Evans, J. H., Luft, J. L., & Shields, M. D. (2003). Budgeting research: Three theoretical perspectives and criteria for selective integration. *Journal of Management Accounting Research, 15*, 3–49.

Dermer, J. D. (1975). The interrelationship of intrinsic and extrinsic motivation. *Academy of Management Journal, 18*, 125–129.

Ettredge, M. L., Bedard, J. C., & Johnstone, K. M. (2004). *Audit time budgeting dynamics and fixed fee constraints.* Working paper. University of Kansas.

Gist, W. E., & Davidson, R. A. (1999). An exploratory study of the influence of client factors on audit time budget variances. *Auditing: A Journal of Practice & Theory, 18*(1), 101–116.

Govindarajan, V. (1986). Appropriateness of accounting data in performance evaluation: An empirical examination of environmental uncertainty as an intervening variable. *Accounting, Organizations and Society, 9*(2), 125–135.

Hair, J. F., Jr., Anderson, R. E., Tatham, D. L., & Black, W. C. (1998). *Multivariate data analysis.* Upper Saddle River, NJ: Prentice-Hall.

Hofstede, G. H. (1967). *The game of budget control.* Assen: Van Gorcum.

Houston, R. W. (1999). The effects of fee pressure and client risk on audit seniors' time budget decisions. *Auditing: A Journal of Practice & Theory, 18*(2), 70–86.

Kaplan, S. E., & Reckers, P. M. J. (1985). An examination of auditor performance evaluation. *The Accounting Review, 60*(3), 477–488.

Kelley, T., & Margheim, L. (1990). The impact of time budget pressure, personality, and leadership variables on dysfunctional auditor behavior. *Auditing: A Journal of Practice & Theory, 9*(1), 21–42.

Kenis, I. (1979). Effects of budgetary goal characteristics on managerial attitudes and performance. *The Accounting Review, 54*(4), 707–721.

Kruetzfeldt, R. W., & Wallace, W. A. (1986). Error characteristics in audit populations: Their profile and relationship to environmental factors. *Auditing: A Journal of Practice & Theory, 6*(1), 20–43.

Margheim, L., & Pany, K. (1986). Quality control, premature signoff, and underreporting of time: Some empirical findings. *Auditing: A Journal of Practice and Theory, 5*(1), 50–63.

McNair, C. J. (1991). Proper compromises: The management control dilemma in public accounting and its impact on auditor behavior. *Accounting, Organizations and Society, 16*(7), 635–653.

Meyers, R. (1986). *Classical and modern regression with applications.* Boston, MA: Duxbury Press.

O'Keefe, T. B., King, R. D., & Gaver, K. M. (1994). Audit fees, industry specialization, and compliance with GAAS reporting standards. *Auditing: A Journal of Practice and Theory, 13*(2), 40–55.

Onsi, M. (1977). Factor analysis of behavior variables affecting budgetary slack. *The Accounting Review, 52*, 535–548.

Pasewark, W. R., & Strawser, J. R. (1994). Subordinate participation in audit budgeting decisions: A comparison of decisions influenced by organizational factors to decisions conforming with the Vroom–Jago model. *Decision Sciences, 25*(2), 281–299.

Ponemon, L. A. (1992). Auditor underreporting of time and moral reasoning: An experimental lab study. *Contemporary Accounting Research, 9*(1), 171–189.

Public Oversight Board of the SEC Practice Section (POB). (2000). *The panel on audit effectiveness report and recommendations.* Stamford, CT: POB.

Selto, F. H., & Widener, S. K. (2004). Relevance of management accounting research. *Advances in Management Accounting, 12*, 1–36.

Swieringa, R. J., & Moncur, R. H. (1974). *Some effects of participative budgeting on managerial behavior.* New York: National Association of Accountants.

Viator, R. E., & Pasewark, W. R. (2005). Mentorship separation tension in the accounting profession: The consequences of delayed structural separation. *Accounting, Organizations and Society, 30*(4), 371–387.

Vroom, V. H., & Jago, A. G. (1987). *The new leadership: Managing participation in organizations.* Englewood Cliffs, NJ: Prentice-Hall.

Williams, J. J., Macintosh, N. B., & Moore, J. C. (1990). Budget-related behavior in public sector organizations: Some empirical evidence. *Accounting, Organizations and Society, 15*(3), 221–246.

APPENDIX A. FACTORS POTENTIALLY AFFECTING AUDIT BUDGET ACCURACY: DERIVED FROM PRIOR RESEARCH

Subordinate Participation (SUBPART – Factor 1) – the degree to which the audit senior utilizes input from audit staff when preparing the budget.
Source: We use four questions from Vroom and Jago (1987). Like several other studies, Vroom and Jago attempt to measure the construct "participation" to determine its influence on budget performance.

Control over Budget Formation (BUDFORM – Factor 2) – the degree to which the audit senior believes that he or she can autonomously influence the budget.
Source: We use five questions from Kenis (1979). Similar to other studies, Kenis found that greater control over budget formation was positively associated with budget performance. These five questions focus on whether firm culture permits an audit senior to exercise autonomy and authority over the budget process.

Influence of Superior (INFSUP – Factor 3) – the degree to which the budget reflects the intentions of the superior rather than the audit senior.
Source: We use three questions from Govindarajan (1986). Building on other studies, Govindarajan finds that budget performance improves when a superior permits a subordinate to alter and approve the budget.

Usefulness of Budget in Personal Development (PERSDEV – Factor 4) – the perceived usefulness of budgets in determining a leadership role within the firm.
Source: We use four questions from Govindarajan (1986). These questions were originally developed by Swieringa and Moncur (1974) and Bruns and Waterhouse (1975). Govindarajan finds that when managers believe the budget is useful in their development as individuals, budgetary performance improves.

Role of Budget in Personal Motivation (PERSMOT – Factor 5) – the degree to which the attainment of budget goals influences a sense of personal accomplishment.
Source: We use three questions from Dermer (1975). Dermer finds that personal accomplishment, growth, and satisfaction derived from achieving budget goals is highly correlated with performance relative to the budget.

Clarity of Budget Goals (BUDGOAL – Factor 6) – a clear understanding of budget goals.
Source: We use three questions from Kenis (1979). Kenis finds that clear budget goals are helpful in determining a sense of priorities; consequently, clear budget goals have a strong influence on budget performance.

Use of Budgets for Evaluation (BUDEVAL – Factor 7) – the degree to which budget achievement is used to motivate and evaluate employee performance within the firm.
Source: We use four questions from Kenis (1979). Swieringa and Moncur (1974), Bruns and Waterhouse (1975), and Williams, Macintosh, and Moore (1990) investigate the relationships between employee performance evaluation and budget performance with mixed results. Statements by the Commission on Auditors' Responsibilities (1978) and the Panel on Audit Effectiveness (POB, 2000) concerning potential relationship between audit quality and the evaluative process prompted us to include three additional questions specifically related to audit budgets.

Budget Importance (BUDIMP – Factor 8) – the perception that the budget is necessary.
Source: We use three questions from Hofstede (1967). The general notion within this line of research is that "important" budgets are associated with higher budgetary achievement.

Budget Slack (BUDSLACK – Factor 9) – the extent to which the audit senior budgets unneeded hours to make budget achievement less difficult.
Source: We use three questions from Onsi (1977) and create four audit-specific questions. The budget slack literature is extensive but inconclusive. Intuitively, more slack reduces budget variance and budget overruns because budgeters consume the slack whenever slack is available. Theoretically, various predictions between budget slack and budget performance can be made.

APPENDIX B. FACTORS POTENTIALLY AFFECTING AUDIT BUDGET ACCURACY: DERIVED FROM DISCUSSIONS WITH AUDIT PARTNERS AND AUDIT MANAGERS

Weakness of Client Controls (CLICONT – Factor 10)
Several partners and managers noted that deficiencies in the client's internal controls often resulted in unplanned audit investigations. We requested information about continuing clients to eliminate control issues that would likely be corrected in an initial audit. We attempt to capture the construct "weak client controls" using four questions that relate to the discovery of audit exceptions, the adequacy of internal controls, and documentation of evidence.

Client Cooperation (CLICOOP – Factor 11)
Several partners and managers identified situations in which the audit was delayed by the firm's inability to gain access to needed evidence or client personnel. Conversely, some firm members mentioned situations in which the client specifically accommodated the audit staff (often to minimize audit fees). We designed five questions to measure the degree to which the client was concerned with providing access and documentation required to complete an audit.

Staff Effectiveness (STAFFEFF – Factor 12)
Several partners and managers noted that, although hiring practices are generally effective in identifying reliable staff, staff quality differences do exist. Intuitively, high quality staff members might reduce the possibility of going over budget. We created seven questions to measure this construct.

Budget Training (BUDTRAIN – Factor 13)
One of the authors asked several partners and managers about budget training during one-on-one interviews. Although most firm representatives indicated that formal budget training is relatively limited, informal training (i.e., "this is how you budget") does exist. We created five questions to control for any effects that budgetary training might have on budget accuracy.

THE MULTIPLE ROLES OF PARTICIPATIVE BUDGETING ON JOB PERFORMANCE

Vincent K. Chong, Ian R. C. Eggleton and Michele K. C. Leong

ABSTRACT

This paper examines the multiple roles (i.e., cognitive, motivational and value attainment) of participative budgeting and the combined effects of these three roles on subordinates' job performance. Specifically, this paper proposes that participative budgeting affects job performance via three intervening variables, namely role ambiguity, organizational commitment and job satisfaction. The responses of 74 senior-level managers, drawn from a cross-section of the Australian financial services sector, to a questionnaire survey were analyzed by using a path analytic technique. The results support the multiple roles of participative budgeting and the indirect effect of participative budgeting on subordinates' job performance through role ambiguity, organizational commitment and job satisfaction.

INTRODUCTION

The relationship between participative budgeting and subordinates' job-related outcomes (e.g., subordinates' job performance) is one of the most researched

Advances in Accounting, Volume 22, 67–95
Copyright © 2006 by Elsevier Ltd.
All rights of reproduction in any form reserved
ISSN: 0882-6110/doi:10.1016/S0882-6110(06)22004-2

topics in management accounting (see Shields & Shields, 1998; Covaleski, Evans, Luft, & Shields, 2003).[1] To date, the empirical studies on participative budgeting have generally been focused on the motivational and/or cognitive roles of participative budgeting on subordinates' job performance. The motivational role of participative budgeting suggests that subordinates' participation in the budget-setting process induces them to accept and commit to their budget goals, thereby enhancing their job performance (see, e.g., Nouri & Parker, 1998; Chong & Chong, 2002a; Wentzel, 2002; Chong & Leung, 2003). The cognitive role of participative budgeting, on the other hand, suggests that subordinates' participation in the budget-setting process provides them with the opportunity to gather, exchange and disseminate job-relevant information to facilitate their decisions, which in turn, improved their job performance (e.g., Chenhall & Brownell, 1988; Kren, 1992; Magner, Welker, & Campbell, 1996; Chong, 2002; Chong & Chong, 2002a).[2]

Prior studies (e.g., Shields & Shields, 1998; Chong, Eggleton, & Leong, 2005; see also Locke & Scheweiger, 1979; Locke & Latham, 1990) have suggested value attainment as the third role of participative budgeting. A review of the prior accounting literature reveals that the value attainment role of participative budgeting has been recognized, but no studies have explicitly tested it within the cognitive and motivational models (see the appendix). Shields and Shields (1998), for example, suggested that the value attainment role of participative budgeting is theorized to affect subordinate's job satisfaction. They, however, did not attempt to empirically test the value attainment role of participative budgeting. Shields and Shields (1998, p. 59) argued that by allowing subordinates to participate in the budget-setting process would increase the likelihood that they will " ... experience self-respect and feelings of equality arising from the opportunity to express his or her values." Chong et al. (2005) advanced the participative budgeting literature by incorporating the value attainment role of participative budgeting into the *cognitive* model. They found that the joint effect of value attainment and cognitive roles of participative budgeting significantly improved subordinates' job performance.

Despite the recognition of the three mechanisms (i.e., cognitive, motivational and value attainment) by which participative budgeting will bring about the benefits of increased subordinates' job performance, to date no studies have attempted to explicitly examine the existence of these three mechanisms of participative budgeting in a single study, and the combined impacts of these three roles of participative budgeting on subordinates' job performance. This existing gap in the accounting literature constitutes the motivation for our study.

This study proposes that participative budgeting affects subordinates' job performance via three intervening variables: role ambiguity, organizational commitment and job satisfaction. The proposed theoretical model (see Fig. 1) incorporates the effects of cognitive, motivational and value attainment roles of participative budgeting on subordinates' job performance. We propose that the cognitive effect of participative budgeting reduces role ambiguity (Link 1, Fig. 1), the motivational effect of participative budgeting increases subordinates' organizational commitment (Link 2, Fig. 1) and the value attainment effect of participative budgeting increases subordinates' job satisfaction (Link 3, Fig. 1). Specifically, we propose that participative budgeting reduces subordinates' role ambiguity by providing them with clear information regarding their role expectations, and methods for fulfilling their role expectations and performance (Chenhall & Brownell, 1988; Chong & Bateman, 2000). We argue that participative budgeting increases subordinates organizational commitment because the opportunity to participate in the budget-setting process enhances their sense of control, trust and identification with the organization (see Nouri & Parker, 1998; Shields & Shields, 1998). We further suggest that participative budgeting also increases subordinates level of job satisfaction because the process of participation allows them to experience self-respect and feelings of equality (see Nouri & Parker, 1998; Shields & Shields, 1998). In addition, our study

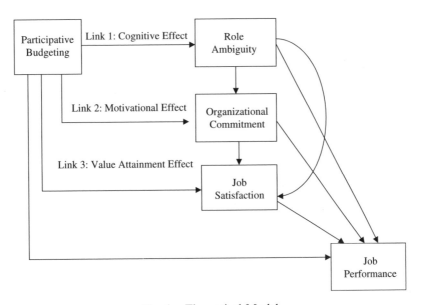

Fig. 1. Theoretical Model.

proposes that participative budgeting increases job performance indirectly via role ambiguity, organizational commitment and job satisfaction.

The remainder of the paper is structured as follows. In the next section, the research model is presented. Subsequent sections address the research method, results, conclusion and limitations of the study.

RESEARCH MODEL AND THEORETICAL DEVELOPMENT

The Cognitive Effect Hypothesis: The Relationship between Participative Budgeting and Role Ambiguity

The first hypothesis is concerned with the cognitive role of participative budgeting. Specifically, it is related to the relationship between participative budgeting and role ambiguity.[3] Prior empirical studies (Jackson & Schuler, 1985; Chenhall & Brownell, 1998) and role theory (see Kahn, Wolfe, Quinn, Snoek, & Rosenthal, 1964) support a negative association between participative budgeting and role ambiguity. For example, Jackson and Schuler (1985) found that higher level of participation leads to lower role ambiguity. Chenhall and Brownell (1988), on the other hand, found that participative budgeting was negatively associated with role ambiguity. The cognitive mechanism assumes that participative budgeting provides subordinates the opportunity to share their local and specialized knowledge with their peers and superiors, and permit open discussion of preferred means-end approaches (Kren & Liao, 1988; Magner et al., 1996; Shields & Shields, 1998; Chong, 2002; Chong & Chong, 2002a). Magner et al. (1996) argued that the act of participation allows subordinates to interact with their superiors, where subordinates can ask questions to clarify their role expectations and work strategies. Chong and Chong (2002a, p. 69) argued that " ... the act of participation provides an opportunity for subordinates to gather, exchange and disseminate job-relevant information to enhance their decision making process." Hence, it is proposed that participative budgeting provides subordinates' the opportunity to share information between a subordinate and superior (Shields & Shields, 1998), and the availability of information will aid to clarify subordinates' role expectations, methods of fulfilling their role expectations and performance. Thus, we propose that *the cognitive role of participative budgeting is expected to reduce subordinates' levels of role ambiguity*. Stated formally, the following hypothesis is tested:

H1. Participative budgeting is negatively associated with role ambiguity.

The Motivational Effect Hypothesis: The Relationship between
Participative Budgeting and Organizational Commitment

The second hypothesis is concerned with motivational role of participative budgeting. Specifically, it is regarding the relationship between participative budgeting and organizational commitment. Existing theory and empirical evidence (e.g., Nouri & Parker, 1996a, 1996b, 1998) suggest that participative budgeting is positively associated with organizational commitment.[4] For example, Nouri and Parker (1998) argued that when the subordinates become involved in the budget setting, they become better acquainted with the budget goals, thereby increases their association, not only with budget objectives but also with all organizational goals. Participative budgeting allows the subordinates to better understand the budget-target-setting process (Nouri & Parker, 1998). Shield and Shields (1998, p. 59) suggested that the process of budgetary participation will increase subordinates' " ... trust, sense of control and ego-involvement with the organization which then jointly cause less resistance to change and more acceptance of and commitment to, the budget decision." Thus, we propose that *the motivational role of participative budgeting is expected to increase subordinates' levels of organizational commitment.* Accordingly, the following hypothesis is tested:

H2. Participative budgeting is positively associated with organizational commitment.

The Value Attainment Effect Hypothesis: The Relationship between
Participative Budgeting and Job Satisfaction

The third hypothesis is concerned with the value attainment role of participative budgeting. The notion of the value attainment role of budgetary participation suggests that by allowing subordinates to participate in the budget-setting process will increase the likelihood that they will feel satisfied with their *values* (French, Israel, & As, 1960; Strauss, 1963; Lowin, 1968; Locke & Schweiger, 1979).[5] It is suggested that participative budgeting helps to increase the subordinates' self-esteem and enhances their job satisfaction. It is argued that the value attainment role of participative budgeting affects job satisfaction and morale of subordinates in the organization (Shields & Shields, 1998). In other words, participative budgeting provides subordinates the opportunity to attain their values (Locke, 1976). Shields and Shields (1998, p. 59), for example, theorized that the act of participation allows subordinates to " ... experience self respect and feelings of equality arising from the opportunity to express his or her values." Chong et al. (2005) found that the value attainment role of participative budgeting was positively related with subordinates' job satisfaction. Thus, it can be concluded that *the value attainment role of participative budgeting is expected to increase subordinates' levels of job satisfaction*. Accordingly, the following hypothesis is tested:

H3. Participative budgeting is positively associated with job satisfaction.

The Relationship between Role Ambiguity and Organizational Commitment

Subordinates' role ambiguity is costly for the organization in terms of the required behaviors or performance levels (Kahn et al., 1964; Rizzo, House, & Lirtzman, 1970). As noted earlier, the cognitive role of budgetary participation is expected to reduce subordinates' levels of role ambiguity, while motivational role of participative budgeting is expected to increase subordinates' levels of organizational commitment. Taken together, we propose that if subordinates have clear information regarding their role expectations and performance (i.e., low role ambiguity), they are more likely to experience a sense of control, reduced resistance to change, reduced anxiety and a fuller grasp of the methods to be used in accomplishing their job (French, et al., 1960; Vroom, 1964; see also Shields & Shields, 1998). Thus, it can be concluded that when subordinates experience *low* role ambiguity, we expect that role ambiguity is associated with *high* organizational commitment. On the other hand, when subordinates experience *high* role ambiguity, we expect that role ambiguity is associated with *low* organizational commitment. Taken together, it is concluded that *subordinates' role ambiguity is negatively associated with organizational commitment*.

The Relationship between Role Ambiguity and Job Satisfaction

It is argued that high role ambiguity causes lower productivity, tension, dissatisfaction and psychological withdrawal from the work group (Rizzo et al., 1970; Van Sell, Brief & Schuler, 1981). Prior empirical studies (Jackson & Schuler, 1985; Chenhall & Brownell, 1988; Rebele & Michaels, 1990; Chong & Bateman, 2000; Fisher, 2001) suggested that high level of role ambiguity reduces subordinates' levels of job satisfaction. Fisher (2001) found that role ambiguity was negatively associated with auditors' job satisfaction. Findings reported from the marketing literature have paralleled these results (see Brown & Peterson, 1993; Rhoads, Singh, & Goodell, 1994). For example, Brown and Peterson (1993), in their meta study, found correlation of −0.36 between role ambiguity and job satisfaction. Therefore, the consensual view emerging from these findings is that role ambiguity has significant dysfunctional (negative) effect on job satisfaction. Thus, it is concluded that *role ambiguity is negatively associated with job satisfaction.*

The Relationship between Organizational Commitment and Job Satisfaction

Several accounting studies (e.g., Aranya, Lachman, & Amernic, 1982; Aranya, Kushnir, & Valency, 1986; Bline, Duchon, & Meixner, 1991; Gregson, 1992; Kalbers & Fogarty, 1995; Pasewark & Strawser, 1996; Poznanski & Bline, 1997; Ketchand & Strawser, 1998) have observed a positive relationship between organizational commitment and job satisfaction. Mixed results are reported regarding the causal relationship between organizational commitment and job satisfaction. For example, numerous researchers (e.g., Porter, Steers, Mowday, & Boulian, 1974; Bartol, 1979; Johnston, Parasuraman, Futrell, & Black, 1990; Brown & Peterson, 1993) have argued that job satisfaction precedes organizational commitment. These studies argue that job satisfaction causes organizational commitment because it is more specific, less stable and more rapidly formed (Williams & Hazer, 1986). However, other studies (Farrell & Rusbult, 1981; Bateman & Strasser, 1984) suggest that organizational commitment is an antecedent of job satisfaction. Our study attempts to test the *three* mechanisms (cognitive, motivational and value attainment) by which participative budgeting will bring about the benefits of increased subordinates' job satisfaction, therefore, we theorize that organizational commitment increases job satisfaction in our theoretical model (see Fig. 1). Thus, it is concluded that *higher level of organizational commitment is associated with increased subordinates' job satisfaction.*

The Relationship between Job Satisfaction and Job Performance

Numerous prior accounting studies (see, e.g., Choo & Tan, 1997; Poznanski & Bline, 1997; Chong et al., 2005) have found that job satisfaction is an *antecedent* to job performance.[6] Chong et al. (2005), for example, found that there is a positive relationship between job satisfaction and job performance. Franken (1982) claims that a dissatisfied subordinate is more likely than a highly satisfied subordinate to decide simply not to perform in his or her job. Franken (1982, p. 451) argues that "*job* dissatisfaction is likely to lead to ... simply poor *job* performance" (emphasis added in italics). In addition, it has generally been assumed that a subordinate who is satisfied with his or her job will perform better (Locke, 1986; Katzell, Thompson, & Guzzo, 1992). These studies attribute such findings to the fact that subordinates, who are highly satisfied with their job, are more likely to exert additional effort to perform. It is suggested that increased effort leads to improved job performance (Brown & Peterson, 1994; see also Bonner & Sprinkle, 2002).[7] Thus, we propose that higher level of job satisfaction is associated with increased subordinates' job performance.

The Indirect Effect Hypothesis: The Relationship between Participative Budgeting and Job Performance

As noted earlier, the cognitive role of participative budgeting is expected to reduce subordinates' levels of role ambiguity (i.e., hypothesis H1). The motivational and value attainment roles of participative budgeting are expected to increase subordinates' organizational commitment (i.e., hypothesis H2) and job satisfaction (i.e., hypothesis H3), respectively. It is proposed that subordinates' role ambiguity, in turn, is negatively associated with organizational commitment and job satisfaction. Furthermore, it is proposed that higher organizational commitment is associated with increased subordinates' job satisfaction; and job satisfaction, in turn, is positively associated with job performance. Taken together, it is suggested that participative budgeting affects subordinates' job performance mainly through the influence it has on role ambiguity, organizational commitment and job satisfaction. Thus, we postulate that *participative budgeting is indirectly associated with job performance through subordinates' role ambiguity, organizational commitment and job satisfaction.* This idea is formally expressed in the following hypothesis:

H4. There is an indirect relationship between participative budgeting and job performance through role ambiguity, organizational commitment and job satisfaction.

METHOD

Sample

This study employs a survey method to collect data. A questionnaire was administered to a total of 141 senior-level managers from firms randomly drawn from *Kompass Australia* (1999) business directory. An initial tele-phone call to each of the senior manager was made to ensure that they were the appropriate person to receive the questionnaire. They were asked the following two questions: (1) Are budgets used in your organization?" and (2) "Do you have any budget-setting responsibilities?" These two questions were asked to ensure that the respondents surveyed were involved in the budget-setting process.[8] To enhance our response rate, each respondent was promised a gift voucher of 15.00 Australian dollars if the questionnaire was returned. In addition, each questionnaire was pre-coded to enable non-respondent to be traced and follow-up to be executed. A reminder letter and another copy of the questionnaire were sent to those who had not responded after four weeks. The response rate to the mail-out was 77 (54 percent).[9] Three incomplete questionnaires were excluded from the study resulted in 74 usable responses for our final data analysis. The managers surveyed had been employed in their respective firms and held their current position for an average of 10.9 years and 4.8 years, respectively. The average age of the respondents was 41 years.

Measurement of Variables

Participative budgeting was measured by a three-item, seven-point Likert-type scale adapted from Milani (1975). Previous accounting studies have used similar items in their studies (e.g., Kren, 1992; Magner et al., 1996). A factor analysis of the three items was subjected to a varimax rotation. The results indicate satisfactory construct validity (Kerlinger, 1964; Kerlinger & Lee, 2000). The three items were found to be loaded above 0.5 levels on the first factor and explained 81.59 percent of the total variance. The Cronbach alpha coefficient (Cronbach, 1951) for participative budgeting was 0.89, which indicates satisfactory internal reliability for the scale (Nunnally, 1967).

Role ambiguity was measured by a six-item, seven-point Likert-type scale developed by Rizzo et al. (1970). This instrument has been used in prior accounting studies (Chenhall & Brownell, 1988; O'Connor, 1995; Chong & Bateman, 2000). A factor analysis of the six items was subjected to a varimax rotation. The results indicate satisfactory construct validity. The six items were found to be loaded above 0.5 levels on the first factor and explained 63.66 percent of the total variance. The Cronbach alpha coefficient of 0.86 was observed in this study, which indicates satisfactory level of internal reliability.

Organizational commitment was measured by a nine-item, seven-point Likert-type short-form scale from Mowday, Steer, and Porter (1979). This instrument has been used by numerous prior studies (see, e.g., Nouri, 1994; Nouri & Parker, 1996a, 1996b, 1998). A factor analysis of the scale showed two factors with the first factor explaining 40.92 percent and the second factor 28.62 percent of the total variance. In order to be consistent with previous studies (e.g., Nouri & Parker, 1996a, 1996b, 1998), our study used the composite score of the nine items. The Cronbach alpha coefficient for organizational commitment was 0.90, which indicates high internal reliability for the scale.

Job satisfaction was measured by a two-item, seven-point Likert-type scale developed by Dewar and Werbel (1979). A factor analysis of the two items was subjected to a varimax rotation. The results indicate satisfactory construct validity. The two items were found to be loaded above 0.5 level on the first factor and explained 89.09 percent of the total variance. The Cronbach alpha coefficient for job satisfaction was 0.88, which indicates satisfactory internal reliability for the scale.

Job performance was measured by a single-item scale, which asked respondents to rate their overall performance from "well below average" to "well above average" on a fully anchored seven-point Likert-type scale. The use of this scale is consistent with numerous prior accounting studies (e.g., Merchant, 1981, Brownell & Merchant, 1990; Mia & Chenhall, 1994; Dunk, 1995).

RESULTS

Table 1 shows the descriptive statistics for the variables used in the study and Table 2 presents the Pearson correlation matrix for the variables used in this study.

The results shown in Table 2 suggest there is a negative and significant correlation between participative budgeting and role ambiguity ($r = -0.498$,

Table 1. Descriptive Statistics.

Variable	Mean	Standard Deviation	Theoretical Range	Actual Range
Participative Budgeting (PB)	5.140	1.564	1–7	2.00–7.00
Role Ambiguity (RA)	1.978	0.778	1–7	1.00–4.00
Organizational Commitment (OC)	5.024	0.997	1–7	2.00–6.44
Job Satisfaction (JS)	5.574	1.113	1–7	1.00–7.00
Job Performance (JP)	5.980	0.952	1–7	2.00–7.00

Table 2. Correlation Matrix.

Variables	PB	RA	OC	JS	JP
PB	1.000				
RA	−0.498**	1.000			
OC	0.267*	−0.385**	1.000		
JS	0.347**	−0.451**	0.749**	1.000	
JP	0.265*	−0.348**	0.186	0.338**	1.000

*Correlation is significant at the 0.05 level (2-tailed).
**Correlation is significant at the 0.01 level (2-tailed).

$p < 0.01$), supporting hypothesis H1. This result supports the cognitive role of participative budgeting and prior empirical accounting studies (e.g., Chenhall & Brownell, 1988; Kren, 1992; Magner et al., 1996). The results shown in Table 2 further suggest that there are positive and significant correlations between participative budgeting and (1) organizational commitment ($r = 0.267$, $p < 0.05$, hypothesis H2), and (2) job satisfaction ($r = 0.347$, $p < 0.01$, hypothesis H3). These results confirm the motivational role and value attainment effects of participation budgeting, thus supporting hypotheses H2 and H3.

To test for hypothesis H4, a path analysis technique (Alwin & Hauser, 1975; Ahser, 1983) was used. The indirect effects of participative budgeting on job performance consist of the following paths and are computed based on the values of path coefficients in Table 3:

Path 1	PB	→	RA	→	JP		=	−0.498	×	−0.220		=	0.110
Path 2	PB	→	RA	→	JS	→ JP	=	−0.498	×	−0.146	× 0.342	=	0.025
Path 3	PB	→	OC	→	JP		=	0.099	×	−0.178		=	−0.018
Path 4	PB	→	OC	→	JS	→ JP	=	0.099	×	0.667	× 0.342	=	0.023
Path 5	PB	→	JS	→	JP		=	0.097	×	0.342		=	0.033

Total Indirect Effect = 0.173

These results suggest the relationship between participative budgeting and job performance consist two effects. First, there is a direct effect of 0.085 (see Table 3) and second there is an indirect effect of 0.173. It is suggested that an indirect effect in excess of an absolute value of 0.05 may be considered meaningful (see Bartol, 1983, p. 309; Lau & Tan, 2003). These results suggest that role ambiguity, organizational commitment and job satisfaction mediates *fully* the relationship between participative budgeting and job performance.[10] A graphical presentation of the results is shown in Fig. 2.

Table 3.   Path Analysis Results.

Dependent Variable	Independent Variable	Path Coefficient	*t*-Value	*p*-Value
RA	PB	−0.498	−4.876	0.000
OC	PB	0.099	0.789	0.433
	RA	−0.336	−2.672	0.009
JS	PB	0.097	1.100	0.275
	RA	−0.146	−1.588	0.117
	OC	0.667	8.087	0.000
JP	PB	0.085	0.664	0.509
	RA	−0.220	−1.641	0.105
	OC	−0.178	−1.079	0.284
	JS	0.342	1.992	0.050

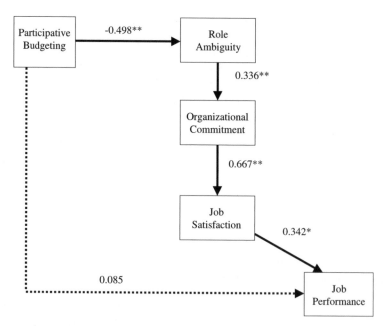

*   Coefficient is significant at the 0.05 level (2-tailed)
**Coefficient is significant at the 0.01 level (2-tailed)

Fig. 2.   Path Coefficients.

Taken together, these results support hypothesis H4, which states that there is an indirect relationship between participative budgeting and job performance through role ambiguity, organizational commitment and job satisfaction.

CONCLUSION AND LIMITATIONS

The objective of this study is to test the *three* mechanisms (i.e., cognitive, motivational and value attainment) in which participative budgeting influences on subordinates' job performance. The results of this study provide some insight into the *process* of the influence of the cognitive, motivational and value attainment role of participative budgeting on subordinates' job performance. Specifically, the cognitive role of participative budgeting reduces subordinates' levels of role ambiguity (see hypothesis H1). This result is consistent with our theoretical expectation and prior empirical studies (e.g., Chenhall & Brownell, 1988). The results of this study reveal that participative budgeting exerts the motivational effect which increases subordinates' levels of organizational commitment (see hypothesis H2). This finding is consistent with our theoretical expectations and prior studies (e.g., Nouri & Parker, 1998). Finally, our study confirms that the value attainment of participative budgeting enhanced subordinates' job satisfaction (see hypothesis H3). Taken together, the results of this study reveal that participative budgeting *indirectly* affects subordinates' job performance via role ambiguity, organizational commitment and job satisfaction (see hypothesis H4).

The results of this study advance the literature in participative budgeting in a number of ways. First, this study attempts to ascertain if there is support for the three mechanism (i.e., cognitive, motivational and value attainment) of participative budgeting. As noted, the results of this study pertaining to the three roles of participative budgeting are supportive of our theoretical expectation.

Second, the results of this study reveal that the *combined effects* of cognitive, motivational and value attainment roles of participative budgeting significantly improved subordinates' job performance. This study provides additional empirical evidence to support the robustness of the theories and results found in prior studies that examined the *cognitive* role (e.g., Kren, 1992; Magner et al., 1996; Chong, 2002; Chong & Chong, 2002a), *motivational* role (e.g., Nouri & Parker, 1998; Chong & Chong, 2002a; Chong & Leung, 2003) and *value attainment* role (e.g., Chong et al., 2005) of participative budgeting on subordinates' job performance.

Third, the results of this study have some practical implications to management. This study helps management to better understand: (1) the effect of cognitive role of participative budgeting in reducing role ambiguity, (2) the motivational effect of participative budgeting in increasing subordinates' organizational commitment, and (3) the value attainment effect of participative budgeting in increasing subordinates' job satisfaction. Taken together, the results of the study assist managers to understand and appreciate the importance of allowing subordinates to get involved in the budget-setting process.

There are a number of limitations in this study. First, our sample was selected from the financial services sector. Hence, caution should be undertaken if our results should be used to generalize other industries (e.g., manufacturing or retailing). Future research to compare the various industries may be worthwhile. Second, this study used a survey method. As cross-section survey method does not prove causal direction between variables. The causal relationships between variables may be different from what were proposed in our study. For example, mixed results are reported regarding the relationship between organizational commitment and job satisfaction. Several studies (e.g., Porter et al., 1974; Aranya et al., 1982; Harrell, Chewning, & Taylor, 1986; Lachman & Aranya, 1986a, 1986b; McGregor, Killough, & Brown, 1989) had viewed organizational commitment as a predictor of job satisfaction. Other research (e.g., Ferris & Aranya, 1983; Aranya et al., 1986; Meixner & Bline, 1989) had considered job satisfaction to be a predictor of organizational commitment. In addition, Harrell (1990) found reciprocal relationship between organizational commitment and job satisfaction. Thus, alternative empirical methods such as experimental study may be used to provide more substantial information of the direction of causality.

Third, our study may suffer from the problem of "survivorship bias" as our sample was randomly selected from senior-level managers. Our results revealed that the managers surveyed in our study had been employed in their firms for about 11 years. Therefore, the likelihood of role ambiguity is likely to be low, job satisfaction and organizational commitment are likely to be high; and consequently, job performance is likely to be high.[11] Future research may replicate our study by relying on sample drawn from lower or middle-level managers who held budget-setting responsibility.

Finally, our study has focused on an examination of the consequences of participative budgeting without considering its antecedents, despite many criticisms of this approach (see Shields & Young, 1993; Shields & Shields, 1998). For example, Shields and Shields (1998, p. 50) suggest that future studies on participative budgeting "would be more complete and reliable if they also include causal antecedents to participative budgeting in addition to its effects". Thus, it is proposed that future research should consider incorporating the antecedents (such as perceived environmental uncertainty, task uncertainty and information asymmetry) of participative budgeting.

NOTES

1. Participative budgeting refers to a " ... process whereby subordinates are given the opportunity to get involved in and have influence on the budget setting process" (Brownell, 1982a, p. 124).

2. Empirical studies that examined the motivational role of budgetary participation have generally relied on the expectancy theory (Brownell & McInnes, 1986) or goal-setting theory (Chong & Chong, 2002a; Wentzel, 2002; Chong & Leung, 2003); while studies that examined the cognitive role of budgetary participation have relied on the agency theory (Shields & Young, 1993), attribution theory (Nouri et al., 1999), information-processing theory (Kren, 1992; Magner et al., 1996) and role theory (Chenhall & Brownell, 1988; Chong & Bateman, 2000).

3. *Role ambiguity* is defined as " ... the extent to which clear information is lacking regarding: (a) the expectations associated with a role, (b) methods for fulfilling role expectations and/or (c) the consequences of role performance" (Chenhall & Brownell, 1988, p. 326).

4. Meyer, Allen, and Gellatly (1990) suggested that organizational commitment can be conceptualized in the following ways: (1) affective and (2) continuance commitment. *Continuance commitment* relates to perceived costs as a result of leaving the organization (Becker, 1960). *Affective* ("attitudinal") *commitment* is characterized as the acceptance of organizational values or goals and a willingness to exert effort on behalf of the organization (Porter et al., 1974; Angle & Perry, 1981). Our study uses the *affective* conceptualization of organizational commitment.

5. Pinder (1984, p. 95) suggests that " ... values are those things that a person believes are conducive to his/her welfare", while Locke (1983, p. 1034) claims that " ... a value is what a person consciously or subconsciously desires, wants, or seeks to attain". As noted earlier, subordinates' values may include: (1) the opportunity to express their views, (2) the feeling of being treated equally, or (3) the desire for respect or dignity (Argyris, 1952; Davis, 1957). It is suggested that values play an important role in determining job satisfaction (Katzell, 1964).

6. For example, Choo and Tan (1997) found that job satisfaction mediates the relationship between disagreement in budgetary performance evaluation style and job performance. Specifically, they found that when subordinates' preferred budgetary performance evaluation styles disagreed with the superior's preferred budgetary performance evaluation style, this disagreement led to lower levels of job satisfaction and poorer job performance among subordinates.

7. In general, it is suggested that increased effort can either lead to *immediate* performance increases if it is directed toward *current performance*, or lead to *delayed* performance increases if it is directed toward *learning* (see Bonner & Sprinkle, 2002).

The focus of this study is to investigate the increased effort, which is directed toward current performance (i.e., immediate performance) rather than directed toward learning (i.e., delayed performance).

8. Our respondents occupy the following job titles or positions: business development manager, financial accountant, human resources manager, operation manager, marketing manager and division manager.

9. We tested for non-response bias by the approach suggested by Oppenheim (1966, p. 34). We found no statistically significant differences in the mean scores between the early and late responses.

10. According to Baron and Kenny (1986) a *full* mediation occurs if a significant relationship (i.e., a significant zero-order correlation between the independent variable (participative budgeting) and the dependent variable (job performance) becomes insignificant after controlling for the effect of the intervening variable. On the other hand, if the relationship between the independent variable and the dependent variable is still significant, after controlling for the effects of the intervening variable, a *partial* mediation is deemed to have occurred.

11. A test revealed that there were no statistically significant correlations between our independent variables and dependent variable with our respondents' tenures.

ACKNOWLEDGMENTS

We appreciate the helpful comments and suggestions of Phil Reckers (Editor), the Associate Editor, and participants of the research seminar at the University of Western Australia, the 2003 Accounting and Finance Association of Australia and New Zealand (AFAANZ) Conference, Brisbane, Australia and the 2004 British Accounting Association (BAA) Annual Conference, York, United Kingdom.

REFERENCES

Ahser, R. (1983). *Causal modelling*. London: Sage.

Alwin, D. F., & Hauser, R. M. (1975). The decomposition of effects in path analysis. *American Sociological Review, 40*, 144–153.

Angle, H. L., & Perry, J. L. (1981). An empirical assessment of organizational commitment and organizational effectiveness. *Administrative Science Quarterly, 26*, 1–14.

Aranya, N. A., Kushnir, T., & Valency, A. (1986). Organizational commitment in a male-dominated profession. *Human Relations, 39*(5), 433–448.

Aranya, N. A., Lachman, R., & Amernic, J. (1982). Accountants job satisfaction: A path analysis. *Accounting, Organizations and Society, 7*(3), 201–215.

Argyris, C. (1952). *The impact of people on budgets*. New York: Controllership Foundation.

Baron, R. M., & Kenny, D. A. (1986). The moderator–mediator variable distinction in social psychological research: Conceptual, strategic and statistical considerations. *Social Psychiatry and Psychiatric Epidemiology, 51*(6), 1173–1182.

Bartol, K. M. (1979). Professionalism as a predictor of organizational commitment, role stress, and turnover: A multidimensional approach. *Academy of Management Journal, 22*(4), 815–822.

Bartol, K. M. (1983). Turnover among DP personnel: A causal analysis. *Communications of the ACM, 26*, 807–811.

Bateman, T. S., & Strasser, S. (1984). A longitudinal analysis of the antecedents of organizational commitment. *Academy of Management Journal, 27*(1), 95–112.

Becker, H. S. (1960). Notes on the concept of commitment. *American Journal of Sociology, 66*(July), 32–42.

Bline, D. M., Duchon, D., & Meixner, W. (1991). The measurement of organizational and professional commitment: An examination of the psychometric properties of two commonly used instruments. *Behavioral Research in Accounting, 3*, 1–12.

Bonner, S. E., & Sprinkle, G. B. (2002). The effects of monetary incentives on effort and task performance: Theories, evidence, and a framework for research. *Accounting, Organizations and Society, 27*, 303–345.

Brown, S. P., & Peterson, R. A. (1993). Antecedents and consequences of salesperson job satisfaction: A meta-analysis and assessment of causal effects. *Journal of Marketing Research, 30*, 63–77.

Brown, S. P., & Peterson, R. A. (1994). The effect of effort on sales performance and job satisfaction. *Journal of Marketing, 58*, 70–80.

Brownell, P. (1981). Participation in budgeting, locus of control and organizational effectiveness. *The Accounting Review, 56*(4), 844–860.

Brownell, P. (1982a). Participation in the budgeting process: When it works and when it doesn't. *Journal of Accounting Literature, 1*, 124–153.

Brownell, P. (1982b). A field study examination of budgetary participation and locus of control. *The Accounting Review, 57*(4), 766–777.

Brownell, P. (1983). The motivational impact of management-by-exception in a budgetary context. *Journal of Accounting Research, 21*(4), 456–471.

Brownell, P. (1985). Budgetary systems and the control of functionally differentiated organizational activities. *Journal of Accounting Research, 23*(2), 502–512.

Brownell, P., & Dunk, A. S. (1991). Task uncertainty and its interaction with budgetary participation and budget emphasis: Some methodological issues and empirical investigation. *Accounting, Organizations and Society, 16*(8), 693–703.

Brownell, P., & Hirst, M. (1986). Reliance on accounting information, budgetary participation, and task uncertainty: Tests of a three-way interaction. *Journal of Accounting Research, 24*(2), 241–249.

Brownell, P., & McInnes, M. (1986). Budgetary participation, motivation and managerial performance. *The Accounting Review, 61*(4), 587–600.

Brownell, P., & Merchant, K. A. (1990). The budgetary and performance influences of product standardization and manufacturing process automation. *Journal of Accounting Research, 28*(2), 388–397.

Chalos, P., & Haka, S. (1989). Participative budgeting and managerial performance. *Decision Sciences, 20*, 334–347.

Chenhall, R. H. (1986). Authoritarianism and participative budgeting: A dyadic analysis. *The Accounting Review, 61*(4), 263–272.

Chenhall, R. H., & Brownell, P. (1988). The effect of participative budgeting on job satisfaction and performance: Role ambiguity as an intervening variable. *Accounting, Organizations and Society, 13*(3), 225–253.

Cherrington, D. J., & Cherrington, J. O. (1973). Appropriate reinforcement contingencies in the budgeting process. *Empirical Research in Accounting: Selected Studies, Supplement to Journal of Accounting Research, 11*, 225–253.

Chong, V. K. (2002). A note on testing a model of cognitive budgetary participation processes using a structural equation modeling approach. *Advances in Accounting, 19*, 27–51.

Chong, V. K., & Bateman, D. (2000). The effects of role stress on budgetary participation and job satisfaction-performance linkages: A test of two different models. *Advances in Accounting Behavioral Research, 3*, 268–276.

Chong, V. K., & Chong, K. M. (2002a). Budget goal commitment and informational effects of budget participation on performance: A structural equation modeling approach. *Behavioral Research in Accounting, 14*, 65–86.

Chong, V. K., & Chong, K. M. (2002b). The role of feedback on the relationship between budgetary participation and performance. *Pacific Accounting Review, 14*(2), 33–55.

Chong, V. K., Eggleton, I. R. C., & Leong, M. K. C. (2005). The effects of value attainment and cognitive roles of budgetary participation on job performance. *Advances in Accounting Behavioral Research, 8*, 213–233.

Chong, V. K., & Leung, S. (2003). Testing a model of the motivational role of budgetary participation on job performance: A goal-setting theory analysis. *Asian Review of Accounting, 11*(1), 1–17.

Choo, F., & Tan, K. B. (1997). A study of the relations among disagreement in budgetary performance evaluation style, job-related tension, job satisfaction and performance. *Behavioral Research in Accounting, 9*, 199–218.

Covaleski, M. A., Evans III, J. H., Luft, J. L., & Shields, M. D. (2003). Budgeting research: Three theoretical perspectives and criteria for selective integration. *Journal of Management Accounting Research, 15*, 3–49.

Cronbach, L. J. (1951). Coefficient alpha and the internal structure test. *Psychometrika, 16*(3), 297–334.

Davis, K. (1957). Management by participation: Its place in today's business world. *Management Review, 46*, 69–79.

Dewar, R., & Werbel, R. M. (1979). Universalistic and contingency predictions of employee satisfaction and conflict. *Administrative Science Quarterly, 24*(3), 426–448.

Dunk, A. S. (1990). Budgetary participation, agreement on evaluation criteria and managerial performance, a research note. *Accounting, Organizations and Society, 15*(3), 171–178.

Dunk, A. S. (1992). The effects of managerial level on the relationship between budgetary participation and job satisfaction. *British Accounting Review, 24*, 207–218.

Dunk, A. S. (1993). The effect of budget emphasis and information asymmetry on the relation between budgetary participation and slack. *The Accounting Review, 68*(2), 400–410.

Dunk, A. S. (1995). The joint effects of budgetary slack and task uncertainty on subunit performance. *Accounting and Finance, 35*(2), 61–75.

Farrell, D., & Rusbult, C. E. (1981). Exchange variables as predictors of job satisfaction, job commitment, and turnover: The impact of rewards, costs, alternatives, and investments. *Organizational Behavior and Human Performance, 27*, 78–95.

Ferris, K. R., & Aranya, N. (1983). A comparison of two organizational commitment scales. *Personnel Psychology, 36*, 87–98.

Fisher, R. T. (2001). Role stress, the type A behavior pattern, and external auditor job satisfaction and performance. *Behavioral Research in Accounting, 13*, 143–170.

Franken, R. E. (1982). *Human motivation.* Monterey, CA: Brooke/Cole Publishing Company.

French, J. R. P., Jr., Israel, J., & As, D. (1960). An experiment on participation on Norwegian factory: Interpersonal dimensions of decision-making. *Human Relations, 13*(1), 3–19.

Frucot, V., & Shearon, W. T. (1991). Budgetary participation, locus of control, and Mexican managerial performance and Job satisfaction. *The Accounting Review, 66*(1), 80–99.

Gregson, T. (1992). An investigation of the causal ordering of job satisfaction and organizational commitment in turnover models in accounting. *Behavioral Research in Accounting, 4*, 80–95.

Gul, F. A., Tsui, J., Fong, S. C. C., & Kwok, H. Y. L. (1995). Decentralisation as a moderating factor in the budgetary participation–performance relationship: Some Hong Kong evidence. *Accounting and Business Research, 25*(98), 107–113.

Harrell, A. (1990). A longitudinal examination of large CPA firm auditors' personnel turnover. *Advances in Accounting, 8*, 233–246.

Harrell, A., Chewning, E., & Taylor, M. (1986). Organizational–professional conflict and the job satisfaction and turnover intentions of internal auditors. *Auditing: A Journal of Practice & Theory, 5*(Spring), 109–121.

Harrison, G. L. (1992). The cross-cultural generalizability of the relation between participants, budget emphasis and job-related attitudes. *Accounting, Organizations and Society, 17*(1), 1–15.

Jackson, S. E., & Schuler, R. S. (1985). A meta-analysis and conceptual critique of research note on role ambiguity and role conflict in work settings. *Organizational Behavior and Human Decision Processes, 36*, 16–78.

Johnston, M. W., Parasuraman, A., Futrell, C. M., & Black, W. C. (1990). A longitudinal assessment of the impact of selected organizational influences on salesperson's organizational commitment during early development. *Journal of Marketing Research, 27*, 333–344.

Kahn, R. L., Wolfe, D. M., Quinn, R. P., Snoek, J. D., & Rosenthal, R. (1964). *Organizational stress: Studies of role conflict and role ambiguity*. New York: Wiley.

Kalbers, L. P., & Fogarty, T. J. (1995). Professionalism and its consequences: A study of internal auditors. *Auditing: A Journal of Practice & Theory, 14*(Spring), 64–68.

Katzell, R. A. (1964). Personal values, job satisfaction, and job behavior. In: H. Borow (Ed.), *Man in a world at work*. Boston: Houghton Mifflin.

Katzell, R. A., Thompson, D. E., & Guzzo, R. A. (1992). How job satisfaction and job performance are and are not linked. In: C. J. Cranny, P. C. Smith & E. F. Stone (Eds), *Job satisfaction: How it affects their performance*. New York: Lexington Books.

Kenis, I. (1979). Effects of budgetary goal characteristics on managerial attitudes and performance. *The Accounting Review, 54*(4), 707–721.

Kerlinger, F. A. (1964). *Foundations of behavioral research*. New York: Holt, Rinehart and Winston.

Kerlinger, F. A., & Lee, H. B. (2000). *Foundations of behavioral research* (4th ed.). South Melbourne, Australia: Wadsworth, Thomson Learning.

Ketchand, A. A., & Strawser, J. R. (1998). The existence multiple measures of organizational commitment and experience-related differences in a public accounting setting. *Behavioral Research in Accounting, 13*, 221–251.

Kompass Australia. (1999). Prahran: Peter Isaacson.

Kren, L. (1992). Budgetary participation and managerial performance: The impact of information and environmental volatility. *The Accounting Review, 67*(3), 511–526.

Kren, L., & Liao, W. M. (1988). The role of accounting information in the control of organizations: A review of the evidence. *Journal of Accounting Literature, 7*(1), 280–309.

Lachman, R., & Aranya, N. (1986a). Evaluation of alternative models of commitments and job attitudes of professionals. *Journal of Occupational Behavior, 7*, 227–243.

Lachman, R., & Aranya, N. (1986b). Job attitudes and turnover intentions among professionals in different work settings. *Organization Studies, 7*(3), 279–293.

Lau, C. M., & Buckland, C. (2000). Budget emphasis, participation, task difficulty and performance: The effect of diversity within culture. *Accounting and Business Research, 31*(1), 37–55.

Lau, C. M., Low, L. C., & Eggleton, I. R. C. (1995). The impact of reliance on accounting performance measures on job-related tension and managerial performance: Additional evidence. *Accounting, Organizations and Society, 20*(5), 359–381.

Lau, C. M., Low, L. C., & Eggleton, I. R. C. (1997). The interactive effect of budget emphasis, participation and task difficulty on managerial performance: A cross-cultural study. *Accounting, Auditing and Accountability Journal, 10*(2), 175–197.

Lau, C. M., & Tan, S. L. C. (1998). The impact of budget emphasis, participation and task difficulty on managerial performance: A cross-cultural study of the financial services sector. *Management Accounting Research, 9*, 163–183.

Lau, C. M., & Tan, S. L. C. (2003). The effects of participation and job-relevant information on the relationship between evaluative style and job satisfaction. *Review of Quantitative Finance and Accounting, 21*, 17–34.

Locke, E. A. (1976). The nature and causes of job satisfaction. In: M. D. Dunnette (Ed.), *Handbook of industrial and organizational psychology*. Chicago: Rand McNally & Company.

Locke, E. A. (1983). The nature and causes of job satisfaction. In: M. D. Dunnette (Ed.), *Handbook of industrial and organizational psychology*. New York: Wiley.

Locke, E. A. (1986). Job attitudes in historical perspective. In: D. Wren (Ed.), *Paper dedicated to the development of modern management*, Academy of Management.

Locke, E. A., & Latham, G. P. (1990). *A theory of goal setting and task performance*. New Jersey: Prentice-Hall.

Locke, E. A., & Schweiger, D. (1979). Participation in decision-making: One more look. In: B. M. Staw (Ed.), *Research in Organizational Behaviour* (Vol. 1), Greenwich, CT: JAI Press.

Lowin, A. (1968). Participative decision making: A model, literature critique, and prescriptions for research. *Organizational Behavior and Human Performance, 3*, 68–106.

Magner, N., Welker, R. B., & Campbell, T. L. (1996). Testing a model of cognitive budgetary participation processes in a latent variable structural equations framework. *Accounting and Business Research, 27*(1), 41–50.

McGregor, C. C., Killough, L. N., & Brown, R. M. (1989). An investigation of organizational professional conflict in Management Accounting. *Journal of Management Accounting Research, 1*(Fall), 104–118.

Meixner, W. F., & Bline, D. M. (1989). Professional and job-related attitudes and the behaviors they influence among government accountants. *Accounting, Auditing and Accountability Journal, 2*(1), 8–20.

Merchant, K. A. (1981). The design of the corporate budgeting system: Influences on managerial behavior and performance. *The Accounting Review, 56*(4), 813–829.

Meyer, J. P., Allen, N. J., & Gellatly, I. R. (1990). Affective and continuance to the organization: Evaluations of measures and analysis of concurrent and time-lagged relations. *Journal of Applied Psychology, 75*(6), 710–720.

Mia, L. (1988). Managerial attitude, motivation and the effectiveness of budgetary participation. *Accounting, Organizations and Society, 13*(5), 465–475.

Mia, L. (1989). The impact of participation in budgeting and job difficulty on managerial performance and work motivation: A research note. *Accounting, Organizations and Society*, *14*(4), 347–357.

Mia, L., & Chenhall, R. H. (1994). The usefulness of management accounting systems, functional, differentiation and managerial effectiveness. *Accounting, Organizations and Society*, *19*(1), 1–13.

Milani, K. (1975). The relationship of participation in budget setting to industrial supervisor performance and attitudes: A field study. *The Accounting Review*, *50*(2), 274–284.

Mowday, R., Steer, R., & Porter, L. (1979). The measurement of organizational commitment. *Journal of Vocational Behaviour*, *14*(2), 224–247.

Nouri, H. (1994). Using organizational commitment and job involvement to predict budgetary slack: A research note. *Accounting, Organizations and Society*, *19*(3), 289–295.

Nouri, H., Kyj, L., & Dunk, A. S. (1999). The effect of performance reporting on budgetary participation: An attribution theory analysis. *Advances in Management Accounting*, *8*, 211–223.

Nouri, H., & Parker, R. J. (1996a). The effect of organizational commitment on the relation between budgetary participation and budgetary slack. *Behavioural Research in Accounting*, *8*, 74–90.

Nouri, H., & Parker, R. J. (1996b). The interactive effect of budget-based compensation, organizational commitment, and job involvement on managers' propensities to create budgetary slack. *Advances in Accounting*, *14*, 209–222.

Nouri, H., & Parker, R. J. (1998). The relationship between budget participation and job performance: The roles of budget adequacy and organizational commitment. *Accounting, Organizations and Society*, *23*(5/6), 467–483.

Nunnally, J. C. (1967). *Psychometric theory*. New York: McGraw-Hill.

O'Connor, N. G. (1995). The influence of organizational culture on the usefulness of budget participation by Singapore–Chinese managers. *Accounting, Organizations and Society*, *20*, 383–403.

Oppenheim, A. N. (1966). *Questionnaire design and attitudes measurement*. London: Heinemann Educational Books, Ltd.

Pasewark, W. R., & Strawser, J. R. (1996). The determinants and outcomes associated with job insecurity in a professional accounting environment. *Behavioral Research in Accounting*, *8*, 91–113.

Pinder, C. C. (1984). *Work motivation*. Glenview, IL: Scott Foresman.

Porter, L. W., Steers, R. W., Mowday, R. T., & Boulian, P. V. (1974). Organizational commitment, job satisfaction, and turnover among psychiatric technicians. *Journal of Applied Psychology*, *59*(5), 603–609.

Poznanski, P. J., & Bline, D. M. (1997). Using structural equation modeling to investigate the causal ordering of job satisfaction and organizational commitment among staff accountants. *Behavioral Research in Accounting*, *9*, 154–171.

Rebele, J. E., & Michaels, R. E. (1990). Independent auditors' role stress: Antecedent, outcome and moderating variables. *Behavioral Research in Accounting*, *2*, 124–153.

Rhoads, G. K., Singh, J., & Goodell, P. W. (1994). The multiple dimensions of role ambiguity and their impact upon psychological and behavioral outcomes of industrial salespeople. *Journal of Personal Selling and Sale Management*, *14*, 1–24.

Rizzo, J. R., House, R. J., & Lirtzman, S. I. (1970). Role conflict and ambiguity in complex organizations. *Administrative Science Quarterly*, *15*(2), 150–163.

Shields, J. F., & Shields, M. D. (1998). Antecedents of participative budgeting. *Accounting, Organizations and Society, 23*(1), 49–76.

Shields, M. D., & Young, S. M. (1993). Antecedents and consequences of participative budgeting: Evidence on the effects of asymmetrical information. *Journal of Management Accounting Research, 5*, 265–280.

Strauss, G. (1963). Some notes on power-equalization. In: H. Leavitt (Ed.), *The social science of organizations: Four perspectives*. Englewood Cliffs, NJ: Prentice-Hall.

Van Sell, M., Brief, A. P., & Schuler, R. S. (1981). Role conflict and role ambiguity: Integration of the literature and directions for future research. *Human Relations, 34*(1), 43–71.

Vroom, V. H. (1964). *Work and motivation*. New York: Wiley.

Wentzel, K. (2002). The influence of fairness perceptions and goal commitment on managers' performance in a budget setting. *Behavioral Research in Accounting, 14*, 247–271.

Williams, L. J., & Hazer, J. T. (1986). Antecedents and consequences of satisfaction and commitment in turnover models: A re-analysis using latent variable structural equation models. *Journal of Applied Psychology, 71*(2), 219–231.

APPENDIX. EMPIRICAL STUDIES ON THE COGNITIVE, MOTIVATIONAL AND VALUE ATTAINMENT ROLES OF PARTICIPATIVE BUDGETING ON DEPENDENT VARIABLES

Study	Method	The Roles of Participative Budgeting	Variables Studied: Independent Variable (IND), Moderating Variable (MOD), Intervening Variable (INV), Antecedent Variable (ANT) and Dependent Variable (DEP)	Results
Cherrington and Cherrington (1973)	Lab experiment	Motivational and value attainment	IND = Participative budgeting and budget-based incentives DEP = Performance and job satisfaction	There is a significant interaction between participative budgeting and budget-based incentives on performance and job satisfaction
Kenis (1979)	Survey	Motivation and value attainment	IND = Participative budgeting DEP = Attitude, motivation, job-related tension and budgetary performance	There is a positive and significant association between participative budgeting and attitude, budget motivation and budgetary performance. There is a negative and significant association between participative budgeting and job-related tension
Brownell (1981)	Lab experiment	Value attainment	IND = Participative budgeting MOD = Locus of control DEP = Performance	There is a significant two-way interaction between participative budgeting and locus of control on performance.
Brownell (1982a)	Survey	Value attainment	IND = Budget emphasis MOD = Participative budgeting DEP = Performance and job satisfaction	There is a significant two-way interaction between participative budgeting and management-by-exception on motivation

APPENDIX (Continued)

Study	Method	The Roles of Participative Budgeting	Variables Studied: Independent Variable (IND), Moderating Variable (MOD), Intervening Variable (INV), Antecedent Variable (ANT) and Dependent Variable (DEP)	Results
Brownell (1982b)	Survey	Value attainment	IND = MOD = Locus of control DEP = Motivation	There is a marginal significant two-way interaction between participative budgeting and locus of control on performance. There is a significant two-way interaction between participative budgeting and locus of control on job satisfaction
Brownell (1983)	Survey	Value attainment	IND = Participative budgeting MOD = Leadership-style DEP = Performance and job satisfaction	There is a significant two-way interaction between participative budgeting and leadership-style on performance and job satisfaction
Brownell (1985)	Survey	Cognitive	IND = Participative budgeting MOD = Functional area DEP = Performance	There is a significant two-way interaction between participative budgeting and functional area on performance
Brownell and Hirst (1986)	Survey	Cognitive	IND = Budget emphasis MOD = Participative budgeting DEP = Job-related tension and performance	There is a marginal significant two-way interaction between participative budgeting and budget emphasis on job-related tension and performance
Brownell and McInnes (1986)	Survey	Motivational	IND = Participative budgeting INV = Motivation DEP = Performance	There is a positive and significant relationship between budgetary participation and performance. There is no significant relationship between participative budgeting and motivation

Study	Method	Theory	Variables	Findings
Chenhall (1986)	Survey	Value attainment	IND = Participative budgeting MOD = Authoritarian DEP = Job satisfaction	There is a significant interaction between participative budgeting and authoritarian dyad on job satisfaction
Chenhall and Brownell (1988)	Survey	Cognitive	IND = Participative budgeting INV = Role ambiguity DEP = Performance and job satisfaction	There is a negative and significant association between participative budgeting and role ambiguity. There is a negative and significant association between role ambiguity performance and job satisfaction
Mia (1988)	Survey	Cognitive	IND = Participative budgeting MOD = Attitude, motivation DEP = Performance	There is a significant interaction between participative budgeting and attitude on performance. There is a significant interaction between participative budgeting and motivation on performance
Mia (1989)	Survey	Cognitive	IND = Participative budgeting MOD = Task difficulty DEP = Performance	There is a significant interaction between participative budgeting and task difficulty on performance
Chalos and Haka (1989)	Lab experiment	Cognitive	IND = Participative budgeting MOD = State information	There is a significant association between participative budgeting and state information on performance
Brownell and Merchant (1990)	Survey	Cognitive	IND = Participative budgeting MOD = Product standardization DEP = Performance	There is a significant interaction between participative budgeting and product standardization on performance
Dunk (1990)	Survey	Cognitive	IND = Participative budgeting MOD = Performance evaluation criteria agreement DEP = Performance	There is a significant interaction between participative budgeting and performance evaluation criteria agreement on performance
Brownell and Dunk (1991)	Survey	Cognitive	IND = Budget emphasis MOD = Task uncertainty, task difficulty, task variability and participative budgeting DEP = Performance	There is a significant three-way interaction between participative budgeting, task uncertainty and budget emphasis on performance. There is a significant three-way interaction between participative budgeting, task difficulty and budget emphasis on performance

APPENDIX (*Continued*)

Study	Method	The Roles of Participative Budgeting	Variables Studied: Independent Variable (IND), Moderating Variable (MOD), Intervening Variable (INV), Antecedent Variable (ANT) and Dependent Variable (DEP)	Results
Frucot and Shearon (1991)	Survey	Value attainment	IND = Participative budgeting MOD = Locus of control DEP = Performance and job satisfaction	There is a marginal significant two-way interaction between participative budgeting and locus of control on performance. There is a positive and significant association between participative budgeting and job satisfaction
Dunk (1992)	Survey	Value attainment	IND = Participative budgeting MOD = Management level DEP = Job satisfaction	There is a significant interaction between participative budgeting and management level on job satisfaction
Harrison (1992)	Survey	Value attainment	IND = Budget emphasis MOD = Participative budgeting, national culture DEP = Job-related tension and job satisfaction	There is a significant interaction between participative budgeting and budget emphasis on job-related tension but not with job satisfaction
Kren (1992)	Survey	Cognitive	IND = Participative budgeting INV = Job-relevant information DEP = Performance	There is a positive and significant association between participative budgeting and job-relevant information
Dunk (1993)	Survey	Cognitive	IND = Budget emphasis MOD = Participative budgeting, information asymmetry DEP = Budgetary slack	There is a significant three-way interaction between budget emphasis, participative budgeting and information asymmetry on budgetary slack
Shields and Young (1993)	Survey	Cognitive	IND = Participative budgeting ANT = Information asymmetry INV = Budget-based incentives DEP = Firm-wide performance	There is a positive association between participative budgeting and budget-based incentives

Study	Method	Theory	Variables	Findings
Dunk (1995)	Survey	Cognitive	IND = Participative budgeting MOD = Information asymmetry DEP = Performance	There is a significant two-way interaction between participative budgeting and information asymmetry on performance
Gul, Tsui, Fong, and Kwok (1995)	Survey	Cognitive	IND = Participative budgeting MOD = Decentralization DEP = Performance	There is a significant two-way interaction between participative budgeting and decentralization on performance
Lau, Low, and Eggleton (1995)	Survey	Cognitive	IND = Budget emphasis MOD = Task uncertainty, task difficulty, task variability and participative budgeting DEP = Performance	There is a significant three-way interaction between participative budgeting, task uncertainty and budget emphasis on performance. There is a significant three-way interaction between participative budgeting, task difficulty and budget emphasis on performance
Lau, Low, and Eggleton (1997)	Survey	Cognitive	IND = Budget emphasis MOD = Task difficulty, participative budgeting and national culture DEP = Performance	There is a significant three-way interaction between participative budgeting, task difficulty and budget emphasis on performance
Lau and Tan (1998)	Survey	Cognitive	IND = Budget emphasis MOD = Task difficulty, participative budgeting and national culture DEP = Performance	There is a significant three-way interaction between participative budgeting, task difficulty and budget emphasis on performance
Nouri and Parker (1998)	Survey	Motivational and cognitive	IND = Participative budgeting INV = Budget adequacy and organizational commitment DEP = Performance	There is a positive and significant association between participative budgeting and budget adequacy and organizational commitment. There is a positive association between participative budgeting and performance through the intervening roles of budget adequacy and organizational commitment
Nouri, Kyj, and Dunk (1999)	Lab experiment	Cognitive	IND = Participative budgeting DEP = Performance	There is a positive and significant association between participative budgeting and performance

APPENDIX (*Continued*)

Study	Method	The Roles of Participative Budgeting	Variables Studied: Independent Variable (IND), Moderating Variable (MOD), Intervening Variable (INV), Antecedent Variable (ANT) and Dependent Variable (DEP)	Results
Chong and Bateman (2000)	Survey	Cognitive	IND = Participative budgeting INV = Role ambiguity and role conflict MOD = Role ambiguity and role conflict DEP = Performance and job satisfaction	There is a negative and significant association between participative budgeting and role ambiguity. There is a negative and significant association between role ambiguity and performance and job satisfaction
Lau and Buckland (2000)	Survey	Cognitive	IND = Budget emphasis MOD = Task difficulty, participative budgeting and national culture DEP = Performance	There is a significant three-way interaction between participative budgeting, task difficulty and budget emphasis on performance
Chong (2002)	Survey	Cognitive	IND = Participative budgeting INV = Role Ambiguity DEP = Job performance and job satisfaction	There is a negative association between participative budgeting and role ambiguity. There is a negative and statistically significant association between job performance and job satisfaction
Chong and Chong (2002a)	Survey	Motivational and cognitive	IND = Participative budgeting INV = Job-relevant information, budget goal commitment DEP = Performance	There is a positive association between participative budgeting and performance through the intervening roles of budget goal commitment and job-relevant information
Chong and Chong (2002b)	Survey	Cognitive	IND = Participative budgeting INV = Feedback DEP = Performance	Participative budgeting and feedback, independently, have no effect on performance. Participative budgeting and feedback together led to higher performance

Wentzel (2002)	Survey	Motivational	IND = Participative budgeting INV = Fairness perceptions, goal commitment DEP = Managerial Performance	There is a positive and significant association between participative budgeting and managerial performance through the intervening roles of fairness perceptions and goal commitment
Chong and Leung (2003)	Survey	Motivational	IND = Participative budgeting INV = Budget goal difficulty, budget goal commitment DEP = Job performance	There is a positive association between participative budgeting and job performance through the intervening roles of budget goal difficulty and budget goal commitment
Lau and Tan (2003)	Survey	Cognitive	IND = Budget emphasis INV = Participative budgeting, job-relevant information DEP Job satisfaction	There is a positive and significant effect of budget emphasis on job satisfaction through the intervening roles of participative budgeting and job-relevant information
Chong et al. (2005)	Survey	Cognitive and value attainment	IND = Participative budgeting INV = Job-relevant information, job satisfaction DEP = Performance	There is a significant positive effect of the value attainment and cognitive roles of participative budgeting on subordinates' job performance

THE IMPACT OF AUDITOR TENURE ON INITIAL BOND RATINGS

Aaron D. Crabtree, Duane M. Brandon and John J. Maher

ABSTRACT

The desirability of mandated auditor rotation represents an ongoing debate in the accounting profession. Proponents assert that audit quality (through auditor independence) is threatened by extended auditor–client relationships. Opponents assert that mandatory auditor rotation will actually decrease audit quality, primarily due to the time required for auditors to learn the nuances of a client's business processes. Our research contributes to this important debate by providing empirical evidence regarding the capital markets effects of audit tenure. Specifically, we examine newly issued bonds over the period 1990–2002 and find auditor tenure to be positively related to ratings received. This finding remains consistent across all sample issues regardless of investment grade, firm performance, or time period. We find no evidence that extended auditor–client relationships result in a decrease in the perceptions of audit quality.

Advances in Accounting, Volume 22, 97–121
Copyright © 2006 by Elsevier Ltd.
All rights of reproduction in any form reserved
ISSN: 0882-6110/doi:10.1016/S0882-6110(06)22005-4

INTRODUCTION

Recent corporate problems with financial reporting have spawned intense scrutiny of the auditor–client relationship. Among the most widely debated issues is the potential for negative consequences to be associated with lengthy auditor–client relationships. A major concern expressed is that extended auditor tenure could lead to reduced auditor independence and, subsequently, has led to calls for mandatory audit firm rotation. Several concerned constituencies have responded by pointing out that mandatory audit firm rotation could conceivably decrease overall audit quality. These opponents of mandatory rotation argue that the costs associated with rotating auditors far outweigh the benefits particularly in light of recently enacted legislation designed to strengthen auditor independence.

Our research contributes to this important debate by providing empirical evidence regarding capital markets effects of audit tenure. Specifically, we examine the effects of audit firm tenure on the *perceptions* of auditor independence as discerned by one clearly identifiable class of sophisticated end-users, bond rating analysts. This context provides a valuable and direct setting in which to examine the effects of auditor tenure on end-user perceptions of auditor independence. Bond rating analysts assign a specific rating to a new issue utilizing all the information they can reasonably obtain about the firm and its future prospects of making the required interest and principle payments as scheduled. A critical component of the information set the analysts' utilize in making this decision is the firm's audited financial statements (Standard & Poors, S&P Rating Group, 2003).

Theory suggests and research shows that factors associated with audit quality affect market participants' perceptions of financial statement information (DeAngelo, 1981; Balvers, McDonald, & Miller, 1988; Beatty, 1989; Menon & Williams, 1991; Teoh & Wong, 1993; Michaely & Shaw, 1995; Muzatko, Johnstone, Mayhew, & Rittenberg, 2004). The level of audit quality, or confidence inspired by the auditor, is directly affected by the level of perceived independence possessed by the auditor (DeAngelo, 1981; Johnstone, Sutton, & Warfield, 2001). Increased auditor tenure has been cited as having a negative or positive effect on the quality of the audit, partially due to its perceived effects on independence. Those espousing a negative effect, such as the popular press, maintain that increased auditor tenure results in decreased auditor independence, thereby decreasing the quality of the audit and increasing the risk of the firm which would be consistent with a lower bond rating. Alternatively, others maintain that increased auditor tenure does not negatively affect independence, but actually leads to a better audit due to a more in-depth understanding of the client and its business which could reduce the actual or perceived risk of the firm, and correspondingly, is consistent with a higher bond rating.

Our research empirically examines the relationship between audit tenure and bond ratings to provide insight into the effects of increased auditor tenure on the perceptions of bond rating analysts. Bond ratings reflect the analysts' perception of the quality of the auditor's examination of the financial statements that support the issue. Higher perceived quality of financial statements, ceteris paribus, should lead to a higher firm bond rating. Ratings assigned to debt are a significant determinant of the ultimate yield the firm has to pay (Ziebart & Reiter, 1992). Higher ratings represent smaller default risk and are consistent with a reduced effective interest rate incurred by the firm. The spread between rating classes typically represents substantial and material interest differences. The use of new bond issues helps ensure rating analysts have performed a current and detailed analysis of the firm's overall future prospects, and consequently, assign a current rating. This "fresh" rating context is more appropriate for examining the effects of audit tenure than using seasoned ratings because the rating itself may be stale. Examining newly issued bonds is also a better context than rating changes because some research has demonstrated that rating changes typically occur after the bulk of firm performance changes have occurred rather than proactively (Goh & Ederington, 1993; Ederington & Goh, 1998). Thus, tests using new bond issues should be more powerful and appropriate here. Our findings provide empirical evidence directly germane to the current debate concerning the effects of audit tenure on audit quality. We utilize this setting to examine the importance of audit tenure in the bond rating decision process, and subsequently obtain insights regarding bond analysts' perceptions concerning auditor independence and audit quality.

We examine newly issued bonds over the period 1990–2002 and find auditor tenure to be positively related to ratings received. This is consistent with the inference that the longer the audit tenure the higher the rating. This finding remains reliable across all sampled issues, regardless of investment grade, firm performance, or time period. Moreover, the results hold true even after we consider detailed information regarding the level of audit and non-audit service fees paid to the client, i.e. for a subsample of firms issuing bonds after the fee data was publicly available.

The remainder of this paper is organized as follows. The next section discusses relevant prior literature and is followed by the development of our hypothesis. This is followed by a description of our research method. Finally, we provide results and conclude with a summary.

LITERATURE REVIEW

Auditor Tenure and Rotation

A substantial portion of the Sarbanes-Oxley Act of 2002 (S-O) is intended to more clearly define and preserve auditor independence. In addition to specific regulations and prohibitions that S-O places on external auditors of public companies and their clients, Section 207 of S-O directed the General Accounting Office (GAO) to conduct a study of the effects of mandatory audit firm rotation to determine its efficacy. Upon completion of the study, the GAO refrained from making specific recommendations, but instead, recommended regulatory agencies to monitor the situation to determine if mandatory rotation is needed in addition to auditor independence safeguards currently in place (GAO, 2003). Furthermore, the GAO recommended audit committees to seriously consider voluntary auditor rotation. Given these important profession-critical recommendations and the possibility of additional future regulation, it is essential to obtain a clear understanding of both the actual and perceived audit quality implications of extended auditor tenure.

Proponents of auditor rotation primarily argue that rotation can remedy the potential reduction in auditor independence and related declines in the quality of financial reporting resulting from lengthy client relationships. This could result from the economic alignment of the auditor with the client as a result of quasi rents and/or a lack of professional skepticism on the part of the auditor as a result of complacency (DeAngelo, 1981; Carcello & Nagy, 2004). This argument is particularly important given that previous research shows negative capital market consequences when audit quality perceptions are compromised by a possible reduction in auditor independence (e.g. Frankel, Johnson, & Nelson, 2002; Francis & Ke, 2003; Brandon, Crabtree, & Maher, 2004). Proponents also assert that, in addition to pressures to retain the client, an extended relationship may cause the auditor to become complacent. This could lead to substandard audits or even acquiescence to client preferences. Proponents say mandatory rotation would bring a "fresh look" at firm financial statements which could increase the likelihood that the auditor will uncover misstatements and/or challenge questionable accounting practices. Moreover, rotation could conceivably lead to audit innovations that allow auditors to audit new clients more efficiently.

Opponents of auditor rotation, generally led by the accounting profession (Melancon, 2002; Copeland, 2002; PricewaterhouseCoopers, 2002), argue that restricting the length of relationships is likely to decrease audit quality. They point out that newly appointed auditors must rely more heavily on client estimates and representation in the initial years of an audit engagement. As auditor tenure increases, the auditor learns more about the client and obtains a more-detailed understanding of its business processes, allowing the auditor to reduce reliance on management estimation and representation resulting in a more effective audit. Managers working for the company to be audited also tend to be opposed to mandatory auditor rotation because of the costs and time commitment associated with bringing new auditors up to speed regarding their company activities and processes. Moreover, new auditors may not have the industry expertise or may not possess the same level of firm-specific knowledge required to audit a new client effectively (Dunham, 2002).

Auditor Tenure and Audit Quality

Prior research has established auditor independence, both in fact and appearance, to be an important aspect of audit quality (DeAngelo, 1981). If auditors appear to lack independence, this increases the perception that they are less objective and therefore less likely to report a discovered misstatement (Lowe & Pany, 1995). For example, both Titman and Trueman (1986) and Datar, Feltham, and Hughes (1991) provide models in which the initial value of an IPO is demonstrated to be an increasing function of audit quality. Further, extant research provides support that there are capital market consequences when the perception of audit quality is compromised by a possible reduction in independence (Frankel et al., 2002; Raghunandan, 2003; Francis & Ke, 2003; Brandon et al., 2004).

Much of the existing empirical research on the effects of auditor tenure on audit quality and independence (both in fact and appearance) provides evidence that audit quality may actually increase with increased tenure (e.g. Ghosh & Moon, 2005; Carcello & Nagy, 2004; Mansi, Maxwell, & Miller, 2004; Myers, Myers, & Omer, 2003). However, other research suggests this may not be the case (e.g. Knapp, 1991; Deis & Giroux, 1992; Davis, Soo, & Trompeter, 2003; Choi & Doogar, 2005). Our research provides useful information relevant to the debate and adds to the existing literature by empirically documenting the association auditor tenure has with new bond ratings.

Studies investigating the effects of auditor tenure on actual audit quality examine a variety of dependent variables and report somewhat inconsistent results. For example, Geiger and Raghunandan (2002) investigate audit reporting failures and find no evidence of impaired audit quality when auditor tenure is longer. In fact, their results indicate that audit failures are more likely to occur in the beginning of the auditor–client relationship. Carcello and Nagy (2004) investigate the relationship between tenure and fraudulent financial reporting and also find that fraudulent reporting is more likely in the early years of the relationship. Furthermore, they report no evidence of a relationship between fraud and longer tenure. On the other side of the debate, Choi and Doogar (2005) find systematic evidence that longer auditor tenure is negatively associated with the likelihood of a going-concern qualification. They find that this negative association is particularly true for non-Big-Five auditors.

Approaching the topic of audit tenure from a different perspective, an alternative stream of research investigates the relation between accounting accruals and auditor tenure. The results of this research are mixed with Myers et al. (2003) and Johnson, Khurana, and Reynolds (2002) finding that longer audit tenure does not decrease audit quality, while Davis et al. (2003) and Deis and Giroux (1992) indicate that audit quality decreases as tenure increases. Another stream of behavioral research investigates whether *perceptions* of audit quality are affected by auditor tenure, and also report inconsistent results (e.g. Shockley, 1981; Knapp, 1991; Chang & Monroe, 2002).

Two recent capital market studies investigate the effects of auditor tenure on market participants' perceptions of audit quality. Ghosh and Moon (2005) report that both earnings response coefficients and seasoned bond ratings are positively related to auditor tenure. These findings are consistent with capital market participants perceiving an increase in audit quality as auditor tenure increases. Mansi et al. (2004) note that auditor tenure has a positive effect on bond yields, but that extended auditor relationships may be more beneficial in situations where default risk is higher.

Overall, the effect of auditor tenure on the perception of auditor independence (and audit quality) has not yet been clarified (e.g. Knapp, 1991; Chang & Monroe, 2002; Ghosh & Moon, 2005; Mansi et al., 2004; Choi & Doogar, 2005). Our research adds to the existing literature regarding perceptions of audit quality. Our analysis allows inferences to be made concerning an important group of informed financial statement users, i.e. bond rating analysts. We utilize a large sample of new bond issues and, thus, examine ratings that are 'fresh' and reflect a current assessment of the issuing firm's financial health and future prospects. We intentionally avoid using seasoned bond ratings because of the substantial time involved in making rating changes. The first step involved with a ratings change is being placed on a credit "watch-list". The time an issue spends on the watch-list varies substantially. The average is over 3 months, with some taking as long as 8 months (Moody's Investor Service, 1998). Part of the reason for the long time an issue spends on the watch-list reflects ratings agencies' reluctance to change ratings until a reversal is unlikely to happen in a the near future (Cantor, 2001). Ratings changes have also been shown to lag changes in a firm's default risk (Loffler, 2003). Therefore, new issue ratings represent the most appropriate vehicle for empirically examining bond rating analysts' current perceptions regarding the effects of audit tenure.

Bond Ratings

Bonds provide an important mechanism by which firms obtain new funds to finance new and continuing activities and projects. Typically, firms raise substantially more "new" funds in the bond market each year than in the equity market. For example, in 2001 companies raised $1,209 billion in the bond market compared to $262 billion in the equity market (Investment Dealer's Digest, IDD Inc., 2002). The assigned rating is important because of what it implies about the bond issue. An immediate implication is the effect it has on the subsequent yield. Higher bond ratings imply a lower required effective interest rate, resulting in lower interest payments. Yield spread between categories can be substantial, resulting in a difference of tens of millions of dollars in interest over the life of the obligation.

In addition to the implications related to interest yield, there are also many regulatory requirements in the United States and abroad that are specified in terms of a firm's assigned bond rating. Several agencies allow investments to be made only in the top rating categories (e.g. Baa3 and above), typically referred to as "Investment Grade" debt. For example, the Federal Reserve Board and the Federal Home Loan Bank System permit their members to invest in corporate debt only with investment grade ratings. The Department of Labor allows pension funds to invest in securities only in top rating categories. In addition, the New York and Philadelphia Stock Exchanges establish margin requirements for mortgage securities depending on their ratings (S&P Rating Group, 2003). The fact that regulatory agencies define requirements partially based on independent ratings indicates the importance and degree to which the rating process is ingrained in the market system.

There is substantial empirical evidence in the finance and accounting literature that establishes the importance and information content of bond ratings and changes in bond ratings. Previous studies have demonstrated evidence of stock price movement and abnormal returns after bond rating changes (Holthausen & Leftwich, 1986; Glascock, Davidson, & Henderson, 1987). Hand, Holthausen, and Leftwich (1992) examine the bond and stock price effects that occur when a firm is placed on Standard & Poor's Credit Watch List, as well as the effects of an actual rating downgrade or upgrade. They conclude that there are both bond and stock price effects associated with all these events. Ziebart and Reiter (1992) provide evidence that bond ratings have a direct impact on bond yields. Dichev and Piotroski (2001) examine the equity market effects of rating changes and show that firms that receive upgrades on their bond ratings outperform firms that receive bond rating downgrades by 10–14% in common stock performance in the year following the bond rating change. Furthermore, they report that current ratings changes predict not only future rating changes, but also changes in the firm's future profitability.

While bond market research often complements and reinforces research performed in the equity markets, the results can differ due to the underlying divergence in the composition of the stakeholders and their contingent claims on the firm. Equity stakeholders are predominantly interested in the uncertain return they will earn from dividends and price appreciation of shares. They are the beneficiary of the residual earnings after all other claims are paid by the firm. This unconstrained upside potential can result in a readiness to engage in high-risk projects. Bondholders, in contrast, because their uppermost gain has been established and defined by the terms of the debt contract, are chiefly interested in protecting the firm's capacity to achieve contractually required interest and principle payments. While management serves the interests of shareholders, the interests of debt-holders are not management's prime consideration. This is referred to by Penman (2004) as the "moral hazard" of debt which can result in decisions having disproportionate consequences for each constituency. This makes the bond market potentially incongruent with the equity market and, therefore, an interesting and important environment in which to analyze issues that are significant to the accounting profession.

Debt ratings provide a particularly useful context in which to examine questions related to the perceptions of auditor independence because bond rating analysts rely extensively upon audited financial information to conduct their fundamental analysis of the company. As part of its process to assign the rating, Standard & Poor's (S&P) requires 5 years of audited financial statements. These financial statements are frequently utilized to develop various ratio guidelines based on profitability and leverage measures that are generally necessary for a firm to achieve in order to attain a particular bond rating. Moreover, S&P's Corporate Ratings Criteria (2003) states "Ratings require audited data, and the rating does not entail auditing a company's financial records" (p. 22) clearly indicating the reliance of bond rating analysts on the external auditors' job of attesting to the reliability of the firm's financial statements. This makes any information that pertains to the quality and/or independence of the auditor of utmost importance to the bond rating agencies whose existence depends on their ability to provide unbiased evaluations of firm default risk. Bonds have different underlying characteristics than a firm's common shares and also represent differential claims to the firm's underlying assets. The differences in fundamental security characteristics make bonds an interesting and important alternative capital market setting in which to explore the perceptions of auditor independence and the corresponding issue of mandatory auditor rotation.

HYPOTHESIS DEVELOPMENT

Similar to IPOs, when a firm issues bonds, analysts are taking a detailed current look at the firm and its future prospects. The literature related to IPOs and audit quality is particularly relevant because audit tenure has shown that pricing is sensitive to audit quality. The IPO market has several features that make it attractive for audit quality research (Muzatko et al., 2004). Generally, there is a great deal of uncertainty concerning actual IPO firm value (Beatty, 1989). In addition, there is very little public information available on a firm prior to the IPO making the initial financial reports and the auditor's opinion of those statements of utmost importance. Audit quality research in this area tends to focus on the "underpricing" of IPO securities. Underpricing is the term coined to indicate the large abnormal returns immediately following the IPO that results from the inherent uncertainty surrounding the IPO (Muzatko et al., 2004). Prior literature posits and generally supports that audit quality reduces the underpricing of a firm's securities by reducing the uncertainty in financial information in relation to the IPO (Balvers et al., 1988; Beatty, 1989; Menon & Williams, 1991; Michaely & Shaw, 1995; Muzatko et al., 2004).

As in the IPO market, research has demonstrated that factors associated with audit quality are significantly associated with a firm's bond rating (Allen, 1994; Brandon et al., 2004). Allen (1994) uses auditor size (Big 8 vs. Non-Big 8) as a proxy for audit quality and finds accounting information associated with Big 8 auditors is significant in explaining municipal bond ratings, while accounting information associated with Non-Big 8 auditors is not significantly associated with municipal bond ratings. Further, classification accuracy for the municipalities that engaged Big-8 auditors is greater than those that did not. More recently, Brandon et al. (2004) examine the relationship between indicators of audit quality and bond ratings and report an inverse relationship between the amount of non-audit fees provided to the client and bond ratings for new corporate issues.

Several studies have examined the effect of auditor tenure on audit quality, both perceived and in-fact. Contrary to opinions and concerns expressed in the popular press, several of these studies find a positive relationship between auditor tenure and proxies for audit quality. The results are somewhat mixed, however, as other studies provide evidence of a negative relationship. The objective of our research is to provide evidence related to perceived audit quality with respect to new bond issues by investigating the existence of an association between auditor tenure and the actual rating assigned. The consequences of perceived questionable audit quality on financial statement users have been well documented in previous literature (e.g. Teoh & Wong, 1993; Allen, 1994; Franz, Crawford, & Johnson, 1998). If financial statement users feel that longer auditor tenure compromises auditor quality, contracting for the firm will be more costly and result in a lower bond rating (Johnstone et al., 2001). Conversely, if financial statement users perceive longer auditor tenure provides the auditor with more client expertise (competence), contracting for the firm will be less costly, and should result in a higher bond rating.

We formulate our research question with this background in mind and attempt to determine what effect, if any, auditor tenure has on the default risk perceptions of a sophisticated set of financial statement users, bond rating analysts. To help provide empirical evidence regarding the issue of audit tenure, and the related issue of mandatory auditor rotation, we investigate the following null hypothesis.

H_0. The number of consecutive years a client has retained an auditor has no effect on the client's bond rating.

Results indicating a significant positive association between tenure and a firm's bond rating would be consistent with the auditor expertise argument espoused by the profession. A negative association would imply support for the concerns raised in the popular press that is based on the belief that auditor rotation would increase the independence and objectivity of auditors.

RESEARCH METHOD

Model Development

Our benchmark model is based on the fundamental groundwork established by Kaplan and Urwitz (1979) and enhanced by other researchers over subsequent years. The Kaplan and Urwitz (KU) model has proven to be robust and is econometrically sound. The model contains six basic independent variables that are economically linked to a firm's bond rating: subordination status of the issue, a measure of firm size, a measure of leverage, a measure of profitability, an indication of the firm's ability to service new debt, and a measure of firm risk. Based on the work of Maher (1987) and Graham, Maher, and Northcut (2001), the benchmark model is enhanced by the inclusion of a net pension variable to incorporate the effects of a firm's defined benefit retirement obligations. We also include issue year indicators to control for year effects. Finally, to control for industry effects, a series of indicator variables are incorporated based on industry classifications found in Fama and French (1997).

Our measure of auditor tenure follows the work of Beck, Frecka, and Solomon (1988); Deis and Giroux (1992); Davis et al. (2003); Myers et al. (2003); and Mansi et al. (2004) and is calculated as the number of consecutive years an auditor has audited the firm's financial statements since 1980.[1] Longer auditor tenure could indicate one of two things as described in previous research, and depending on the perception of the financial statement user: (1) a possible increase in complacency or a decrease in objectivity thus increasing risk or (2) a greater insight into the client's inherent risk and operations increasing expertise, thus decreasing overall risk. An indicator of firm age (AGE), calculated as the number of years the firm has been listed on Compustat since 1980, is also added to the model. The dependant variable (RATING) is the bond rating assigned to a specific debt issue by Moody's Investment Services. The rating is coded with the highest category assigned the highest numerical value (i.e. Aaa = 20, Aa1 = 19, Aa2 = 18, etc.). The basic estimation model takes the following form:

$$
\begin{aligned}
\text{RATINGj} = {} & \beta_0 + \beta_1 \text{SUBj} + \beta_2 \text{SIZEj} + \beta_3 \text{LEVERAGEj} \\
& + \beta_4 \text{PROFITj} + \beta_5 \text{PENSIONj} \\
& + \beta_6 \text{TIMESj} + \beta_7 \text{BETAj} \\
& + \beta_8 \text{AGEj} + \beta_{9-41} (\text{FF1} - 43)\text{j} \\
& + \beta_{42-54} (\text{YEAR90} - 02)\text{j} + \beta_{55} \text{TENUREj} + v_j \qquad (1)
\end{aligned}
$$

where

SUB
1 for subordinated bonds and 0 otherwise. The subordination status is expected to be associated with a higher risk, therefore exhibiting a negative association with bond rating.

SIZE
Log of total assets. Size proxies for, and has, an inverse relationship with default risk. Size is expected to have a positive association with bond rating.

LEVERAGE
Long term debt divided by total assets. Leverage represents the relative amount of debt current incurred by the firm. Leverage is expected to have a negative association with bond rating.

PROFIT
Operating income for the year divided by total assets. Profitability is expected to have a positive association with bond rating.

PENSION
Net pension liability divided by total assets. Pension is a representation of future liabilities. Pension is expected to have a negative association with bond rating.

TIMES
Operating income before interest expense divided by interest expense. Times is expected to have a positive association with bond rating.

BETA
The firms common stock Beta. Firms with a higher beta are considered riskier, hence Beta is expected to have negative association with bond rating.

AGE
The number of years the firm has been listed on Compustat since 1980. Older firms are more stable and Age is expected to have a positive association with bond rating.

FF1-43
Industry indicator variables (0,1) are added as independent variables to the benchmark model to represent the Fama-French industry classifications (minus financial and insurance industries). This procedure has been utilized in the accounting and finance literature to control for industry.

YEAR90-02
Indicator variables (0,1) are included to control for specific year effects.

TENURE
Calculated as the number of consecutive years an auditor has audited the firm's financial statements since 1980.

Sample

We examine new corporate bonds issues rated by Moodys/Mergent's bond rating agency and issued during the time period January 1990 to December 2002. The sample consists of non-financial firms that issue bonds backed solely by the issuer's ability to pay. No convertible bonds, mortgage bonds, asset-backed bonds, or deferred interest bonds are included. This allows us to examine bonds whose ratings are based entirely on the issuing firms default risk and not the risk of another underlying asset or option. As discussed previously, the sample is restricted to new issues because these ratings are ensured to be the result of a detailed and complete recent analysis conducted by the raters.

The initial sample consists of 4,492 new debt issues from firms listed on Compustat. Of those, 247 firms did not have information for Beta available on CRSP and an additional 1,207 did not have the other necessary control variables available (e.g. total assets, long-term debt) on Compustat. This results in a sample of 3,038 new issues during the period 1990–2002. Descriptive statistics for the sample are shown in Panel A of Table 1. The sample contains only 21 bonds that were issued by firms that were not audited by Big 4 auditors which is consistent with extant research indicating a decrease of publicly traded firms using Non-Big 4 auditors (Shu, 2000).[2] Our sample firms are somewhat larger than some of the previous auditor tenure studies

Table 1. Descriptive Statistics.

Variable	Mean	SD	First Quartile	Median	Third Quartile
Panel A: Descriptive Statistics (n = 3,038)					
Total assets (in millions)	13,794	26,229	2,082	5,563	14,125
Long-term debt (in millions)	3,262	5,938	459.0	1,313	3,743
Operating income (in millions)	548	1,036	58.0	230	639
Pension liability (in millions)	2,776	8,582	37.0	517	1,585
SUB	0.07	0.26	0.0	0.0	0.0
SIZE	8.57	1.45	7.64	8.62	9,56
LEVERAGE	0.28	0.17	0.17	0.25	0.36
PROFIT	0.05	0.05	0.02	0.05	0.07
PENSION	0.15	0.18	0.02	0.09	0.20
TIMES	6.61	12.62	2.35	4.37	7.27
BETA	0.95	0.45	0.66	0.96	1.22
AGE	14.98	4.82	12.0	16.0	18.0
TENURE	13.34	5.71	10.0	14.0	18.0

Table 1 (*Continued*)

Rating	Number of Issues	Percentage of Sample
Panel B: Sample Bond Ratings		
Aaa	56	1.84
Aa1	35	1.15
Aa2	85	2.80
Aa3	136	4.48
A1	313	10.30
A2	486	16.00
A3	408	13.43
Baa1	283	9.32
Baa2	523	17.22
Baa3	180	5.92
Ba1	97	3.19
Ba2	70	2.30
Ba3	93	3.06
B1	97	3.19
B2	104	3.42
B3	65	2.14
Caa1	6	0.20
Ca1	1	0.03

Tenure	Frequency	Percentage of Sample
Panel C: Sample Auditor Tenure		
1	104	3.42
2	38	1.25
3	50	1.65
4	102	3.36
5	119	3.92
6	66	2.17
7	91	3.00
8	79	2.60
9	67	2.21
10	150	4.94
11	205	6.75
12	200	6.58
13	184	6.06
14	109	3.59
15	164	5.40
16	171	5.63
17	223	7.34
18	336	11.06
19	232	7.64
20	112	3.69
21	56	1.84
22	124	4.08
23	56	1.84

Table 2. Pearson Correlation Coefficients.

	RATING	SUB	SIZE	LEVERAGE	PROFIT	PENSION	TIMES	BETA	AGE
SUB	−0.52***								
SIZE	0.54***	−0.34***							
LEVERAGE	−0.52***	0.30***	−0.17***						
PROFIT	0.40***	−0.13***	−0.04**	−0.40***					
PENSION	0.24***	−0.15***	0.20***	−0.28***	0.17***				
TIMES	0.16***	−0.03	−0.08***	−0.32***	0.42***	0.06**			
BETA	0.12***	−0.05***	0.18***	−0.08***	−0.01	0.01	0.01		
AGE	0.23***	−0.17***	0.28***	−0.18***	0.17***	0.22***	0.05***	−0.09***	
TENURE	0.29***	−0.18***	0.25***	−0.22***	0.18***	0.26***	0.06	−0.01	0.71***

*Indicates significance at the 10% level;
**Indicates significance at the 5% level;
***Indicates significance at the 1% level.

(Geiger & Raghunandan, 2002; Myers et al., 2003; Mansi et al., 2004) as indicated by firm total assets. In addition, our sample firms, on average, have longer auditor tenure and are older than firms utilized in some previous audit tenure studies. Panel B of Table 1 shows the distribution of the ratings in the sample. The sample consists of 18 different ratings from Aaa to Ca representing a wide range of bond ratings. Of the issues, 2,505 are investment grade (Baa3 or higher) and 533 are non-investment grade. Panel C presents the distribution of auditor tenure for the sample. The sample has a range of 1–23 years. The sample is reasonably well distributed across the years with somewhat higher frequencies of auditor tenure found between 10 and 20 years.

Bivariate correlations for the sample are presented in Table 2. The correlations all show strong relationships between bond ratings and each of the explanatory variables. Auditor tenure, the variable of concern is highly correlated with bond ratings, indicating that longer auditor relationships are associated with higher bond ratings. The correlations also show that firm age and auditor tenure are closely related. However, while these variables have a close relationship, they are not complete substitutes for each other.[3] One variable, pension, has an unexpected sign (positive) in the bivariate correlations. This is likely due to the fact that companies with large pension obligations tend to be large well-established firms. Looked at in isolation, the pension variable can be acting as a proxy for firm size. This is remedied when size is included in the multivariate analyses. Overall, there is nothing extraordinary displayed in the bivariate correlations that prevents us from estimating our regression equations for this sample.

EMPIRICAL RESULTS

Regression Results

Results from the ordered logistic regression for the overall sample are shown in Table 3 with Model 1 providing the results of the benchmark model. The summary statistics of the benchmark model (Psuedo R^2 = 69.82%; Model c = 0.784) indicate a robust model that explains a significant amount of the variation involved in the bond rating decision process. All control variables except times interest earned are significant and have the expected signs.

Model 2 displays the results that include the addition of an independent variable for the primary variable of interest, auditor tenure (TENURE). The results demonstrate that auditor tenure is significant and positively related to a firm's bond rating, indicating that longer auditor tenure has a significant positive impact. This is consistent with the proposition that bond rating analysts perceive greater company expertise for those auditors with longer tenure and is not consistent with the lack of objectivity and loss of independence argument. Alternatively stated, the continued presence of the same auditor is perceived to lower firm default risk, ceteris paribus, as represented by the firm's bond rating.

To further analyze these results, we segment the sample based on the investment grade status of the bond. The segmented sample consists of 533 non-investment grade issues (below Baa3) and 2,505 investment grade issues (Baa3 and above). Results of re-estimating the regression equations for each subsample are presented in Table 4. Tenure has a significant positive association with bond ratings for investment grade firms ($p = 0.0170$) as well as for non-investment grade firms ($p = 0.0077$). These similar results indicate that the relationship between auditor tenure and bond ratings remains consistent across firms regardless of the investment grade status of the issue. With respect to our control variables, both PENSION and AGE no longer indicate significance for the non-investment grade sample. Further examination of the sample reveals that over half of the non-investment grade firms did not have a defined pension benefit or liability (likely to utilize defined contribution plans, e.g. 401K) leading to a reduced significance of this variable. It is difficult to definitively explain the results for the AGE variable for the non-investment grade subsample. We conjecture that it may represent a lower likelihood of an older firm reversing an economic decline relative to a younger firm. The BETA variable is also not significant for the non-investment grade subsample. This is not unusual as BETA has periodically not been found to be significant in various other studies that

Table 3. Logistic Regression Results: Bond Rating Models for 3,038
New Bond Issues from Jan 1990 to Dec 2002.

	Predicted Sign	Model 1 Coefficient (p-Value)[a]	Model 2 Coefficient (p-Value)
SUB	−	−2.68	−2.69
		(<0.0001)	(<0.0001)
SIZE	+	1.04	1.04
		(<0.0001)	(<0.0001)
LEVERAGE	−	−4.87	−4.85
		(<0.0001)	(<0.0001)
PROFIT	+	18.48	18.86
		(<0.0001)	(<0.0001)
PENSION	−	−0.65	−0.68
		(0.0054)	(0.0037)
TIMES	+	−0.002	−0.003
		(0.3380)	(0.2917)
BETA	−	−0.42	−0.43
		(<0.0001)	(<0.0001)
AGE	+	0.06	0.02
		(<0.0001)	(0.0805)
TENURE	+		0.04
			(<0.0001)
Likelihood ratio		3,590.38	3,625.82
Model c		0.784	0.783
Pseudo R^2		69.82%	70.18%

Note:

$$RATINGj = \beta_0 + \beta_1 SUBj + \beta_2 SIZEj + \beta_3 LEVERAGEj$$
$$+ \beta_4 PROFITj + \beta_5 PENSIONj + \beta_6 TIMESj$$
$$+ \beta_7 BETAj + \beta_8 AGEj + \beta_{9-51}(FF1 - 43)j$$
$$+ \beta_{52-64}(YEAR90 - 02)j + \beta_{65}TENUREj + v_j$$

SUB, 1 for subordinated bonds and 0 otherwise; SIZE, log of total assets; LEVERAGE, long-term debt divided by total assets; PROFIT, operating income for the year divided by total assets; PENSION, net pension liability divided by total assets, TIMES, operating income before interest expense divided by interest expense; BETA, the firm's common stock Beta; AGE, the number of years the firm has been listed on Compustat since 1980; TENURE, calculated as the number of consecutive years an auditor has audited the firm's financial statements since 1980 or since the firm has been listed by Compustat.
[a]All p-values are two-tailed. Industry and year indicator variables statistics suppressed.

examined part of the period of our sample (e.g. Crabtree & Maher, 2005; Graham et al., 2001). In summary, our primary findings of a positive association between tenure and bond ratings continue to hold true across the subsamples.

Table 4. Logistic Regression Results: Bond Rating Models for Non-Investment Grade Bond Issues ($n = 533$) and Investment Grade Bond Issues ($n = 2,505$).

	Predicted Sign	Non-Investment Grade Coefficient (p-Value)[a]	Investment Grade Coefficient (p-Value)
SUB	−	−1.72	0.47
		(<0.0001)	(0.3617)
SIZE	+	1.01	0.88
		(<0.0001)	(<0.0001)
LEVERAGE	−	−0.98	−6.56
		(0.0247)	(<0.0001)
PROFIT	+	13.51	18.02
		(<0.0001)	(<0.0001)
PENSION	−	1.06	−0.74
		(0.1706)	(0.0043)
TIMES	+	−0.005	−0.004
		(0.4784)	(0.1986)
BETA	−	−0.07	−0.63
		(0.6830)	(<0.0001)
AGE	+	−0.04	0.02
		(0.0837)	(0.2527)
TENURE	+	0.06	0.03
		(0.0077)	(0.0170)
Likelihood ratio		436.98	1,896.00
Model c		0.830	0.792
Pseudo R^2		57.43%	53.98%

Note:

$$RATINGj = \beta_0 + \beta_1 SUBj + \beta_2 SIZEj + \beta_3 LEVERAGEj$$
$$+ \beta_4 PROFITj + \beta_5 PENSIONj + \beta_6 TIMESj$$
$$+ \beta_7 BETAj + \beta_8 AGEj + \beta_{9-51}(FF1 - 43)j$$
$$+ \beta_{52-64}(YEAR90 - 02)j + \beta_{65} TENUREj + v_j$$

SUB, 1 for subordinated bonds and 0 otherwise; SIZE, log of total assets; LEVERAGE, long-term debt divided by total assets; PROFIT, operating income for the year divided by total assets; PENSION, net pension liability divided by total assets; TIMES, operating income before interest expense divided by interest expense; BETA, the firm's common stock Beta; AGE, the number of years the firm has been listed on Compustat since 1980; TENURE, calculated as the number of consecutive years an auditor has audited the firm's financial statements since 1980 or since the firm has been listed by Compustat.
[a]All p-values are two-tailed. Industry and year indicator variables statistics suppressed.

Additional Analysis

We next segment the sample based on return on assets to determine if financial performance might be driving the primary results. There is some evidence in Mansi et al. (2004) that perceived audit quality may be less critical for higher performing firms. The sample is partitioned based on the firm being classified above or below the industry median Return-on-Assets (ROA). For calculation of the industry ROA, we first grouped all applicable Compustat companies into their respective Fama-French industry groupings. We then calculated the industry ROA median for each industry group. Each firm was placed in one of two subsamples based on whether it was above or below the corresponding industry ROA median performance. The logistic regressions were then re-run for each subsample. Results are reported in Table 5 and indicate auditor tenure is positively related to a firm's bond rating for both samples. These results imply that extended auditor tenure continues to be perceived as a positive factor regardless of industry-relative firm financial performance.[4] Most of the control variables remain significant with the correct sign in the above median sample. The results for the below median sample indicate that PENSION, BETA, and AGE are no longer significant. This is similar to the results for the non-investment grade subsample and is likely due to similar reasons. Importantly, TENURE continues to be reliably associated with the firm's bond rating.

Next, we investigate whether recent accounting scandals (e.g. Enron) and the subsequent collapse of Arthur Andersen has any effect on our results by partitioning our sample into pre- and post-Enron time periods (i.e. 2001). The untabulated results indicate that auditor tenure continues to have a strong positive association with bond rating for bonds issued from 2001 to 2002 ($p<0.0001$) as well as for those issued prior to 2001, i.e. 1990–2000 ($p<0.0001$). This indicates that the impact of auditor tenure on bond ratings did not change as a result of the intense scrutiny the auditing profession received during this period.

Finally, we investigate the possibility that our results are being unduly influenced by other important variables that provide insight into the auditor–client relationship not already captured in our model. We gather and employ detailed information concerning the amount of audit and non-audit service fees (NAS) (e.g. information systems consulting) paid by the client to the financial statement auditor. We obtain this information for those bonds that were issued after the non-audit service fee information was required to be made public in March of 2001. Prior research has indicated that non-audit service fees (Brandon et al., 2004) can influence the perceptions of bond rating analysts regarding the quality of the financial statements and the ultimate bond rating assigned to the firm. To ensure the amount of these fees are not confounding our results, we add two audit fee variables to our model (OTHERFEES, measured by the log of non-audit service fees, and

Table 5. Logistic Regression Results: Bond Rating Models – Sample Is Split Based on the Firm Being Above ($n = 2,194$) or Below ($n = 844$) the Median ROA for Its Particular Fama-French Industry Groupings.

	Predicted Sign	Above Median Coefficient (p-value)[a]	Below Median Coefficient (p-value)
SUB	−	−3.07	−2.28
		(<0.0001)	(<0.0001)
SIZE	+	1.12	1.05
		(<0.0001)	(<0.0001)
LEVERAGE	−	−6.18	−2.68
		(<0.0001)	(<0.0001)
PROFIT	+	13.36	13.70
		(<0.0001)	(<0.0001)
PENSION	−	−0.85	−0.73
		(0.0014)	(0.1907)
TIMES	+	−0.004	0.19
		(0.2408)	(<0.0001)
BETA	−	−0.57	−0.16
		(<0.0001)	(0.3270)
AGE	+	0.02	−0.02
		(0.1049)	(0.3864)
TENURE	+	0.06	0.06
		(<0.0001)	(0.0003)
Likelihood ratio		2574.05	1181.31
Model c		0.798	0.583
Pseudo R^2		69.61%	75.92%

Note:

$$\text{RATINGj} = \beta_0 + \beta_1\text{SUBj} + \beta_2\text{SIZEj} + \beta_3\text{LEVERAGEj}$$
$$+ \beta_4\text{PROFITj} + \beta_5\text{PENSIONj} + \beta_6\text{TIMESj}$$
$$+ \beta_7\text{BETAj} + \beta_8\text{AGEj} + \beta_{9-51}(\text{FF1} - 43)\text{j}$$
$$+ \beta_{52-64}(\text{YEAR90} - 02)\text{j} + \beta_{65}\text{TENUREj} + v_j$$

SUB, 1 for subordinated bonds and 0 otherwise; SIZE, log of total assets; LEVERAGE, long-term debt divided by total assets; PROFIT, operating income for the year divided by total assets; PENSION, net pension liability divided by total assets; TIMES, operating income before interest expense divided by interest expense; BETA, the firm's common stock Beta; AGE, the number of years the firm has been listed on Compustat since 1980; TENURE, calculated as the number of consecutive years an auditor has audited the firm's financial statements since 1980 or since the firm has been listed by Compustat.

[a] All p-values are two-tailed. Industry and year indicator variables statistics suppressed.

AUDITFEES, measured by the log of audit fees) and re-run the regressions for the reduced sample. The non-tabulated results show, consistent with prior literature, that the non-audit service fees are significantly associated with the firm's bond rating. Importantly, the TENURE variable continues to be positively associated with the firm's bond rating even in the presence of other variables that provide insight into the auditor–client relationship.

The overall results of this study reliably demonstrate a positive association between auditor tenure and the actual bond rating assigned to an issue. These results are consistent with the theory that increased auditor tenure is viewed as a positive signal to bond rating analysts regarding the firm's bond rating. This is consistent with the increased auditor expertise theory espoused by the auditing profession.

SUMMARY AND CONCLUSIONS

This study adds to the extant literature by empirically examining how one set of sophisticated financial statement users, bond rating analysts, perceive an important aspect of the auditor–client relationship. Specifically, we investigate the effects that auditor tenure has on the perception of auditor independence by examining the firm's bond rating. Using a relatively large sample of new issues over an extended period of time, we document a significant positive effect of auditor tenure on new bond ratings. Moreover, these results hold true regardless of the level of default risk, time period, or differences in firm financial performance. We contribute knowledgeably to the debate regarding mandatory rotation of financial statement auditors by providing empirical evidence of the systematic inclusion of one aspect of the auditor–client relationship into the bond rating process, and also by documenting the perceptions of an important class of financial statement users regarding this relationship.

This research should be interpreted in light of several limitations. First, our research was conducted in the U.S. where auditor rotation is voluntary. The results of this study, as well as other auditor tenure research on U.S. firms, should be interpreted with this caveat in mind. We do not directly consider a period of mandatory changes. Further, because we investigate the perception of audit quality utilizing archival data, we cannot rule out all possible alternatives consistent with our results. For example, it is possible that the reason we observe a positive association between auditor tenure and initial bond ratings is because bond raters use the length of the auditor–client relationship as a proxy for default risk. Indeed, prior research indicates firms that switch auditors' tend to be firms with higher risk (e.g. Walker, Lewis, & Casterella, 2001). This is not surprising in light of audit firm's strict monitoring of their client risk portfolio (Bedard & Johnstone, 2004). It is logical to expect market participants to utilize this information in their decision making. Moreover, this potential interpretation does not overshadow the fact that we find no evidence that audit quality decreases with extended auditor/client relationships. Some interesting avenues for future research might include re-examining the question in an overseas environment that requires mandatory auditor rotation. Another extension might investigate the effects of audit tenure in a regulated company environment (e.g. utilities), and also examine the same issues for asset-backed and mortgage bonds. These areas would help to shed further light on the effects of audit tenure on the bond rating decision process in these areas. Overall, our results should be of interest to all agencies and constituents that are involved in the ongoing debate concerning mandatory auditor rotation and its effects on the capital market system.

Our research provides relevant and timely evidence to regulators, members of the accounting profession, and firms contracting for audit services. Consistent with most prior literature, we find no evidence that one class of sophisticated financial statement users perceive increased auditor tenure to lead to a decrease in auditor objectivity. In fact, our results are consistent with the auditor expertise argument that users perceive an increase in audit quality. Companies currently considering or practicing voluntary audit firm rotation should consider these results, especially those planning to issue public debt. Finally, the SEC and PCAOB should carefully consider the results of this study, along with other auditor tenure research, as mandatory auditor rotation continues to be debated.

NOTES

1. We also utilize the log transformation of TENURE (Geiger & Raghunandan, 2002) in our analysis and the results are qualitatively similar to those reported in Table 2.

2. Results remain the same when these bonds are removed from the data set.

3. Multicollinearity diagnostics for the model do not indicate a problem with multicollinearity, based on standard regression diagnostics (i.e. Variance Inflation Factor (VIF)<3 and Condition Indices <11).

4. We also split the sample based on raw ROA and re-ran the analyses. All inferences remained the same.

REFERENCES

Allen, A. C. (1994). The effect of large-firm audits on municipal bond rating decisions. *Auditing: A Journal of Practice & Theory, 13*(1), 115–125.

Balvers, R. J., McDonald, B., & Miller, R. E. (1988). Underpricing of new issues and the choice of auditor as a signal of investment banker reputation. *The Accounting Review, 63*(4), 605–622.

Beatty, R. P. (1989). Auditor reputation and the pricing of initial public offerings. *The Accounting Review, 64*(4), 693–709.

Beck, P. J., Frecka, T. J., & Solomon, I. (1988). An empirical analysis of the relationship between MAS involvement and auditor tenure: Implications for auditor independence. *Journal of Accounting Literature, 7*, 65–84.

Bedard, C., & Johnstone, K. M. (2004). Earnings manipulation risk, corporate governance risk, and auditors' planning and pricing decisions. *The Accounting Review, 79*(2), 277–304.

Brandon, D. M., Crabtree, A. D., & Maher, J. J. (2004). Non-audit fees, auditor independence, and bond ratings. *Auditing: A Journal of Practice and Theory, 23*(2), 89–103.

Cantor, R. (2001). Moody's investors service response to the consultative paper issued by the Basel Committee on Banking Supervision and its implications for the rating agency industry. *Journal of Banking and Finance, 25*(1), 171–186.

Carcello, J. V., & Nagy, A. L. (2004). Audit firm tenure and fraudulent financial reporting. *Auditing: A Journal of Practice and Theory, 23*(2), 55–69.

Chang, M., & Monroe, G. S. (2002). *The impact of reputation, audit contract type, tenure, audit fees and other services on auditors' perceptions of audit quality*. Working Paper. University of Western Australia.

Choi, J.H., & Doogar, R. (2005). *Auditor tenure and audit quality: Evidence from going-concern qualifications issued during 1996–2001*. Working Paper. University of Illinois.

Copeland, J. E. (2002). Prepared statement of Mr. James E. Copeland, CPA Chief Executive Officer Deloitte & Touche before the US Senate Committee on Banking, Housing, and Urban Affairs.

Crabtree, A. D., & Maher, J. J. (2005). Earnings predictability, bond ratings, and bond yields. *Review of Quantitative Finance and Accounting, 25*(3), 233–254.

Datar, S. M., Feltham, G. A., & Hughes, J. S. (1991). The role of audits and audit quality in valuing new issues. *Journal of Accounting and Economics, 14*(1), 3–49.

Davis, L. R., Soo, B. S., & Trompeter, G. (2003). *Auditor tenure, auditor independence and earnings management*. Working Paper. Boston College.

DeAngelo, L. E. (1981). Auditor independence, 'low balling', and disclosure regulation. *Journal of Accounting and Economics, 3*(2), 113–127.

Deis, D. R. J., & Giroux, G. A. (1992). Determinants of audit quality in the public sector. *The Accounting Review, 67*(3), 462–479.

Dichev, I. D., & Piotroski, J. D. (2001). The long run stock returns following bond ratings changes. *Journal of Finance, 56*(1), 173–203.

Dunham, K. J. (2002). Firms that want to switch auditors find it takes time, money and faith. *Wall Street Journal Online*, March 15.

Ederington, L. H., & Goh, J. C. (1998). Bond rating agencies and stock analysts: Who knows what when? *Journal of Financial and Quantitative Analysis, 33*(4), 569–585.

Fama, E. F., & French, K. R. (1997). Industry costs of equity. *Journal of Financial Economics, 43*, 153–193.

Francis, J. R., & Ke, B. (2003). *Disclosure of fees paid to auditors and the market valuation of earnings surprises*. Working Paper. Pennsylvania State University.

Frankel, R. M., Johnson, M. F., & Nelson, K. K. (2002). The relation between auditors' fees for non-audit services and earnings quality. *Accounting Review, 77*(Suppl.), 71–114.

Franz, D. R., Crawford, D., & Johnson, E. N. (1998). The impact of litigation against an audit firm on the market value of nonlitigating clients. *Journal of Accounting, Auditing & Finance, 13*(2), 117–134.

Geiger, M. A., & Raghunandan, K. (2002). Auditor tenure and audit reporting failures. *Auditing: A Journal of Practice and Theory*, *21*(1), 67–78.

General Accounting Office (GAO). (2003). *Public accounting firms required study on the potential effects of mandatory audit firm rotation*. Washington, DC.

Ghosh, A., & Moon, D. (2005). Audit tenure and perceptions audit quality. *The Accounting Review*, *80*(2), 585–612.

Glascock, J. L., Davidson, W. N., & Henderson, G. V. (1987). Announcement effects on moody's bond rating changes on equity returns. *Quarterly Journal of Business and Economics*, *26*, 67–78.

Goh, J. C., & Ederington, L. H. (1993). Is a bond rating downgrade bad news, good news, or no news for stockholders? *Journal of Finance*, *48*(5), 2001–2008.

Graham, A., Maher, J. J., & Northcut, W. D. (2001). Environmental liability information and bond ratings. *Journal of Accounting, Auditing and Finance*, *16*, 93–116.

Hand, J. R., Holthausen, R. W., & Leftwich, R. W. (1992). The effect of bond rating agency announcements on bond and stock prices. *Journal of Finance*, *47*, 733–752.

Holthausen, R. W., & Leftwich, R. W. (1986). The effect of bond rating changes on common stock prices. *Journal of Financial Economics*, *17*, 57–90.

IDD Inc. (2002). *Investment dealer's digest.* January 7.

Johnson, V. E., Khurana, I. K., & Reynolds, J. K. (2002). Audit-firm tenure and the quality of financial reports. *Contemporary Accounting Research*, *19*(4), 637–660.

Johnstone, K. M., Sutton, M. H., & Warfield, T. D. (2001). Antecedents and consequences of independence risk: Framework for analysis. *Accounting Horizons*, *15*(1), 1–18.

Kaplan, R. S., & Urwitz, G. (1979). Statistical models of bond ratings. *Journal of Business*, *52*, 231–262.

Knapp, M. C. (1991). Factors that audit committee members use as surrogates for audit quality. *Auditing: A Journal of Practice and Theory*, *10*(1), 35–51.

Loffler, G. (2003). *Avoiding the rating bounce: Why rating agencies are slow to react to new information*. Working Paper. University of Frankfurt.

Lowe, D. J., & Pany, K. (1995). CPA performance of consulting engagements with audit clients: Effects on financial statement users' perceptions and decisions. *Auditing: A Journal of Practice & Theory*, *14*(2), 35–53.

Maher, J. J. (1987). Pension obligations and the bond credit market: An empirical analysis of accounting numbers. *The Accounting Review*, *62*, 785–798.

Mansi, S. A., Maxwell, W. F., & Miller, D. P. (2004). Does auditor quality and tenure matter to investors? Evidence from the bond market. *Journal of Accounting Research*, *42*(4), 755–793.

Melancon, B. (2002). Statement of Barry Melancon, President and CEO, American Institute of Certified Public Accountants to the Committee on Financial Services, US House of Representatives. New York: AICPA.

Menon, K., & Williams, D. (1991). Auditor credibility and initial public offerings. *The Accounting Review*, *66*(2), 313–332.

Michaely, R., & Shaw, W. H. (1995). The choice of going public: Spin-offs vs. carve-outs. *Financial Management*, *24*(3), 5–21.

Moody's Investor Service. (1998). *An historical analysis of Moody's watchlist*. Moody's Global Credit Research.

Muzatko, S. R., Johnstone, K. M., Mayhew, B. W., & Rittenberg, L. E. (2004). An empirical investigation of IPO underpricing and the change to the LLP organization of audit firms. *Auditing: A Journal of Theory and Practice, 23*(1), 53–67.

Myers, J., Myers, L. A., & Omer, T. C. (2003). Exploring the term of the auditor-client relationship and the quality of earnings: A case for mandatory auditor rotation? *The Accounting Review, 78*(3), 779–799.

Penman, S. (2004). *Financial statement analysis and security valuation* (2nd ed.). New York: McGraw-Hill.

PriceWaterhouseCoopers. (2002). Mandatory rotation of audit firms: Will it improve audit quality? New York: PriceWaterhouseCoopers (March 8).

Raghunandan, K. (2003). Nonaudit services and shareholder ratification of auditors. *Auditing: A Journal of Practice & Theory, 22*(1), 155–163.

S&P Rating Group. (2003). *S&P Corporate Ratings Criteria.* New York.

Shockley, R. (1981). Perceptions of auditors' independence: An empirical analysis. *The Accounting Review, 56*(4), 785–800.

Shu, S. (2000). Auditor resignations: Clientele effects and legal liability. *Journal of Accounting and Economics, 29*(2), 173–205.

Teoh, S. H., & Wong, T. J. (1993). Perceived auditor quality and the earnings response coefficient. *The Accounting Review, 68*(2), 346–366.

Titman, S., & Trueman, B. (1986). Information quality and the valuation of new issues. *Journal of Accounting and Economics, 8*(2), 159–172.

Walker, P. L., Lewis, B. L., & Casterella, J. R. (2001). Mandatory auditor rotation: Arguments and current evidence. *Accounting Enquiries, 10*(Spring/Summer), 209–242.

Ziebart, D. A., & Reiter, S. A. (1992). Bond ratings, bond yields, and financial information. *Contemporary Accounting Research, 9*, 252–282.

PROMINENT AUDIT CLIENTS AND THE RELATION BETWEEN DISCRETIONARY ACCRUALS AND NON-AUDIT SERVICE FEES

Carol Callaway Dee, Ayalew Lulseged and Tanya S. Nowlin

ABSTRACT

Using a matched-pair design, we find that for S&P 500 firms, higher proportions of non-audit fees are associated with higher income-increasing accruals; however, this result is not robust to alternative fee measures. For a group of matching small firms, higher fees paid to auditors are associated with higher levels of income-decreasing discretionary accruals (i.e., lead to more negative discretionary accruals). We conclude that (1) the relation between discretionary accruals and fees paid to auditors differs for prominent and less-prominent audit clients, and (2) auditors appear to be more conservative with their less-prominent audit clients from whom they receive large fees.

INTRODUCTION

In 2001, because of concerns over the possible effect non-audit fees may have on auditor independence, the United States Securities and Exchange

Advances in Accounting, Volume 22, 123–148
Copyright © 2006 by Elsevier Ltd.
ISSN: 0882-6110/doi:10.1016/S0882-6110(06)22006-6

Commission (SEC) began requiring companies to disclose amounts paid to auditors for services provided (both audit and non-audit). The availability of U.S. fee disclosures has led to many empirical studies examining the relation between non-audit service fees and auditor independence. Findings in these studies are inconclusive. Frankel, Johnson, and Nelson (2002) find a positive relation between non-audit service fees and earnings management (as proxied by discretionary accruals), consistent with the notion that such fees increase the economic bonding between the auditor and client.[1] However, others have challenged the findings of Frankel et al. (2002).

Ashbaugh, LaFond, and Mayhew (2003, hereafter ALM) conclude there is no evidence that non-audit service fees result in reduced auditor independence, and attribute the results of Frankel et al. (2002) to measurement error in the dependent variable that is correlated with the independent variable. Chung and Kallapur (2003) find no relation between the absolute value of discretionary accruals and either total fees or non-audit service fees scaled by the total revenue of the audit firm. For a sample of financially distressed firms, DeFond, Raghunandan, and Subramanyam (2002) find no relation between either audit fees or non-audit fees and the auditor's propensity to issue a going concern opinion. Reynolds, Deis, and Francis (2004) conclude that the results of Frankel et al. (2002) do not hold after controlling for firm growth.

The contradictory findings in prior research are puzzling and deserving of further investigation. In this paper, we extend prior research by addressing one research design limitation that the aforementioned studies commonly share – not allowing for differing degrees of concern auditors may have about maintaining relationships with their more prominent (larger) and smaller clients.

It is widely believed that audit firms are concerned about maintaining good relationships with their more prominent clients. At Arthur Andersen, for example, powerful, high-paying clients such as those in the Standard and Poors (S&P) 500 were commonly referred to as "Crown Jewels" (Toffler, 2003, p. 62), a fact not lost on the SEC when it investigated Arthur Andersen for its failed audits of Waste Management (Unger, 2001). Lev (2003) writes that examples of fraud and earnings restatements have increasingly involved major corporations. Among the recent wave of accounting failures, some of the most dramatic occurred at S&P 500 firms.[2] However, as highly publicized as these scandals were, they are not necessarily evidence of economic bonding leading to a lack of independence between auditors and their prestigious clients.

In light of the above, we test the hypothesis that, if non-audit service fees increase economic bonding between the auditor and client, evidence of such bonding is most likely to be found among the largest, most influential clients of the auditor. Thus, we take a different approach from prior studies, which for the most part include all client firms regardless of importance. We use a matched-pair design consisting of two groups of firms – a group of prominent firms most likely to have influence with their auditors (proxied by S&P 500 firms), and a matching group of small firms less likely to have such influence.[3]

We find some evidence that for S&P 500 firms, higher proportions of non-audit fees to total fees are positively associated with higher levels of income-increasing discretionary accruals. This result, however, does not hold when we replace the proportion of non-audit fees paid with other fee measures (total fees, audit fees, and non-audit fees.) On the other hand, for the matching small firms, higher fees paid to auditors (regardless of the composition of the fees) are associated with higher levels of income-decreasing discretionary accruals (i.e., lead to more negative discretionary accruals). This indicates that auditors are unyielding with small clients who already have income-decreasing discretionary accruals due to auditor concern for reputation or auditor conservatism.

Overall, our results indicate that the relation between discretionary accruals and fees paid to auditors differs for S&P 500 firms and the matching small firms. However, the current regulatory environment differs from the period covered by our study, largely due to passage of the Sarbanes-Oxley Act of 2002 (SOX, or "the Act"), and thus care should be taken in generalizing our findings. Auditors are now prohibited from providing most non-audit services for their publicly traded audit clients, and those services not expressly forbidden must be approved in advance by the audit committee of the board of directors.[4] The Act likely has reduced the magnitude and proportion of non-audit services auditors provide to their audit clients, while recent, highly publicized audit failures have increased public and regulatory scrutiny of the activities of audit firms.

Our findings, however, are still relevant given the conflicting findings in prior research and the changing nature of the current regulatory environment. The prohibited services delineated in SOX are subject to change – the list of prohibited services includes "any other services that the [Public Company Accounting Oversight] Board determines, by regulation, is impermissible" (Sarbanes-Oxley Act of 2002). Additionally, the SEC has recently empowered an advisory committee to study the effects of securities regulations, including SOX, on smaller public companies. We believe our results showing the relation between discretionary accruals and fees paid to auditors differs for prominent and less-prominent clients provides an empirical benchmark in the SECs continued consideration of prohibited non-audit services, and is particularly relevant given the SEC's new task force on smaller public companies. Finally, our research extends the literature on the association between auditor decision-making and client influence by exploring a new dimension – the effects of client importance on the association between discretionary accruals and non-audit fees – that has not been previously addressed.

The next section describes the research design and methodology used in the study. We then present our results and conclude.

RESEARCH DESIGN AND METHODOLOGY

We use a matched-sample research design (large vs. small clients) to test our hypothesis that evidence of bonding between the auditor and client, if it exists, is most likely to be found among the largest, most influential clients of the auditor. This design will allow us to test directly the mediating impact that the size of the client might have on the relation between our measures of client influence and proxies for client earnings-management activities.

S&P 500 firms are large, and thus generate enormous fees (both audit and non-audit) for their auditors. As a group, the S&P 500 firms account for approximately 70–75% of the total U.S. market capitalization. Therefore, we choose S&P 500 firms as representatives of the large and influential clients of auditors. For each S&P 500 firm in our sample, we select a matching small firm using the following procedure. We sort all Compustat firms by two-digit SIC code, audit firm, and market value of equity. We choose the firm with the smallest market value of equity that (1) has the same two-digit SIC code and auditor as the S&P 500 firm, (2) has the data available for our analyses, and (3) did not change auditors from 1999 to 2000.

As outlined above, our objective is to test whether the association between the degree of economic bonding between client and auditor and the level of earnings management is mediated by the importance of the client. This requires identifying proxies for (1) the degree of economic bonding between client and auditor and (2) the degree of earnings management by the client.

We use the ratio of non-audit fees to total fees (FEERATIO) as our primary proxy for the degree of economic bonding between the client and the auditor. This measure is consistent with prior research (e.g. Frankel et al., 2002) and also allows us to shed light on the concerns of the SEC regarding the impact increasing proportions of non-audit fees have on auditor independence. However, some researchers (e.g. ALM; Kinney & Libby, 2002) have expressed concern about using FEERATIO as a proxy for economic bonding as it does not take into account the scale effects of the fees paid by clients. Chung and Kallapur (2003, p. 933) also state that "it is difficult to interpret the non-audit to total fees ratio within DeAngelo's (1981) framework as a proxy for auditors' incentives to compromise independence." ALM argue that total fees (the sum of audit and non-audit fees) better captures the degree of economic bonding between the client and the auditor. To address these concerns and as a robustness check, we use other fee-related measures including total fees, audit fees, and non-audit fees as alternative proxies for the economic dependence of the auditor on the client.

As in ALM and Frankel et al. (2002), discretionary accruals is our primary proxy for the degree of earnings management. However, we also estimate logistic regression models using alternative proxies of earnings management as dependent variables. These models test the relation between the degree of economic bonding between client and auditor and the likelihood of meeting or beating two earnings benchmarks – prior year's earnings, and analysts' forecasts.

Discretionary Accruals Model

We estimate discretionary accruals using a method to control for firm performance discussed in Kothari, Leone, and Wasley (2005).[5] The model controls for firm performance by including lagged return on assets in the regression. We first estimate the following current accrual model cross sectionally, separately by two-digit SIC code and size group (S&P 500 and small firm group):

$$CA_{ijt}/A_{ijt-1} = \beta_0(1/A_{ijt-1}) + \beta_1(\Delta REV_{ijt}/A_{ijt-1})$$
$$+ \beta_2(INCB4EX_{ijt-1}/A_{ijt-1}) + e_{ijt} \qquad (1)$$

where i, t, and j are firm, year, and industry subscripts, respectively; CA equals income before extraordinary items plus depreciation and amortization minus operating cash flows; A equals total assets; ΔREV equals net revenues in period t minus net revenues in period $t-1$; INCB4EX equals income before extraordinary items; and e equals unexpected portion of total accruals.

Next, we use the parameter estimates, by industry and size group, from Eq. (1) to estimate the expected current accruals for each firm in the two size groups:

$$\text{Expected}\,CA_{it}/A_{it-1} = \hat{\beta}_0(1/A_{it-1}) + \hat{\beta}_1(\Delta REV_{it}/A_{it-1})$$
$$+ \hat{\beta}_2(INCB4EX_{it-1}/A_{it-1}) + e_{it} \qquad (2)$$

Finally, we calculate performance-adjusted discretionary accruals as

$$REDCA = (CA_{it}/A_{it-1}) - (\text{Expected}\,CA_{it}/A_{it-1}) \qquad (3)$$

REDCA and the absolute value of REDCA are then used as dependent variables in a pooled cross-sectional regression model we estimate to test our hypothesis that (a) discretionary accruals increase as fees paid (or the proportion of non-audit fees paid) to auditors increase, and (b) the association between the two variables is mediated by the size group to which the firm belongs. As in ALM, we control for various factors including lagged accruals, firm size (natural log of market value of equity), client's involvement in merger and financing activities, leverage, growth, litigation, institutional ownership, presence of prior loss, and cash flows. In addition, we include an asset growth variable (Reynolds et al., 2004) and industry dummy variables (Chung & Kallapur, 2003).

Thus, our test equation is

$$DA = \beta_0 + \beta_1 SP500 + \beta_2 FEEMEASURE + \beta_3 FEEMEASURE^* SP500 + \beta_4 L1ACCRUAL$$
$$+ \beta_5 LnMVE + \beta_6 MERGER + \beta_7 FINANCING + \beta_8 LEVERAGE + \beta_9 MB$$
$$+ \beta_{10} LITIGATION + \beta_{11} INST + \beta_{12} LOSS + \beta_{13} CFO + \beta_{14} ASSETGROW$$
$$+ \beta_{15} IND2 + \beta_{16} IND3 + \beta_{17} IND4 + \beta_{18} IND5 + \beta_{19} IND7 + \varepsilon \qquad (4)$$

where

DA	=	Discretionary accrual measure, either REDCA or the absolute value of REDCA.
SP500	=	An indicator variable equal to one if the firm is a member of the S&P 500; zero otherwise.
FEEMEASURE	=	The measure of economic bonding between client and auditor, equal to either the ratio of non-audit fees to total fees, the natural log of total fees, the natural log of audit fees, or the natural log of non-audit fees.

FEEMEASURE *SP500	=	The product of FEEMEASURE and SP500.
LlACCRUAL	=	Prior year's current accruals, equal to income before extraordinary items plus depreciation and amortization minus operating cash flows, scaled by beginning of year total assets.
Ln MVE	=	The natural log of market value of equity at the end of 2000 (a size proxy).
MERGER	=	Dummy variable equal to one if the firm engaged in a merger or acquisition in the current year (as identified in Compustat footnote code AFTNT 1); zero otherwise.
FINANCING	=	One if MERGER is not equal to one and either one or both of the following conditions apply: long-term debt increased by 20% or more, or number of shares outstanding increased by 10% or more after controlling for stock splits; zero otherwise.
LEVERAGE	=	Total debt divided by total assets.
MB	=	Market value of equity plus book value of debt, scaled by book value of assets.
LITIGATION	=	One if the firm is in a high-litigation industry; zero otherwise. "High litigation industries are those with SIC codes of 2833–2836, 3570–3577, 3600–3674, 5200–5961, and 7370." (ALM, p. 624).
INST	=	Percentage of shares held by institutional investors at the beginning of the calendar year.
LOSS	=	Dummy variable equal to one if the firm reports a net loss; zero otherwise.
CFO	=	Cash flows from operations, scaled by total assets at the beginning of the year.
ASSETGROW	=	Ending total assets minus beginning total assets, divided by beginning total assets.
IND2, IND3, IND4, IND5, IND7	=	Indicator variables equal to one if the firm's SIC code is between 2000 and 2999, 3000 and 3999, 4000 and 4999, 5000 and 5999, 7000 and 7999, respectively; zero otherwise.

Benchmark Tests Models

We estimate the following logistic regression models to test the relation between the degree of economic bonding between client and auditor and the likelihood of meeting or beating two earnings benchmarks – prior year's earnings, and analysts' forecasts.

$$\text{INCREASE or SURPRISE} = \beta_0 + \beta_1 \text{SP500} + \beta_2 \text{FEEMEASURE} + \beta_3 \text{FEEMEASURE*SP500}$$
$$+ \beta_4 \text{LITIGATION} + \beta_5 \text{MB} + \beta_6 \text{LnMVE} + \beta_7 \text{INST}$$
$$+ \beta_8 \text{LOSS} + \beta_9 \text{REDCA} + \beta_{10} \text{IND2} + \beta_{11} \text{IND3} + \beta_{12} \text{IND4}$$
$$+ \beta_{13} \text{IND5} + \beta_{14} \text{IND7} + \varepsilon \qquad (5)$$

where $\text{INCREASE} = 1$ if change in net income scaled by beginning market value of equity is between 0 and 0.02, zero otherwise; $\text{SURPRISE} = 1$ if annual earnings per share equals or exceeds analysts' forecasts by \$0.01 or less, zero otherwise; and all other variables are as previously defined.

Sample Selection

As noted earlier, we use S&P 500 firms as proxies for prominent audit clients. We identify S&P 500 firms that meet the sample selection criteria outlined below. We gather data on audit fees and non-audit service fees from proxy statements. We begin with an initial sample of all 408 firms from the S&P 500 that filed proxy statements under the SEC's revised audit fee disclosure rules by September 1, 2001. As in other studies using accounting accruals, we exclude firms in the financial (SIC 6000–6999) and electric utility industries (SIC 4900–4999).[6] This exclusion reduces the sample to 297 firms. We exclude 16 firms that are missing necessary financial data on Compustat, two firms whose proxies omit fee data, and five firms with non-big five auditors. This reduces the sample to 274.

Using the cross-sectional Jones (1991) model to estimate discretionary accounting accruals requires classification of firms by their industry membership using two-digit SIC codes. Owing to the sensitivity of cross-sectional discretionary accrual models to a small number of observations, we exclude 56 firms who are in two-digit SIC codes containing fewer than five firms, reducing the sample to 218. Twelve firms that changed auditors are excluded from the sample because auditor changes can affect discretionary accruals (DeFond & Subramanyam, 1998). We exclude four firms that were highly influential in the regression analyses, identified by examining DFFITS, DFBETAS, and studentized residuals (Belsley, Kuh, & Welsch, 1980).[7] These exclusions reduce the sample to 202 firms.

For each S&P 500 firm in our sample, we select a matching small firm. To choose the matching firms, we sort all Compustat firms by two-digit SIC code, audit firm, and market value of equity. We choose the firm with the smallest market value of equity that (1) has the same two-digit SIC code and auditor as the S&P 500 firm, (2) has the data available for our analyses, and (3) did not switch auditor from 1999 to 2000. Our purpose in choosing the smallest matching firm is to create the greatest size contrast with the matching S&P 500 firm, which should increase the power of our tests. We are unable to find an appropriate match for 10 of the S&P 500 firms.[8] Thus, our final sample consists of 192 S&P 500 firms and 192 matching small firms.

RESULTS

Descriptive Statistics

Table 1 presents descriptive statistics. The S&P 500 firms are financially healthier than the small firms, with higher operating cash flows and fewer loss firms. By design, the S&P 500 firms are much larger than the matching firms, as evidenced by mean and median values of total assets and market value of equity. Further, the mean (median) audit fees paid by the S&P 500 firms of $2.366 million ($1.476 million) are over 10 times the mean (median) fees of $176,000 ($133,000) paid by the matching firms. This is consistent with prior research that shows audit fees are highly associated with the size of the client firm (Maher, Tiessen, Colson, & Broman, 1992; Palmrose, 1986; Francis, 1984).

For the S&P 500 firms, the mean non-audit fee of $7.298 million is three times the size of the audit fee ($2.366 million); the median non-audit fee of $3.101 million is double the median audit fee ($1.476 million). The mean (median) fee ratio is 66.3% (68.2%). In other words, non-audit fees, on average, account for roughly two-thirds of the total fees that these firms paid to their auditors in 2000. For the matching small firms, however, non-audit fees account for slightly more than one-third of the total fees paid to the auditor, with mean (median) FEERATIO of 37.6% (37.9%). For the combined sample, mean (median) values of FEERATIO of 51.9% (54.9%) are comparable to but slightly higher than those of ALM, Frankel et al. (2002), and Reynolds et al. (2004).

Table 1. Descriptive Statistics.

Variable	SP 500 Firms (N = 192)			Matching Firms (N = 192)			All Firms (N = 384)		
	Mean	Med.	Std.	Mean	Med.	Std.	Mean	Med.	Std.
REDCA	0.016	0.005	0.069	-0.028	-0.009	0.173	-0.006	0.000	0.133
Abs REDCA	0.046	0.027	0.054	0.110	0.056	0.136	0.078	0.038	0.108
CA	0.008	0.009	0.068	-0.057	-0.017	0.198	-0.025	0.001	0.151
LIACCRUAL	-0.008	-0.001	0.068	-0.305	-0.021	1.675	-0.156	-0.007	1.193
AUDIT	2.366	1.476	2.303	0.176	0.133	0.155	1.271	0.428	1.964
NON-AUDIT	7.298	3.101	10.492	0.218	0.071	0.599	3.758	0.670	8.224
TOTAL	9.664	4.831	12.072	0.394	0.213	0.676	5.029	1.078	9.718
FEERATIO	0.663	0.682	0.166	0.376	0.379	0.210	0.519	0.549	0.237
ASSETS	11,492.21	5,717.60	15,350.57	157.817	50.599	282.477	5,825.01	989.007	12,237.36
MVE	24,596.19	8,539.79	44,429.18	68.738	15.059	222.932	12,332.47	802.818	33,692.96
MERGER (0,1)	0.307	0.00	0.463	0.109	0.00	0.313	0.208	0.00	0.407
FINANCING (0,1)	0.339	0.00	0.474	0.349	0.00	0.478	0.344	0.00	0.476
LEVERAGE	0.572	0.595	0.184	0.604	0.549	0.555	0.588	0.580	0.413
MB	3.156	2.186	2.637	1.276	0.928	1.232	2.216	1.378	2.261
LITIGATION	0.286	0.00	0.453	0.302	0.00	0.460	0.294	0.00	0.456
INST	0.641	0.660	0.138	0.192	0.136	0.189	0.416	0.451	0.279
LOSS (0,1)	0.078	0.00	0.269	0.589	1.000	0.493	0.333	0.00	0.472
CFO	0.149	0.128	0.102	-0.049	0.019	0.239	0.050	0.080	0.209
ASSETGROW	0.211	0.076	0.442	0.054	-0.025	0.772	0.132	0.034	0.633

Note: REDCA = Performance-adjusted discretionary accrual measure.

Abs REDCA = Absolute value of REDCA.

CA = Current accruals, equal to income before extraordinary items plus depreciation and amortization minus operating cash flows.

L1ACCRUAL = Prior year's CA.

AUDIT = Fees paid by company for audit work (as indicated in proxy statement), in millions of dollars.

NON-AUDIT = Fees paid by company to auditor for non-audit work (as indicated in proxy statement), in millions of dollars.

TOTAL = The sum of audit fees and non-audit fees.

FEERATIO = Ratio of NON-AUDIT to TOTAL.

ASSETS = Total assets in millions of dollars.

MVE = Market value of equity at the end of 2000, in millions of dollars.

MERGER = Dummy variable equal to one if the firm engaged in a merger or acquisition in the current year (as identified in Compustat footnote code AFTNT 1); zero otherwise.

FINANCING = One if MERGER is not equal to one and either one or both of the following conditions apply: long term debt increased by 20% or more, or number of shares outstanding increased by 10% or more after controlling for stock splits; zero otherwise.

LEVERAGE = Total debt divided by total assets.

MB = Market value of equity plus book value of debt, scaled by book value of assets.

LITIGATION = One if the firm is in a high-litigation industry; zero otherwise. "High litigation industries are those with SIC codes of 2833–2836, 3570–3577, 3600–3674, 5200–5961, and 7370." (ALM, p. 624).

INST = Percentage of shares held by institutional investors at the beginning of the calendar year.

LOSS = Dummy variable equal to one if the firm reports a net loss, zero otherwise.

CFO = Cash flows from operations, scaled by total assets at the beginning of the year.

ASSETGROW = Ending total assets minus beginning total assets, divided by ending total assets.

The median REDCA of 0.5% for the S&P 500 firms is closely comparable to that of 0.53% reported in ALM; however, the mean REDCA of 1.6% for the S&P 500 firms is much higher than the mean value of −0.66% in ALM. Similarly, the mean (median) REDCA of −2.8% (−0.9%) for the matching small firms is smaller (i.e., more negative) than the mean (median) reported in ALM. Although we use different sample selection criteria, the mean (median) REDCA of −0.6% (0.0%) for the pooled sample of firms (S&P 500 plus matching small firms) is closely comparable to, albeit slightly lower than, the mean (median) REDCA value of −0.66% (0.53%) reported in ALM.

Regression Results

Table 2 presents regression results from Eq. 4 using various fee-based proxies for the degree of economic bonding between the client and the auditor. Standard diagnostic tests reveal no multicollinearity problems and the White statistics do not reject the joint hypothesis that the models are well specified and homoscedastic (Belsley et al., 1980; White, 1980). All p-values reported are two-tailed.

In the REDCA model, FEERATIO is negatively significant (p-value 0.001), while the coefficient on the interaction term FEERATIO*SP500 is strongly positive (p-value 0.004). The negative association between FEE-RATIO and REDCA suggests that auditors do not give much flexibility to (or are more strict toward) their smaller clients that pay higher proportion of non-audit fees. This interpretation is consistent with the reputation protection hypothesis proposed by Reynolds and Francis (2001). The positive coefficient on the interaction term (FEERATIO*SP500) is consistent with the prediction that the relation between FEERATIO and signed discretionary accruals differs between large and small firms. The partial derivative with respect to FEERATIO = 0.041 ($\beta_2 + \beta_3$) for the S&P 500 firms and is insignificant, suggesting the auditors are not influenced by higher proportions of non-audit fees paid by their prominent clients.

Similar to our results using FEERATIO, the alternative fee measures LnTOTAL, LnAUDIT, and LnNON-AUDIT are significantly negatively related to REDCA. Thus, for the small firms, we find that all measures of fee dependence are associated with income-decreasing earnings management. In the REDCA models that include the interaction of LnTOTAL, LnAUDIT, and LnNON-AUDIT with SP500, we find that the coefficient on the interaction terms is positive in all cases but significant only for LnTOTAL (p-value 0.022). Overall, the results using alternative fee-based

Table 2. Association between Alternative Fee Measures and Discretionary Accruals.

N = 384	Dependent Variable = REDCA				Dependent Variable = abs REDCA			
Fee Measure	FEERATIO	ln TOTAL	ln AUDIT	ln NON-AUDIT	FEERATIO	ln TOTAL	ln AUDIT	ln NON-AUDIT
Intercept	0.025	0.430	0.417	0.083	0.149	−0.062	0.017	0.094
	(0.511)	(0.001)	(0.009)	(0.145)	(0.001)	(0.519)	(0.892)	(0.015)
SP500	−0.147	−0.438	−0.281	−0.132	0.051	0.205	0.191	0.051
	(0.006)	(0.019)	(0.202)	(0.095)	(0.208)	(0.153)	(0.262)	(0.570)
FEEMEASURE	−0.157	−0.041	−0.042	−0.011	0.090	0.022	0.014	0.009
	(0.001)	(0.000)	(0.003)	(0.016)	(0.010)	(0.010)	(0.193)	(0.001)
FEEMEASURE*SP500	0.198	0.030	0.020	0.008	−0.028	−0.013	−0.012	−0.001
	(0.004)	(0.022)	(0.231)	(0.208)	(0.600)	(0.216)	(0.358)	(0.867)
L1ACCRUAL	−0.012	−0.011	−0.009	−0.010	0.013	0.012	0.011	0.013
	(0.039)	(0.055)	(0.100)	(0.203)	(0.003)	(0.005)	(0.010)	(0.003)
Ln MVE	0.012	0.019	0.020	0.013	−0.015	−0.019	−0.015	−0.017
	(0.031)	(0.005)	(0.003)	(0.069)	(0.001)	(0.001)	(0.004)	(0.001)
MERGER	−0.016	−0.015	−0.015	−0.017	0.033	0.033	0.035	0.033
	(0.331)	(0.371)	(0.365)	(0.338)	(0.010)	(0.011)	(0.008)	(0.011)
FINANCING	0.007	0.002	0.002	0.005	−0.011	−0.008	−0.009	−0.010
	(0.639)	(0.877)	(0.917)	(0.751)	(0.330)	(0.461)	(0.443)	(0.375)
LEVERAGE	−0.046	−0.032	−0.027	−0.042	0.022	0.014	0.016	0.019
	(0.007)	(0.064)	(0.126)	(0.093)	(0.083)	(0.296)	(0.224)	(0.133)
MB	−0.005	−0.007	−0.008	−0.005	0.007	0.008	0.007	0.008
	(0.174)	(0.072)	(0.060)	(0.129)	(0.018)	(0.009)	(0.038)	(0.009)
LITIGATION	0.002	−0.004	−0.004	0.001	0.058	0.061	0.061	0.058
	(0.916)	(0.829)	(0.809)	(0.968)	(0.001)	(0.001)	(0.001)	(0.001)
INST	0.025	0.035	0.017	0.024	−0.067	−0.068	−0.061	−0.069
	(0.537)	(0.403)	(0.693)	(0.515)	(0.033)	(0.034)	(0.060)	(0.030)
LOSS	−0.098	−0.089	−0.088	−0.099	0.010	0.005	0.007	0.011
	(0.000)	(0.000)	(0.000)	(0.001)	(0.483)	(0.745)	(0.642)	(0.453)

Table 2. (Continued)

N = 384	Dependent Variable = REDCA				Dependent Variable = abs REDCA			
Fee Measure	FEERATIO	ln TOTAL	ln AUDIT	ln NON-AUDIT	FEERATIO	ln TOTAL	ln AUDIT	ln NON-AUDIT
CFO	-0.119	-0.122	-0.129	-0.125	-0.070	-0.069	-0.069	-0.066
	(0.004)	(0.003)	(0.002)	(0.110)	(0.028)	(0.031)	(0.031)	(0.038)
ASSETGROW	0.031	0.027	0.026	0.030	-0.001	0.001	0.001	0.001
	(0.006)	(0.016)	(0.024)	(0.010)	(0.924)	(0.865)	(0.962)	(0.965)
Adjusted R^2	0.184	0.187	0.177	0.177	0.270	0.267	0.256	0.277
$\beta_2 + \beta_3$	0.041	-0.011	-0.022	-0.003	0.062	0.009	0.002	0.008
	(0.443)	(0.266)	(0.074)	(0.654)	(0.130)	(0.227)	(0.805)	(0.189)

Note:

$$REDCA \text{ or } absREDCA = \beta_0 + \beta_1 SP500 + \beta_2 FEEMEASURE + \beta_3 FEEMEASURE*SP500 + \beta_4 L1ACCRUAL$$
$$+ \beta_5 LnMVE + \beta_6 MERGER + \beta_7 FINANCING + \beta_8 LEVERAGE + \beta_9 MB + \beta_{10} LITIGATION + \beta_{11} INST$$
$$+ \beta_{12} LOSS + \beta_{13} CFO + \beta_{14} ASSETGROW + \beta_{15} IND2 + \beta_{16} IND3 + \beta_{17} IND4 + \beta_{18} IND5 + \beta_{19} IND7 + \varepsilon$$

p-values (two-tailed) are below the parameter estimates. Ln TOTAL, Ln AUDIT, and Ln NON-AUDIT equal the natural logarithm of TOTAL, AUDIT, and NON-AUDIT, respectively. "Fee measure" takes the value FEERATIO, Ln TOTAL, Ln AUDIT, or Ln NON-AUDIT as indicated in the column heading. FEEMEASURE*SP500 equals the indicated fee measure multiplied by SP500. IND2, IND3, IND4, IND5, and IND7 are included in the regression but omitted from the table for brevity. All other variables are as previously defined.

proxies for economic bonding are generally consistent with the results we find with FEERATIO.

In the pooled model with AbsREDCA as the dependent variable, FEE-RATIO is significantly positive (*p*-value 0.010), while the interaction term FEERATIO*SP500 is insignificant (*p*-value 0.600). We find similar results when using the alternative fee measures. Again, in all cases using Abs-REDCA as the dependent variable, $\beta_2 + \beta_3$ is insignificant; there is no association between fee proxies and accruals for the S&P 500 firms. Overall, these results suggest that the association between auditor fee dependence proxies and discretionary accruals differs for the prominent and small clients.

In examining the association between proxies for economic bonding and discretionary accruals, ALM stress the need for distinguishing between income-increasing and income-decreasing accruals.

> While income-decreasing accruals can be interpreted as a form of biased financial reporting, income-decreasing accruals also reflect a conservative application of generally accepted accounting principles (GAAP). Typically, regulators and financial statement users are more concerned with the opportunistic application of GAAP than the conservative application of GAAP, with the opportunistic application of GAAP more likely signaling problems with auditor independence (ALM, p. 613).

To address these concerns, Table 3 presents results after dividing firms into two groups – those with positive values of REDCA and those with negative values of REDCA. The dependent variable is AbsREDCA. For positive values of REDCA, none of the fee measures is significant. However, $\beta_2 + \beta_3$ is marginally significant (*p*-value 0.108) when the dependent measure is FEERATIO. When we separately examine firms with negative values of REDCA, all fee measures are positive and significant, while $\beta_2 + \beta_3$ is positive but insignificant. These findings, which are consistent with those of ALM, suggest that results for the AbsREDCA model in Table 2 are primarily driven by income-decreasing discretionary accruals for the non-prominent audit clients.

The model in Table 3 constrains the coefficient estimates on the control variables to be the same for the S&P 500 firms and the matching small firms. To relax this assumption, we conduct sensitivity analysis by dividing firms into four categories – S&P 500 firms with positive (negative) discretionary accruals, and matching small firms with positive (negative) discretionary accruals. Table 4, panel A presents results for positive discretionary accruals. For the S&P 500 firms, FEERATIO is positively related to discretionary accruals (*p*-value 0.005), consistent with the notion that the auditors permit more income-increasing accruals when prominent clients pay higher

Table 3. Association between Alternative Fee Measures and Absolute Value of Discretionary Accruals, Conditional on Sign of Discretionary Accruals.

Dependent Variable: Abs REDCA

	Positive Discretionary Accruals (N = 195: 109 S&P 500, 86 Matching)				Negative Discretionary Accruals (N = 189: 83 S&P 500, 106 Matching)			
	FEE RATIO	ln TOTAL	ln AUDIT	ln NON-AUDIT	FEE RATIO	ln TOTAL	ln AUDIT	ln NON-AUDIT
Intercept	0.158	0.174	0.231	0.142	0.125	-0.196	-0.148	0.084
	(0.000)	(0.149)	(0.093)	(0.003)	(0.009)	(0.178)	(0.452)	(0.158)
SP500	-0.022	0.015	0.117	0.006	0.091	0.313	0.172	0.063
	(0.664)	(0.935)	(0.542)	(0.955)	(0.139)	(0.150)	(0.530)	(0.640)
FEEMEASURE	-0.006	-0.002	-0.008	0.002	0.123	0.033	0.030	0.009
	(0.897)	(0.873)	(0.511)	(0.612)	(0.018)	(0.008)	(0.094)	(0.020)
FEEMEASURE*SP500	0.083	0.001	-0.006	0.002	-0.110	-0.021	-0.012	-0.003
	(0.198)	(0.912)	(0.664)	(0.809)	(0.175)	(0.166)	(0.566)	(0.784)
L1ACCRUAL	0.009	0.009	0.009	0.009	0.046	0.051	0.047	0.042
	(0.019)	(0.019)	(0.022)	(0.013)	(0.100)	(0.068)	(0.097)	(0.129)
Ln MVE	-0.011	-0.011	-0.005	-0.013	-0.014	-0.019	-0.019	-0.016
	(0.029)	(0.103)	(0.431)	(0.024)	(0.039)	(0.013)	(0.018)	(0.036)
MERGER	0.033	0.033	0.035	0.033	0.041	0.037	0.037	0.038
	(0.017)	(0.017)	(0.012)	(0.018)	(0.074)	(0.105)	(0.116)	(0.102)
FINANCING	-0.005	-0.005	-0.006	-0.005	-0.017	-0.014	-0.015	-0.017
	(0.681)	(0.663)	(0.630)	(0.666)	(0.364)	(0.439)	(0.410)	(0.354)

	(1)	(2)	(3)	(4)	(5)	(6)	(7)	(8)
LEVERAGE	-0.031	-0.031	-0.022	-0.031	0.064	0.053	0.053	0.057
	(0.041)	(0.060)	(0.169)	(0.054)	(0.002)	(0.010)	(0.013)	(0.005)
MB	0.009	0.009	0.006	0.010	0.005	0.006	0.006	0.005
	(0.013)	(0.029)	(0.124)	(0.010)	(0.293)	(0.196)	(0.232)	(0.274)
LITIGATION	0.047	0.045	0.044	0.045	0.066	0.070	0.070	0.063
	(0.001)	(0.002)	(0.002)	(0.002)	(0.004)	(0.002)	(0.002)	(0.005)
INST	-0.047	-0.048	-0.057	-0.049	-0.060	-0.070	-0.053	-0.059
	(0.225)	(0.233)	(0.155)	(0.216)	(0.206)	(0.151)	(0.284)	(0.215)
LOSS	-0.050	-0.053	-0.051	-0.051	0.050	0.041	0.041	0.049
	(0.003)	(0.002)	(0.002)	(0.002)	(0.032)	(0.078)	(0.083)	(0.039)
CFO	-0.137	-0.140	-0.145	-0.136	-0.014	-0.008	-0.006	-0.016
	(0.001)	(0.001)	(0.000)	(0.001)	(0.777)	(0.869)	(0.897)	(0.733)
ASSETGROW	0.008	0.008	0.007	0.009	-0.019	-0.014	-0.010	-0.016
	(0.320)	(0.337)	(0.402)	(0.302)	(0.330)	(0.456)	(0.622)	(0.414)
Adjusted R^2	0.250	0.239	0.248	0.241	0.367	0.373	0.359	0.367
$\beta_2 + \beta_3$	0.077	-0.001	-0.014	0.004	0.013	0.012	0.018	0.006
	(0.108)	(0.971)	(0.174)	(0.619)	(0.841)	(0.310)	(0.240)	(0.481)

Note:

$$AbsREDCA = \beta_0 + \beta_1 SP500 + \beta_2 FEEMEASURE + \beta_3 FEEMEASURE*SP500 + \beta_4 L1ACCRUAL$$
$$+ \beta_5 LnMVE + \beta_6 MERGER + \beta_7 FINANCING + \beta_8 LEVERAGE + \beta_9 MB + \beta_{10} LITIGATION + \beta_{11} INST$$
$$+ \beta_{12} LOSS + \beta_{13} CFO + \beta_{14} ASSETGROW + \beta_{15} IND2 + \beta_{16} IND3 + \beta_{17} IND4 + \beta_{18} IND5 + \beta_{19} IND7 + \varepsilon$$

p-values (two-tailed) are below the parameter estimates. FEEMEASURE takes the value FEERATIO, Ln TOTAL, Ln AUDIT, or Ln NON-AUDIT as indicated in the column heading. FEEMEASURE * SP500 equals the indicated fee measure multiplied by SP500. IND2, IND3, IND4, IND5, and IND7 are included in the regression but omitted from the table for brevity. All other variables are as previously defined.

Table 4. Association between Alternative Fee Measures and Absolute Value of Discretionary Accruals, Conditional on Sign of Discretionary Accruals and Group.

	S&P 500 Firms ($N = 109$)				Matching Firms ($N = 86$)			
	FEERATIO	ln TOTAL	ln AUDIT	ln NON-AUDIT	FEERATIO	ln TOTAL	ln AUDIT	ln NON-AUDIT
Panel A: Positive Discretionary Accruals								
Intercept	0.043	0.088	0.295	0.044	0.195	0.173	0.268	0.172
	(0.521)	(0.413)	(0.007)	(0.626)	(0.001)	(0.293)	(0.158)	(0.014)
FEEMEASURE	0.103	0.003	-0.020	0.007	0.044	0.002	-0.007	0.003
	(0.005)	(0.745)	(0.039)	(0.261)	(0.485)	(0.873)	(0.694)	(0.535)
L1ACCRUAL	-0.133	-0.122	-0.097	-0.132	0.009	0.008	0.008	0.009
	(0.115)	(0.170)	(0.260)	(0.134)	(0.100)	(0.127)	(0.148)	(0.105)
Ln MVE	-0.003	-0.005	0.007	-0.008	-0.015	-0.013	-0.009	-0.014
	(0.503)	(0.468)	(0.313)	(0.222)	(0.232)	(0.350)	(0.487)	(0.246)
MERGER	0.032	0.031	0.032	0.031	-0.031	-0.021	-0.022	-0.023
	(0.008)	(0.014)	(0.008)	(0.013)	(0.497)	(0.618)	(0.608)	(0.587)
FINANCING	-0.006	-0.008	-0.008	-0.007	0.006	0.009	0.007	0.008
	(0.631)	(0.539)	(0.519)	(0.570)	(0.808)	(0.725)	(0.773)	(0.748)
LEVERAGE	-0.061	-0.061	-0.056	-0.067	-0.013	-0.015	-0.010	-0.013
	(0.077)	(0.099)	(0.324)	(0.066)	(0.650)	(0.623)	(0.745)	(0.649)
MB	0.005	0.006	0.003	0.006	-0.007	-0.007	-0.009	-0.006
	(0.156)	(0.147)	(0.515)	(0.096)	(0.598)	(0.609)	(0.498)	(0.662)
LITIGATION	0.045	0.040	0.039	0.041	0.024	0.027	0.025	0.027
	(0.003)	(0.009)	(0.009)	(0.007)	(0.394)	(0.335)	(0.377)	(0.339)
INST	-0.042	-0.052	-0.046	-0.052	-0.025	-0.028	-0.027	-0.031
	(0.359)	(0.279)	(0.326)	(0.272)	(0.746)	(0.720)	(0.725)	(0.688)
LOSS	-0.001	-0.023	-0.022	-0.016	-0.063	-0.063	-0.062	-0.061
	(0.971)	(0.366)	(0.373)	(0.529)	(0.012)	(0.012)	(0.015)	(0.015)
CFO	-0.091	-0.118	-0.147	-0.104	-0.196	-0.193	-0.193	-0.187
	(0.248)	(0.155)	(0.068)	(0.208)	(0.003)	(0.003)	(0.003)	(0.005)
ASSETGROW	0.029	0.041	0.030	0.040	-0.003	-0.002	-0.003	-0.002
	(0.125)	(0.034)	(0.126)	(0.034)	(0.826)	(0.837)	(0.783)	(0.857)
Adjusted R^2	(0.366)	(0.308)	(0.339)	(0.317)	(0.189)	(0.184)	(0.185)	(0.188)

	S&P 500 Firms (N = 83)				Matching Firms (N = 86)			
	FEERATIO	Ln TOTAL	Ln AUDIT	Ln NON-AUDIT	FEERATIO	Ln TOTAL	Ln AUDIT	Ln NON-AUDIT
Panel B: Negative Discretionary Accruals								
Intercept	0.010	−0.014	−0.052	−0.004	0.282	−0.233	−0.297	0.219
	(0.808)	(0.776)	(0.414)	(0.921)	(0.002)	(0.252)	(0.295)	(0.027)
FEEMEASURE	0.006	0.003	0.007	0.002	0.140	0.051	0.058	0.010
	(0.757)	(0.431)	(0.217)	(0.444)	(0.042)	(0.004)	(0.026)	(0.051)
LIACCRUAL	0.009	0.010	0.017	0.010	0.073	0.083	0.079	0.067
	(0.863)	(0.835)	(0.724)	(0.844)	(0.054)	(0.027)	(0.039)	(0.077)
Ln MVE	0.001	−0.002	−0.003	−0.001	−0.028	−0.037	−0.036	−0.027
	(0.899)	(0.737)	(0.493)	(0.785)	(0.021)	(0.003)	(0.006)	(0.028)
MERGER	0.011	0.010	0.009	0.010	0.071	0.068	0.062	0.065
	(0.243)	(0.285)	(0.343)	(0.269)	(0.116)	(0.125)	(0.173)	(0.152)
FINANCING	0.003	0.003	0.003	0.003	−0.044	−0.040	−0.036	−0.043
	(0.716)	(0.710)	(0.730)	(0.724)	(0.161)	(0.192)	(0.243)	(0.165)
LEVERAGE	−0.007	−0.011	−0.020	−0.009	0.059	0.032	0.035	0.054
	(0.792)	(0.651)	(0.444)	(0.702)	(0.087)	(0.370)	(0.334)	(0.117)
MB	−0.004	−0.004	−0.004	−0.004	0.021	0.035	0.031	0.019
	(0.039)	(0.065)	(0.077)	(0.057)	(0.235)	(0.059)	(0.100)	(0.275)
LITIGATION	0.029	0.028	0.038	0.028	0.071	0.078	0.083	0.070
	(0.016)	(0.017)	(0.017)	(0.018)	(0.059)	(0.034)	(0.027)	(0.066)
INST	−0.051	−0.052	−0.052	−0.053	−0.047	−0.086	−0.065	−0.053
	(0.060)	(0.048)	(0.047)	(0.048)	(0.574)	(0.307)	(0.446)	(0.530)
LOSS	0.046	0.045	0.045	0.045	0.037	0.023	0.024	0.041
	(0.001)	(0.001)	(0.001)	(0.001)	(0.326)	(0.530)	(0.523)	(0.281)
CFO	0.251	0.255	0.259	0.255	−0.016	0.007	0.018	−0.015
	(0.001)	(0.001)	(0.001)	(0.001)	(0.824)	(0.915)	(0.797)	(0.831)
ASSETGROW	−0.024	−0.022	−0.021	−0.003	−0.009	−0.002	0.013	−0.005
	(0.008)	(0.015)	(0.026)	(0.013)	(0.818)	(0.954)	(0.738)	(0.889)
Adjusted R^2	(0.441)	(0.446)	(0.454)	(0.446)	(0.339)	(0.370)	(0.346)	(0.337)

Note:

$$AbsREDCA = \beta_0 + \beta_1 FEEMEASURE + \beta_2 LIACCRUAL + \beta_3 LnMVE + \beta_4 MERGER + \beta_5 FINANCING$$
$$+ \beta_6 LEVERAGE + \beta_7 MB + \beta_8 LITIGATION + \beta_9 INST + \beta_{10} LOSS + \beta_{11} CFO$$
$$+ \beta_{12} ASSETGROW + \beta_{13} IND2 + \beta_{14} IND3 + \beta_{15} IND4 + \beta_{16} IND5 + \beta_{17} IND7 + \varepsilon$$

p-values (two-tailed) are below the parameter estimates. FEEMEASURE takes the value FEERATIO, Ln TOTAL, Ln AUDIT, or Ln NON-AUDIT as indicated in the column heading. IND2, IND3, IND4, IND5, and IND7 are included in the regression but omitted from the table for brevity. All other variables are as previously defined.

Table 5. Logit Model, Probability of Small Earnings Increase or Meeting or Beating Analysts' Forecast.

	Dependent Variable: INCREASE (N = 378)				Dependent Variable: SURPRISE (N = 271)			
	FEERATIO	In TOTAL	In AUDIT	In NON-AUDIT	FEERATIO	In TOTAL	In AUDIT	In NON-AUDIT
Intercept	−5.090	4.248	8.936	−4.433	−3.150	3.845	8.508	−2.343
	(0.001)	(0.410)	(0.161)	(0.020)	(0.007)	(0.451)	(0.208)	(0.262)
SP500	0.078	−5.813	−10.008	1.894	−1.728	−9.145	−12.052	−2.967
	(0.957)	(0.325)	(0.156)	(0.511)	(0.225)	(0.120)	(0.102)	(0.331)
FEEMEASURE	0.001	−0.881	−1.336	−0.124	−0.278	−0.601	−1.062	−0.077
	(0.999)	(0.053)	(0.023)	(0.459)	(0.873)	(0.163)	(0.077)	(0.663)
FEEMEASURE*SP500	−1.057	0.393	0.751	−0.191	1.209	0.602	0.872	0.151
	(0.617)	(0.371)	(0.183)	(0.372)	(0.557)	(0.164)	(0.135)	(0.506)
LITIGATION	0.056	−0.079	−0.120	0.055	−1.408	−1.450	−1.486	−1.407
	(0.901)	(0.863)	(0.791)	(0.904)	(0.005)	(0.004)	(0.003)	(0.005)
MB	0.279	0.140	0.126	0.199	0.179	0.160	0.119	0.188
	(0.004)	(0.184)	(0.241)	(0.052)	(0.029)	(0.087)	(0.211)	(0.036)
Ln MVE	0.472	0.833	0.867	0.658	0.508	0.581	0.695	0.487
	(0.001)	(0.001)	(0.001)	(0.001)	(0.001)	(0.003)	(0.001)	(0.005)

INST	-0.649	-0.416	-0.351	-0.714	-2.230	-1.836	-1.848	-2.096
	(0.542)	(0.703)	(0.750)	(0.505)	(0.036)	(0.087)	(0.087)	(0.049)
LOSS	-1.908	-1.806	-1.804	-1.850	-0.949	-1.002	-0.991	-0.975
	(0.007)	(0.011)	(0.011)	(0.011)	(0.139)	(0.121)	(0.127)	(0.131)
REDCA	-0.731	-1.044	-1.452	-0.994	-0.839	-0.913	-1.149	-0.706
	(0.720)	(0.605)	(0.472)	(0.629)	(0.692)	(0.668)	(0.591)	(0.739)
Pseudo R^2	0.368	0.383	0.386	0.375	0.204	0.208	0.212	0.203

Note:

$$INCREASE \text{ or } SURPRISE = \beta_0 + \beta_1 SP500 + \beta_2 FEEMEASURE + \beta_3 FEEMEASURE * SP500$$
$$+ \beta_4 LITIGATION + \beta_5 MB + \beta_6 LnMVE + \beta_7 INST + \beta_8 LOSS$$
$$+ \beta_9 REDCA + \beta_{10} IND2 + \beta_{11} IND3 + \beta_{12} IND4 + \beta_{13} IND5 + \beta_{14} IND7 + \varepsilon$$

p-values (two-tailed) are below the parameter estimates. INCREASE equals one if change in net income scaled by beginning market value of equity is between 0 and 0.02, zero otherwise. SURPRISE = 1 if annual earnings per share equals or exceeds analysts' forecasts by $0.01 or less, and zero otherwise. FEEMEASURE takes the value FEERATIO, Ln TOTAL, Ln AUDIT, or Ln NONAUDIT as indicated in the column heading. FEEMEASURE * SP500 equals the indicated fee measure multiplied by SP500. IND2, IND3, IND4, IND5, and IND7 are included in the regression but omitted from the table for brevity. All other variables are as previously defined.

proportions of non-audit fees. However, the result is not robust to alternative fee measures. In fact, LnAUDIT is negatively related to discretionary accruals (p-value 0.039). This result seems to indicate that, at least for the S&P 500 firms, the relation between fees and discretionary accruals is sensitive to the type of fee paid to the auditor.

Table 4, panel B presents results for firms with negative discretionary accruals. None of the fee measures is significant for the S&P 500 firms. For the matching small firms, FEERATIO, LnTOTAL, LnAUDIT, and LnNON-AUDIT are all significantly positive. Because the dependent variable is AbsREDCA, this indicates that, for small firms, fees paid to auditors are associated with larger (more negative) income-decreasing discretionary accruals.

Taken as a whole, Tables 2–4 indicate that the relation between discretionary accruals and fees paid to auditors differs for S&P 500 firms and the matching small firms. We find some evidence in Table 4 that S&P 500 firms who pay large proportions of non-audit fees to their auditors have larger income-increasing discretionary accruals. However, the result for the S&P 500 firms is not robust to alternative fee measures. On the other hand, for the matching small firms, fees paid to auditors (regardless of the composition of the fees) are associated with larger (more negative) income-decreasing discretionary accruals. This indicates that auditors are unyielding with small clients who already have income-decreasing discretionary accruals (due to auditor concern for reputation or auditor conservatism).

Logistic Regression Results

To check the robustness of our findings in the discretionary accrual model and consistent with Frankel et al. (2002) and ALM, we estimate models using alternative proxies of earnings management as dependent variables. Table 5 presents results from a logistic regression model that specifies the likelihood of having a small positive earnings increase or narrowly beating analysts' forecasts as a function of the variable of interest (fee-based proxies for the economic bonding between the client and the auditor) and other control variables.

In the earnings increase model (INCREASE), FEERATIO, and ln NON-AUDIT are insignificant while ln TOTAL and ln AUDIT are significantly negative. The interaction term (FEEMEASURE*SP500) is insignificant regardless of the fee proxy used. Results in the earnings surprise model (SURPRISE) are similar to those of the earnings increase model. The only exception is that ln TOTAL, which was negatively significant in the earnings increase model, is no longer significant. Taken together, the results from the INCREASE and SURPRISE models, which are consistent with the findings in ALM, suggest that heightened economic bonding between the client and the auditor does not increase the likelihood of clients narrowly beating earnings benchmarks.

CONCLUSION

We test the hypothesis that, if non-audit service fees increase economic bonding between the auditor and the client, evidence of such bonding is most likely to be found among the auditor's largest, most influential clients. Using a matched sample design, we find some evidence that higher proportions of non-audit fees are associated with higher levels of income-increasing accruals for S&P 500 firms (our proxy for prominent firms). However, this finding does not hold when we use other fee measures as the dependence proxy. Alternatively, for matching small firms, higher fees paid to auditors (regardless of the composition of the fees) are positively associated with higher income-decreasing discretionary accruals (i.e., lead to larger negative discretionary accruals). Thus, our results indicate that the relation between discretionary accruals and fees paid to auditors differs for S&P 500 firms and the matched group of small firms (matched on industry and auditor). Our findings provide an empirical benchmark in the SEC's continued consideration of prohibited non-audit services, and are particularly applicable given the SEC's new task force on smaller public companies.

The time period of our study is prior to the passage of SOX, and thus care should be taken in generalizing our findings. The Act likely has reduced the magnitude and proportion of non-audit services auditors provided to their audit clients, while recent, highly publicized audit failures have increased public and regulatory scrutiny of the activities of audit firms. Future research may explore whether and how these changes have affected the relation between discretionary accruals and client–auditor economic bonding. Our conjecture is that these environmental changes will weaken the positive association we find between positive discretionary accruals and the non-audit fee ratio for the S&P 500 firms. On the other hand, we expect that our finding for the smaller firms, which is consistent with the notion that auditors are unyielding with small clients who already have income-decreasing discretionary accruals, will hold or even strengthen further in the post-SOX era.

NOTES

1. By "economic bonding", we mean the importance of the client to the auditor, which has also been referred to in the literature as "economic dependence" or "client influence" (DeAngelo, 1981; Chung & Kallapur, 2003).

2. Examples include Cendant, Waste Management, McKesson HBOC, Rite Aid, W.R. Grace, Xerox, Health South, Worldcom (now MCI), Tyco, Gateway, Global Crossing, and Enron.

3. Prominent clients such as members of the S&P 500 may have greater influence on the auditor than smaller clients for many reasons. First, because larger clients generate greater fees, the auditor has more to lose if such clients choose to switch auditors. Thus the auditor has a higher economic incentive to go along with the accrual decisions of its prominent clients. Second, prominent clients bring prestige and may serve as a promotional tool for the auditor to use in attracting new clients. On the other hand, loss of a prominent client generates negative press coverage, public attention and can lead to the loss of other clients of the auditor.

4. The prohibited services are "(1) bookkeeping or other services related to the accounting records or financial statements of the audit client; (2) financial information systems design and implementation; (3) appraisal or valuation services, fairness opinions, or contribution-in-kind reports; (4) actuarial services; (5) internal audit outsourcing services; (6) management functions or human resources; (7) broker or dealer, investment adviser, or investment banking services; (8) legal services and expert services unrelated to the audit; and (9) any other service that the Board determines, by regulation, is impermissible" (Sarbanes-Oxley Act of 2002).

5. For further discussion of the consequences of not controlling for firm performance, please see Kothari et al. (2005) and ALM.

6. Computing total and discretionary accruals used in the empirical models is problematic for financial firms due to their unique financial statement reporting requirements (Becker, DeFond, Jiambalvo, & Subramanyam, 1998). We exclude utilities because incentives to manage earnings may differ for firms in regulated industries as compared to firms in unregulated industries (Becker et al., 1998).

7. DFFITS is a statistic that measures the change in predicted value of a particular observation if that observation is eliminated from the regression calculation. DFBETAS measures how parameter estimates change if a particular observation is eliminated. (see Belsley et al., 1980, pp. 11–16).

8. Some two-digit SIC codes do not have enough small firms to provide matches for the large firms (matching on auditor as well). For example, during our sample period, PricewaterhouseCoopers audited three S&P 500 firms that were members of a particular two-digit SIC code. However, they did not audit any small firms in this SIC code; thus, the three large firms had to be excluded from the sample.

ACKNOWLEDGEMENTS

We thank Phil Reckers (the editor), an associate editor, and two anonymous reviewers for their comments. Additionally, we are grateful for comments received from workshop participants at the 2002 American Accounting Association mid-year auditing section conference, Florida State University, Rutgers University-Camden, Temple University, and Virginia Commonwealth University, particularly Lisa Gaynor, Greg Gerard, Hassan R. HassabElnaby, Bill Hillison, Jagan Krishnan, Emeka Nwaeze, Amal Said, Jayaraman Vijayakumar, and Benson Wier. We thank Bob Russ for his research assistance. We thank Thomson Financial for providing Institutional Brokers Estimate System data as part of its broad academic program to encourage earnings expectations research.

REFERENCES

Ashbaugh, H., LaFond, R., & Mayhew, B. (2003). Do non-audit services compromise auditor independence? Further evidence. *The Accounting Review, 78*(July), 611–639.

Becker, C., DeFond, M., Jiambalvo, J., & Subramanyam, K. (1998). The effects of audit quality on earnings management. *Contemporary Accounting Research, 15*(Spring), 1–24.

Belsley, W., Kuh, F., & Welsch, R. (1980). *Regression diagnostics: Identifying influential data and sources of collinearity.* New York: Wiley.

Chung, H., & Kallapur, S. (2003). Client importance, non-audit services, and abnormal accruals. *The Accounting Review, 78*(October), 931–955.

DeAngelo, L. (1981). Auditor size and audit quality. *Journal of Accounting and Economics, 3,* 183–199.

DeFond, M., Raghunandan, K., & Subramanyam, K. (2002). Do non-audit service fees impair auditor independence? Evidence from going concern audit opinions. *Journal of Accounting Research, 40*(September), 1247–1274.

DeFond, M., & Subramanyam, K. (1998). Auditor changes and discretionary accruals. *Journal of Accounting and Economics, 25*(February), 35–67.

Francis, J. (1984). The effect of audit firm size on audit prices: A study of the Australian market. *Journal of Accounting and Economics, 6*(August), 133–151.

Frankel, R., Johnson, M., & Nelson, K. (2002). The relation between auditors' fees for non-audit services and earnings management. *The Accounting Review, 77*(Suppl.), 71–105.

Jones, J. (1991). Earnings management during import relief investigations. *Journal of Accounting Research, 29*(Autumn), 193–228.

Kinney, W., & Libby, R. (2002). Discussion of the relation between auditors' fees for non-audit services and earnings management. *The Accounting Review, 77*(Suppl.), 107–114.

Kothari, S., Leone, A., & Wasley, C. (2005). Performance matched discretionary accrual measures. *Journal of Accounting and Economics, 39,* 163–197.

Lev, B. (2003). Corporate earnings: Facts and fiction. *Journal of Economic Perspectives, 17*(Spring), 27–50.

Maher, M., Tiessen, P., Colson, R., & Broman, A. (1992). Competition and audit fees. *The Accounting Review, 67*(January), 199–211.

Palmrose, Z.-V. (1986). Audit fees and auditor size: Further evidence. *Journal of Accounting Research, 24*(Spring), 97–110.

Reynolds, J., Deis, D., & Francis, J. (2004). Professional service fees and auditor objectivity. *Auditing: A Journal of Practice and Theory, 23*, 29–52.

Reynolds, J., & Francis, J. (2001). Does size matter? The influence of large clients on office-level auditor reporting decisions. *Journal of Accounting and Economics, 30*, 375–400.

Sarbanes-Oxley Act of 2002. (2002). Pub. L. No. 107–204, § 201, 116 STAT. 771.

Toffler, B. (2003). *Final accounting*. New York: Random House, Inc.

Unger, L. (2001). *Speech by SEC Acting Chairman: This Year's Proxy Season: Sunlight shines on auditor independence and executive compensation*. Remarks delivered at the Center for Professional Education, Inc. Washington, DC, June 25, 2001. Available from http:// www.sec.gov/news/speech/spch502.htm

White, H. (1980). A heteroskedasticity-consistent covariance matrix estimator and a direct test for heteroskedasticity. *Econometrica, 48*, 817–838.

THE IMPACT OF TAX SERVICES ON AUDITORS' FRAUD-RISK ASSESSMENT

Michael Favere-Marchesi

ABSTRACT

This study examined whether providing tax services to an audit client affects auditors' fraud-risk assessment. A case was administered to audit partners and senior managers of small- and medium-sized firms that provide both audit and tax services. Participants were asked to assess the risk of fraudulent financial reporting for a hypothetical audit client. The provision of tax services and the size of the client fees in relation to the audit partner's annual billings were varied and participants were randomly assigned to three experimental conditions.

Consistent with expectations, auditors whose firm also provided tax services to the audit client reported a significantly lower fraud-risk assessment than auditors whose firm provided no tax services to the audit client. Further, with the provision of tax services to the audit client, auditors' fraud-risk assessment was inversely related to the relative size of the client fees.

INTRODUCTION

In the aftermath of Enron, WorldCom and other financial failures, the U.S. Securities and Exchange Commission (SEC) adopted new auditor independence

Advances in Accounting, Volume 22, 149–165
ISSN: 0882-6110/doi:10.1016/S0882-6110(06)22007-8

rules required by the Sarbanes-Oxley Act of 2002 (SOX). These rules ban audit firms from providing audit clients specific non-audit services (NAS), which the SEC believes, could compromise auditors' objectivity. While SOX did not ban the provision of tax services to audit clients, the SEC cautioned that such services could impair independence. In fact, the U.S. Senate Banking Committee recently examined the need to bar audit firms from providing tax services to the public companies they audit (U.S. Senate Committee on Banking, Housing, and Urban Affairs, 2003). Several large companies have now taken steps to divorce some tax services from the audit in order to avoid the appearance of conflict. For example, Pepsico's policy now states that, while their auditors continue to provide tax compliance services, they are no longer authorized to perform tax-planning services. Recently, the Public Company Accountability Oversight Board has adopted new ethics and independence rules that prevent accountants from providing tax shelter advice to their public company audit clients (PCAOB, 2005).

While SOX rules apply only to public companies, its concepts could cascade to the audits of private companies, and substantial limitations on tax services could have serious economic effects on small businesses and accounting firms. Motivated by concerns over compromised auditors' objectivity and potential further restrictions on the type of NAS audit firms may offer to their audit clients, this study explored whether tax services provided by a small- to medium-sized CPA firm to a non-public registrant affect auditors' fraud-risk assessment. Further, the study examined whether the size of fees paid by the client relative to the audit partner's billings also affect auditors' fraud-risk assessment when the CPA firm provides tax services.

A case was administered to audit partners and senior managers of small- and medium-sized firms that provide both audit and tax services. The case included financial and background information of a hypothetical audit client. The background information contained several red flags of potential fraudulent financial reporting. The nature of the client–firm relationship was included in a separate section, allowing for the variation of both the nature of services provided to the client and the size of the client fees in relation to the audit partner's annual billings. Participants were asked to assess the client's risk of fraudulent financial reporting.

The results are consistent with expectations that both the provision of tax services and the size of the client fees in relation to the audit partner's billings affect the participants' fraud-risk assessment. Auditors whose firm also provided tax services to the audit client reported a significantly lower fraud-risk assessment than auditors whose firm provided no tax services to the audit client. Further, when providing tax services, auditors' fraud-risk assessment decreased as the relative client fees increased from 20% to 30% of the audit partner's annual billings.

The next section presents a review of the literature and research hypotheses. The subsequent two sections describe the research methodology and results of the study, respectively. The final section discusses findings and their implications.

BACKGROUND AND HYPOTHESIS DEVELOPMENT

The debate over whether auditors' judgment can remain objective when audit firms provide tax services to their audit clients is not new. For example, Mautz and Sharaf (1961, p. 223) stated that the "performance of (non-audit) and auditing for the same client by the same accountants (is) a combination of incompatible services."

Regulatory Concerns

In 1978, the SEC adopted Accounting Series Release No. 250, which required the disclosure of NAS provided by auditors, the percentage of non-audit fees to audit fees and a statement as to whether the Board of Directors had reviewed and approved NAS. In response to SEC's concerns over auditors' objectivity, the Public Oversight Board (POB, 1993) issued recommendations for strengthening independence. However, the POB's (2000) Panel on Audit Effectiveness could not agree about the effects of NAS on auditors' objectivity. Following the Panel's report, the SEC proposed rules to ban auditors from providing many NAS. The profession vigorously argued against the rules since the POB had found no evidence that NAS impair auditors' objectivity, and because such ban could affect the entire profession, including auditors of non-public companies (PCPS, 2000). Different rules instituted by the SEC (2001) and the American Institute of Certified Public Accountants (AICPA) (2003) led to differences in rules of independence between public and non-public companies.

Research Studies

Prompted by regulatory concerns over auditors' independence, several research studies reported that the provision of NAS to audit clients affects auditor's objectivity. Emby and Davidson (1998) noted that auditors are less likely to insist on the disclosure of a contingent liability when the contractual and financial arrangements of the engagement give the client more economic power. Sharma and Sidhu (2001) found that auditors tend not to issue a going-concern qualification to clients generating high proportions of NAS fees to total fees and concluded that audit independence might be impaired for economic reasons such as the provision of substantial NAS. Firth (2002) reported that higher consultancy fees paid to the auditor translate into a more likely "clean" audit report. Finally, Frankel, Johnson, and Nelson (2002) concluded that auditors are more likely to condone earnings management when audit clients pay large non-audit fees.

Contrary to these prior studies, Kinney, Palmrose, and Scholtz (2004) presented evidence of a negative association between tax services and public company restatements, suggesting that tax services provided by audit firms improve the quality of the public company audit.

Sarbanes-Oxley Act

Following some high-profile cases of fraudulent financial reporting, the SEC (2003) adopted new auditor independence rules. Originating from the belief that substantial revenues from NAS could compromise auditors' objectivity, these rules prohibit accounting firms from providing, together with the audit of a public client, certain NAS. While SOX allows the provision of tax services to an audit client by the same firm, the SEC Adopting Release (SEC, 2003) cautioned audit committees to be careful that such services do not impair independence. In fact, the significant concern about auditors' objectivity prompted the U.S. Senate Banking Committee to examine the need for barring certain additional services provided by external auditors, including tax services, to the public companies they audit (U.S. Senate Committee on Banking, Housing, and Urban Affairs, 2003). At the same time, the Conference Board's Commission on Public Trust and Private Enterprises released its 2003 best practice suggestions, which recommend that accounting firms limit themselves to audit and closely related services. While Kinney et al. (2004) provided an interesting empirical linkage between the provision of tax services and public company restatements, there is still no evidence as to whether the provision of tax services to non-public audit clients affects auditors' objectivity. Several factors drive the need to examine this segment of the audit market.

While SOX rules apply only to public registrants, the AICPA (2002) is concerned that SOX concepts may cascade to the state level and the audits of non-public companies most often audited by small- and medium-sized firms. Substantial limitations on tax services, offered by accountants to privately owned audit clients, could have serious economic effects on small businesses and accounting firms. Some have argued that limiting an auditor's ability to provide tax services to audit clients would result in less-independent review of tax strategies and less transparency for investors (Ernst & Young, 2003). Auditors today are much more tax focused than in the past, since many firms provide tax awareness programs that alert auditors to instances when clients can benefit from adopting new tax strategies (Temple, 1992). For example, during the auditor's review of the organizational structure and related parties, the auditor might consider the possibility of merging multiple C corporations into one S corporation, adopting an employee stock ownership plan (ESOP), which offers numerous financial and tax advantages, or reconsidering the client's plans for succession and related estate and gift tax concerns.

According to the Small Business Administration (2003), over 99% of accounting firms qualify as small businesses with less than $3 million in revenues and the great majority of all accounting firms consist of one office. Because auditors in small- and medium-sized firms often assist in tax work, study of auditors' objectivity in this segment of the audit market is important. For example, auditors in small- and medium-sized firms often use tax accrual checklists – a reminder list for auditors to see that the tax consequences of potentially significant events have been considered by the client in making the income tax accrual – and tax-savings checklists – an idea-triggering device to identify tax planning and saving matter for clients (Primoff, 1992). Hence, this study specifically focused on the provision of tax services to non-public companies by small- and medium-sized firms.

Auditors' Objectivity

As a proxy measure of auditors' objectivity, this study used fraud-risk assessment.

Fraud-risk assessment is a particularly relevant task for auditors of small- and medium-sized audit firms. While newsworthy fraudulent financial reporting usually involves large public companies (e.g., Enron and World-Com), a study by COSO (1998) revealed that most companies committing financial statement fraud are relatively small (less than $100 million in total assets) and private companies (78% were not listed on the New York or American Stock Exchanges), audited by auditors of small- and medium-sized firms. One of SOX's main arguments for new independence rules was that the provision of NAS creates economic dependency on the part of the auditors and threatens their objectivity in performing audit services

(U.S. Senate Report 107–205).[1] Hence, this study specifically examines whether auditors' fraud-risk assessment is affected when small- and medium-sized firms provide tax services to their non-public audit clients. If the previous argument holds, the provision of tax services will have a negative impact on auditors' fraud-risk assessment as stated in the first hypothesis.

H1. Auditors whose firm also provides tax services to an audit client will have a lower fraud-risk assessment than will auditors whose firm provides no tax services to the audit client.

Some studies have examined whether the size of the NAS (in relation to audit fees) affects auditors' objectivity. Sharma and Sidhu (2001) found that auditors are less likely to issue a going-concern qualification to clients generating higher proportions of NAS fees to total fees, while DeFond, Raghunandan, and Subramanyam (2002) reported no association between going-concern opinions and either total fees or audit fees. Reynolds, Deis, and Francis (2004) noted a positive association between the relative level of NAS fees and discretionary accruals, while Antle, Gordon, Narayanamoorthy, and Zhou (2002) did not find a positive relationship between NAS fees and abnormal accruals.

Tax services are one of the most lucrative NAS provided by audit firms at all levels. For example, according to Tyco's 2001 proxy statement, in addition to $13 million its auditors earned on the audit engagement, the firm was paid even more – $18 million – for tax work. While previous research has not specifically examined the size of client fees in relation to an audit partner's annual billings, Emby and Davidson (1998) and Sharma and Sidhu (2001) both lend credibility to the notion that auditors' independence is inversely related to the client's economic power.

Some expectations can also be formed from recent regulatory developments. Specifically, the SEC (2003) believes that compensating an audit partner for selling NAS creates a conflict that compromises the partner's independence and objectivity. Hence, an accountant's independence is threatened if, at any point during the audit engagement period, an audit partner earns or receives compensation based on selling to the audit client any services, other than audit, review or attest services (SEC, 2003). Obviously, this rule is also not applicable to the audits of non-public clients and, in this setting, audit partners may be rewarded for and indeed focus on selling NAS. Such arrangements may create a financial self-interest that could threaten auditors' objectivity. Small- and medium-sized firms thus warrant a specific examination since tax services account for almost half of the fees collected by those firms (PCPS, 2003).

The mixed research results previously identified suggest a lack of consistent evidence and preclude the development of a directional hypothesis to test the impact of the relative size of a client's fees on the objectivity of auditor's fraud-risk judgments. However, SEC concerns over threats to auditors' objectivity caused by audit firms providing tax services to their audit clients merit an examination and form the basis of the following research question:

> When providing tax services, are changes in the size of the client fees in relation to the audit partner's annual billings associated with changes in the auditors' fraud-risk assessment?

RESEARCH METHOD

Participants

Two U.S. state societies of CPAs solicited potential participants from small- and medium-sized firms within their jurisdiction. To ensure familiarity with the task of fraud-risk assessment, audit partners and senior managers were randomly selected from the listings of potential participants prepared by the state societies. Participants were instructed to work individually and assured of the confidentiality of their responses. In total, 70 audit partners and 20 senior managers participated in the experiment.[2] On average, participants had 18 years of audit experience and reported having detected fraudulent financial reporting on 2% of their audit engagements.

Experimental Task and Procedures

The task was the assessment of the risk of fraudulent financial reporting for a hypothetical non-public audit client described in an experimental case. The researcher developed the case with the senior audit partner of a medium-sized firm, who provided participants for pilot testing. The researcher personally administered the experiment in several group meetings at the office of the state societies. Prior to the experiment, participants were told to assume the role of an audit partner newly assigned to the audit engagement of a continuing non-public client. Participants were told that this study examined auditors' fraud-risk assessment and data collected in the debriefing questionnaires showed that all participants had considered the risk of fraudulent financial reporting when reading the background information of the experimental case.

Following instructions, the case materials consisted of background information on the company with selected financial information and a brief synopsis about the industry. The background information contained several potential "red flags" identified by the AICPA's SEC Practice Section Detection and Prevention of Fraud Task Force (1999) and indicative of an *increased* risk of fraudulent financial reporting.[3] Specifically, the company had a Board of Directors dominated by insiders and directors with significant equity ownership. It had not yet been profitable since coming out of its development stage, had new and unproven products, and was vulnerable to rapidly changing technology. It planned to raise additional capital through public offerings of common stock and was having trouble meeting restrictive debt covenants.[4]

The next section contained a description of the client–firm relationship. All participants were informed that this was the third year their firm had been engaged to perform the audit of the company. Further, their firm was able to maintain the amount of audit fees relatively stable because of the strong relationship it had developed with management, and few adjustments had been necessary in the previous two years. Additional wording differed among the three versions of the instrument. In the first version (*no tax, 20%*), participants were told that their firm provided *only* audit services to this client representing 20% of the audit partner's annual billings and that another local CPA firm prepared the client's tax returns. In the second version (*tax, 20%*), participants were told that, in addition to audit services, their firm also prepared the tax returns of this client representing 20% of the audit partner's annual billings. The third version (*tax, 30%*) contained the same information as the second version, except that the client represented 30% of the audit partner's annual billings.[5]

The thresholds of 20% and 30% were based on recommendations by the Mid-size CA Firms Forum of BC (2002) to the Exposure Draft of the Canadian Institute of Chartered Accountants on new Independence Standards.[6] The Forum recommended a "size criteria," by which the prohibition of providing NAS to audit clients would apply if the client fees represented 25% or more of an individual partner's billings. This threshold seemed to suggest that independence threats would be minimal when the client represented less than 25% of an individual partner's billings. Thus, this study adopted thresholds of 20% and 30% to investigate whether there were any significant differences in fraud-risk assessment due to the size of the client fees.

The participants' fraud-risk assessment was used as the dependent variable for the testing of the hypothesis and follow-up analysis for the research question related to the size of the client fees. Following this task, participants completed a debriefing questionnaire. While few participants would have found additional information useful in assessing the risk of fraudulent financial reporting, none of the participants expressed reservations about the clarity of the case instructions.

RESULTS

Manipulation checks revealed that 100% of the participants correctly read the background information and properly encoded the experimental condition to which they had been assigned. For example, in the debriefing questionnaire, participants were asked whether the background information had mentioned NAS provided to the client by their audit firm; if participants answered positively, they had to identify the type of NAS provided from a given list, which included tax services. Additionally, all participants whose firm provided tax services correctly quantified the relative size of the client's fees.

Descriptive Statistics

In the debriefing questionnaire, participants were asked to assess the rate of fraudulent financial reporting in all types of companies (not just the hypothetical client) and the percentage of their audit engagements on which fraudulent financial reporting had been detected. These data were used to examine any differences among the three groups in their baseline expectations of fraudulent financial reporting and their task-specific experience, factors that might have influenced their fraud-risk assessment on the hypothetical case. A one-way analysis of variance (ANOVA) was conducted to determine whether those two factors were homogeneous across the three experimental conditions. ANOVA results revealed no significant differences in general expectation of fraudulent financial reporting ($F = 0.636$; $p = 0.532$) or in task-specific experience ($F = 0.839$; $p = 0.436$).

Hypothesis Test

To test the hypothesis, an analysis of covariance (ANCOVA) was used with the participants' fraud-risk assessment as the dependent variable, and general expectation of fraudulent financial reporting and task-specific experience as covariates.[7] Table 1 shows there is a significant difference in the average fraud-risk assessment rate between the three experimental conditions ($F = 36.69$; $p = 0.000$).

Table 2 shows the results of multiple comparison procedures using Tamhane's T2.[8] Holding the client fees constant at 20% of the audit partner's billings, the fraud-risk assessment of auditors whose firm provided tax services (12.8%) was significantly lower than that of auditors whose firm only provided audit services (22.1%), supporting H1.

Table 1.   Client's Risk of Fraudulent Financial Reporting (Cell $n = 30$).

Groups	Provision of Tax Services	Client Fees (Percentage of Partner's Annual Billings)	Risk of Fraudulent Financial Reporting Mean[a] (SD)
1	No	20	22.1% (14.3%)
2	Yes	20	12.8% (14.5%)
3	Yes	30	4.5% (14.6%)

Source	df	Mean Square	F-Value	Significance
ANCOVA ($n = 90$)				
Model	5	478786	78.22	0.000
Between groups	3	224544	36.69	0.000
General expectation of fraud	1	275619	45.03	0.000
Task-specific experience	1	17086	2.79	0.098

[a]Means adjusted for the covariates (general expectation of fraud and task-specific experience).

Table 2.   Tamhane's T2 Test of Multiple Comparisons-Dependent Variable: Client's Risk of Fraudulent Financial Reporting.

(I) Version	(J) Version	Mean Difference (I-J)	Standard Error	Significance
No tax services (20% of partner's annual billings)	Tax services (20% of partner's annual billings)	9.3%[a]	20.28	0.000
No tax services (20% of partner's annual billings)	Tax services (30% of partner's annual billings)	17.6%[a]	20.55	0.000
Tax services (20% of partner's annual billings)	Tax services (30% of partner's annual billings)	8.3%[a]	20.93	0.000

[a]The mean difference is significant at the 0.05 level.

Research Question

When the audit firm also provided tax services, auditors' fraud-risk assessment was significantly lower when the client represented 30% of the audit partner's annual billings (4.0%) rather than only 20% of the audit partner's annual billings (12.8%).

Additional Analysis

Additional analysis was conducted with respect to task-specific experience.[9] Task-specific experience was measured by the percentage of audit engagements on which fraudulent financial reporting had been detected. It was expected that auditors with more task-specific experience would have developed higher skepticism, resulting in higher fraud-risk assessment. Specific task experience ranged from 0% to 15%, with an average of 2.3%. Participants were then classified into two groups at the median – less than 2% ($n = 52$) and 2% or more ($n = 38$). As expected, an independent samples t-test revealed that the fraud-risk assessment of auditors with *more* task-specific experience (17.4%) was significantly higher ($t = 2.897$; $p = 0.005$) than that of auditors with *less* task-specific experience (10.1%), reflecting an increased skepticism for more experienced auditors when confronted with red flags indicative of *increased* fraud risk. Fig. 1 shows fraud-risk assessment as a function of experimental condition and task-specific experience. Task-specific experience seems to play a lesser role on auditors' fraud-risk assessment as the economic dependency on the client increases.

An ANCOVA was run with fraud-risk assessment as dependent variable, experimental group and task-specific experience as main factors, and general expectation of fraudulent financial reporting as covariate. As expected, significant main effects were found for experimental group ($F = 48.00$; $p = 0.000$) and task-specific experience ($F = 15.53$; $p = 0.000$). Furthermore, a significant interaction occurred between experimental group and task-specific experience ($F = 3.68$; $p = 0.029$).

DISCUSSION AND CONCLUSION

This study examined whether the provision of tax services by small- and medium-sized audit firms affected auditors' fraud-risk assessment. Auditors whose firm also provided tax services to an audit client had a lower fraud-risk assessment than auditors whose firm provided only audit services. This finding lends credibility to the continued concerns over the potential impairment of auditors' objectivity that may result when independence of audit firms is threatened by their economic dependence on the provision of NAS to audit clients. Indeed, a few high-profiles cases of fraudulent financial reporting have been associated with the provision of tax services. For example, former SEC Chief Accountant Lynn E. Turner wondered how the auditors of Tyco International could have overlooked a misstatement

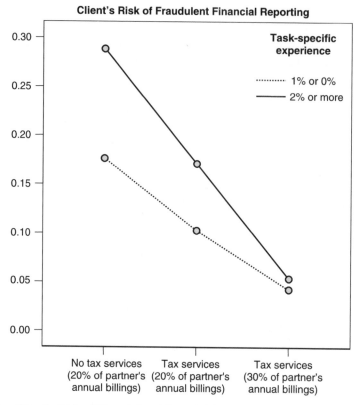

Fig. 1. Client's Risk of Fraudulent Financial Reporting by Experimental Conditions and Task-Specific Experience.

caused by charging $41 million of a $96 million loan-forgiveness scheme to the balance sheet account for "accrued federal income tax," while being deeply involved in efforts to boost earnings by reducing the company's tax bill (Byrnes & Symonds, 2002). More recently, the U.S. Department of Justice is considering a criminal indictment against KPMG for selling questionable tax shelters, prompting SEC officials to privately discuss steps to take if one of the Big Four accounting firms should collapse.[10]

An important caveat to this conclusion is that audit quality could conceivably be improved by auditors having knowledge of the client's tax situation. While the specifics of this case was limited to the routine preparation of the client's tax returns, greater knowledge of the client gained through providing other tax services might cause an audit partner to assess a lower risk of fraudulent financial reporting. The argument can be made that, as more work is done on a client, the audit firm acquires better knowledge of the client, which in turn might increase the audit partner's confidence that any potential problem related to fraudulent financial reporting will be uncovered. Indeed, some have remarked that audit quality is improved when the auditor has extensive knowledge of the client's tax situation (U.S. Chamber of Commerce, 2003). Hence, auditors' fraud-risk assessments could be lower when their firm provides tax services since partners may justifiably feel more comfortable about fraud risk when their own firm (rather than another firm) provides such services. Whether this increased level of confidence in the detection of fraudulent financial reporting can translate ex-ante into a lower fraud-risk assessment is an empirical question to be addressed by future research.

Further, when providing tax services, auditors' fraud-risk assessment decreased as the size of the client fees in relation to the audit partner's annual billings increased. A reduction in fraud-risk assessment with a related increase in relative client fees may be construed as arising from auditors' impaired objectivity due to greater economic dependency on the client. However, it is conceivable in some cases that, when a specific client makes up a larger part of the audit partner's billing base, the partner may spend more time with this client and thus feel more confident about the client's risks of fraudulent financial reporting. Finally, while task-specific experience also had a significant effect on auditors' fraud-risk assessment, it played a lesser role on the auditors' assessment as economic dependency on the client increased.

The study design may have induced a demand effect – results due to participants' expectation of desired behavior in the research setting – because participants were told that the purpose of the study was to investigate fraudulent financial reporting and the only question to which the participants responded was the client's risk of fraudulent financial reporting. However, if there was a demand effect, and participants thought that tax work and economic dependency on a client would be expected to make them less objective, the results would have gone in the opposite direction of those found here.

This study is a first step in addressing an under-researched area – the application of SOX in a non-public audit setting – that is clearly a concern right now in many areas of the profession (PCPS, 2004; Tschopp, Wells, & Barney, 2004). Further research should attempt to determine the underlying cause of the participants' reduced fraud-risk assessment observed in this study (i.e., greater confidence in ability or impaired objectivity in judgment). If the provision of additional services translates in greater auditors' confidence in their ability to uncover fraud, then SOX's restrictions in the scope of services provided to audit clients may have been the wrong remedy for greater auditor objectivity. However, if the provision of additional services does impair auditors' objectivity, then stricter safeguards are justified. For example, in France, statutory laws require a total separation between the audit function and the providers of NAS. Audits are performed by members of the Institute of Statutory Auditors (*Compagnie Nationale des Commissaires aux Comptes – CNCC*), while tax services and other NAS are rendered by qualified independent accountants who are members of the *Ordre des Experts Comptables et des Comptable Agréés* (OECCA). French accountants often belong to both bodies; however, when functioning as statutory auditors, they are not allowed to provide other services and, in order to maintain their independence, any remuneration from the client company other than for the audit is strictly prohibited. Further research could also establish whether such a separation of functions had resulted over time in a decreased rate of fraudulent financial reporting.

Safeguards created by the profession or within a firm's own systems and procedures may equally reduce threats of auditors' objectivity. Hence, future research could examine whether some of these safeguards can be associated with increased auditors' objectivity in small- and medium-sized firms.

NOTES

1. Goldman and Barlev (1974) suggested that, when auditors provide highly specialized services such as information system design, they exert more power vis-à-vis the client and enjoy greater audit independence because of the high cost of changing firm in case of disagreements. Conversely, when auditors perform more routine services such as tax return preparation, they lack a crucial source of power and are more vulnerable to client's pressures in case of disagreements.

2. Because of the limited availability of audit partners of small- and medium-sized firms, 20 senior managers were used to assume the role of partners in order to complete the pool of 90 participants, sufficient to obtain statistical significance with three experimental conditions. An examination of the experience level of those senior managers and a comparison of results between partners and senior managers found no significant differences between those two subject pools, which were combined for analysis purposes.

3. Closely held private companies and public companies are equally likely to experience fraud; only the motives and timing are slightly different, and red flags would be similar (Lundelius, 2003).

4. Participants did not raise any objections to the mention of the experimental private company planning to raise the needed capital through additional public offerings of common stock. In casual discussions with the researcher after the administration of the experiment, several participants mentioned they had interpreted the

wording as meaning that the company was planning to sell more stock to individuals outside the company (since insiders owned only 15% of the outstanding shares) without going public or that the company was considering an initial public offering.

5. The efficient use of costly participants and the limited availability of participants caused a fourth experimental condition – no tax services for an audit client making up 30% of the audit partner's annual billing (*no tax, 30%*) – to be omitted from the design. Hence, the 1 × 3 design did not allow the examination of a potential interaction between "tax services" and "fee size". Nevertheless, the main effects between the three experimental conditions were strong enough to draw conclusions about the independent impact of the two variables under study.

6. The Mid-size CA Firms Forum of BC comprises 26 medium-size accounting firms in British Columbia, responsible for 650 public company audits, 1,200 private company audits, 600 governmental or not-for-profit entity audits, and 6,000 review engagements.

7. Tests of normality and homogeneity of variances were performed. Because of the relatively small cell sample size, a Kruskal–Wallis test was also conducted and results were consistent with ANCOVA results.

8. Tamhane's T2 is a conservative pair wise comparison test based on a *t*-test, and appropriate when the variances in all groups are unequal. The test of homogeneity of variances showed a Levene statistic of 15.502 ($p = 0.000$).

9. General audit experience was analyzed separately, and ranged from 7 to 30 years, with an average of 18 years. Participants were classified into two groups – less than 20 years and 20 years or more of general audit experience. Independent samples *t*-test indicated that there were no significant differences in fraud-risk assessment between those two groups ($t = 0.034$; $p = 0.973$).

10. Deborah Solomon and Diya Gullapalli, "SEC Weighs Steps if KPMG Fails," *Wall Street Journal*, 22 June 2005, sec. C, p. 1.

ACKNOWLEDGEMENTS

I thank the auditors who participated in this study. I acknowledge the helpful comments of Craig Emby, Alec Gelardi, Phil Reckers, participants at the 2004 SFU Faculty of Business Research Seminar, and the Associate Editor and three anonymous reviewers. The SFU President's Research Grant Program provided financial support for the study.

REFERENCES

American Institute of Certified Public Accountants (AICPA). (1999). *Practice Alert No.94-4: Acceptance and Continuance of Audit Clients*. New York, NY: AICPA (SEC Practice Section Detection and Prevention of Fraud Task Force).

American Institute of Certified Public Accountants (AICPA). (2002). *Chairs corner: December 2002*. New York, NY: AICPA.

American Institute of Certified Public Accountants (AICPA). (2003). Rule 101–103: Perform-
    ance of Nonattest Services. *AICPA Code of Professional Conduct.* New York, NY:
    AICPA.
Antle, R., Gordon, E. A., Narayanamoorthy, G., & Zhou, L. (2002). *The Joint determination of
    audit fees, non-audit fees, and abnormal accruals.* Working paper, Yale University.
Byrnes, N., & Symonds, W. C. (2002). Is the avalanche headed for pricewaterhouse? *Business
    Week, 14*(October), 45–46.
COSO. (1998). *Fraudulent financial reporting: 1987–1997 – An analysis of U.S. public companies.*
    New York, NY: Committee of Sponsoring Organizations of the Treadway Commission.
DeFond, M. L., Raghunandan, K., & Subramanyam, K. R. (2002). Do non-audit service fees
    impair auditor independence? evidence from going concern audit opinions. *Journal of
    Accounting Research, 40*(4), 1247–1274.
Emby, C., & Davidson, R. A. (1998). The effects of engagement factors on auditor independence:
    Canadian evidence. *Journal of International Accounting, Auditing & Taxation, 7*(2), 163–179.
Ernst & Young. (2003). Comments on File No. S7-49-02 proposed rule: Strengthening the
    commission's requirements regarding auditor independence. New York.
Firth, M. (2002). Auditor-provided consultancy services and their associations with audit fees
    and audit opinions. *Journal of Business Finance & Accounting, 29*(5 & 6), 661–693.
Frankel, R. M., Johnson, M. F., & Nelson, K. K. (2002). The relation between auditors' fees for
    nonaudit services and earnings management. *The Accounting Review, 77*(Supplement),
    71–105.
Goldman, A., & Barlev, B. (1974). The auditor–firm conflict of interests: Its implications for
    independence. *The Accounting Review, 49*(4), 707–718.
Kinney, W. R., Jr., Palmrose, Z.-V., & Scholtz, S. (2004). Auditor independence, non-audit
    services, and restatements: Was the U.S. government right? *Journal of Accounting Re-
    search, 42*(3), 561–588.
Lundelius, C. R., Jr. (2003). *Financial reporting fraud: A practical guide to detection and internal
    control.* New York, NY: AICPA.
Mautz, R. K., & Sharaf, H. A. (1961). *The philosophy of auditing.* Sarasota, FL: American
    Accounting Association.
Mid-size CA Firms Forum of BC. (2002). Comments on exposure draft of the Canadian
    institute of chartered accountants (CICA): Proposed independence standards. Ontario,
    TO: CICA.
Primoff, W. M. (1992). *Year-end accounting and auditing advantage. The CPA Journal Online.
    January.* New York, NY: The New York State Society of CPA.
Private Companies Practice Section (PCPS). (2000). "Trickle-down effect" Of New SEC Rules
    could soak small firms too. *The Practicing CPA* 24 (6). The AICPA Alliance for CPA
    Firms. New York, NY: AICPA.
Private Companies Practice Section (PCPS). (2003). *PCPS/TSCPA National MAP Survey for
    2003. The AICPA alliance for CPA firms.* New York, NY: AICPA.
Private Companies Practice Section (PCPS). (2004). *PCPS Update January. The AICPA al-
    liance for CPA firms.* New York, NY: AICPA.
Public Company Accounting Oversight Board (PCAOB). (2005). *Ethics and independence rules
    concerning independence, tax services, and contingent fees. PCAOB File No. 2005–02.*
    Washington, DC: PCAOB.
Public Oversight Board (POB). (1993). *In the public interest: A special report by the public
    oversight board of the SEC practice section.* Stamford, CT: POB.

Public Oversight Board (POB). (2000). *The panel on audit effectiveness report and recommendations.* Stamford, CT: POB.

Reynolds, J. K., Deis, D. R., & Francis, J. R. (2004). Professional service fees and auditor objectivity. *Auditing: A Journal of Practice and Theory, 23*(1), 29–52.

Sharma, D. S., & Sidhu, J. (2001). Professionalism vs. commercialism: The association between non-audit services (NAS) and audit independence. *Journal of Business Finance & Accounting, 28*(5 & 6), 595–629.

Small Business Administration (2003). Comments on File No. S7-49-02 proposed rule: Strengthening the commission's requirements regarding auditor independence. Washington, DC.

Temple, R. M. (1992). *Auditors as business advisors: Logical extension of SAS 55. The CPA Journal Online. January.* New York, NY: The New York State Society of CPA.

Tschopp, D. J., Wells, S. C., & Barney, D. K. (2004). *Financial debacles and state regulation: Boards of public accountancy and the 'cascade effect' of Sarbanes–Oxley. The CPA Journal Online. July.* New York, NY: The New York State Society of CPA.

U.S. Chamber of Commerce (2003). Comments on File No. S7-49-02 proposed rule: Strengthening the commission's requirements regarding auditor independence. Washington, D.C.

U.S. Securities and Exchange Commission (SEC). (2001). *Final Rule: Revision of the Commission's Auditor Independence Requirements.* 17 CFR Parts 210 and 240 [Release Nos. 33-7919; 34-43602; 35-27279; IC-24744; IA-1911; FR-56; File No. S7-13-00]. Washington, DC: Securities and Exchange Commission.

U.S. Securities and Exchange Commission (SEC). (2003). *Final Rule: Strengthening the Commission's Requirements Regarding Auditor Independence.* 17 CFR PARTS 210, 240, 249 and 274 [Release Nos. 33-8183; 34-47265; 35-27642; IC-25915; IA-2103, FR-68, File No. S7-49-02]. Washington, DC: Securities and Exchange Commission.

U.S. Senate Committee on Banking, Housing, and Urban Affairs. (2003). *The implementation of the Sarbanes-Oxley act and restoring investor confidence.* Washington, DC: United States Senate.

ACQUISITION OF IPO FIRMS: CASH-FLOW-BASED MEASURES OF OPERATING INEFFICIENCY

Maretno A. Harjoto and Howard F. Turetsky

ABSTRACT

This study examines the impact of accounting-based measures of operating inefficiency on the aftermarket acquisition of an IPO. Prior IPO studies have not incorporated efficiency measures. Utilizing survival analysis, we find strong empirical evidence that the probability of acquisition is increased significantly when the IPO is inefficiently managed, measured by lower ratios of cash flow from continuing operations. When we compare the cash flow measures to conventional accrual assessments of operating inefficiency, we find that the accrual measures are not significant, while the cash flow measures maintain their significance. Moreover, our findings support the "inefficient management rationale" for acquisition.

1. INTRODUCTION

The first significant stage in the evolution and potential longevity of a public company is the initial public offering (IPO). Subsequent to the IPO, a firm can survive independently, fail outright, or be the subject of an acquisition (Jain & Kini, 1999). While the study of corporate acquisition, in general, is

Advances in Accounting, Volume 22, 167–199

Copyright © 2006 by Elsevier Ltd.
ISSN: 0882-6110/doi:10.1016/S0882-6110(06)22008-X

common, the acquisition of an IPO is relatively unexplored in the literature. This study expands the extant, but limited, research examining the factors influencing the aftermarket acquisition of an IPO. We especially consider the impact of operating efficiency on IPO acquisition; prior IPO studies have not incorporated efficiency measures. In particular, we focus on the role of accounting-based inefficiency measures in explaining the acquisition of IPOs.

Consistent with Theodossiou, Kahya, Saidi, and Philippatos (1996) as well as an acquisition hypothesis often stated in the literature (Palepu, 1986), we believe that inefficiently managed firms are popular acquisition candidates, despite their lower comparable profitability and probable financially distressed condition. Firms with "know how" recognize the opportunity to realize upside market value potential through acquisition succeeded by the elimination of inefficiencies and the remedy of financial distress, referred to as the "inefficient management rationale" for acquisition. Accordingly, we theorize that an inefficiently managed IPO firm, as gauged by accounting-based proxies, is a likely acquisition candidate.

Especially, based on prior literature, we examine the role of cash-flow-based measures of inefficiency on the potential subsequent acquisition of the IPO. Mulford and Comiskey (1996) state that operating efficiency is reflected in the three areas of accounts receivable, inventory, and accounts payable, which in turn affect operating cash flow. We consider a firm's cash flow from continuing operations as a relevant accounting measure of a firm's operating performance. Giacomino and Mielke (1993) suggest that cash flow from operating activities should be a firm's primary focus in performance evaluation. While stating that cash-flow-based ratios provide additional information over traditional financial ratios, they specifically categorize three cash flow ratios as "efficiency" measurements. Accordingly, we gauge the efficiency of a firm over time by the relative magnitude of its cash flow from continuing operations.

Pursuant to Giacomino and Mielke (1993), we explicitly measure a firm's operating efficiency using (1) the ratio of cash flow from continuing operations to total assets and (2) the ratio of cash flow from continuing operations to sales.[1,2] We hypothesize that the efficiently managed IPO, characterized by relatively higher operating-cash-flow-based ratios, is less likely to be acquired. Conversely, consistent with the "inefficient management rationale," we hypothesize that the inefficiently managed IPO, reflected by lower ratios of cash flow from continuing operations, over time, is a likelier acquisition target.[3]

Incremental to testing whether our cash-flow-based inefficiency measures are significant precursors for the acquisition of the IPO, our study makes a supporting contribution by considering alternative (to cash flow) accounting-based measures of inefficiency. We compare cash flow measures to the conventional accrual (specifically income-based and inventory-based) assessments of operating inefficiency. Overall, we compile risk profiles, rooted in cash-flow-based measures of operating inefficiency, for IPO firms, examining their longevity and potential acquisition. Throughout our tests, we initially control for IPO characteristics that potentially impact the longevity of the IPO. Then, consistent with prior research efforts (e.g. Palepu, 1986; Clayton & Fields, 1991; Fama & French, 1992; Loughran & Ritter, 1995; Theodossiou et al., 1996; Hensler, Rutherford, & Springer, 1997; Jain & Kini, 1999), we also control for the effect that firm-specific attributes and market perceptions have on the likelihood that an IPO will be acquired.

Utilizing this risk framework, we track firms on a quarterly basis, after the IPO for evidence of acquisition within a five-year window.[4] Our ex ante selection approach (absent knowledge of whether the IPO is subsequently acquired) improves upon conventional sampling techniques, where an ex post sample of acquired firms is "matched" with a control set of similar non-acquired firms.[5] Further, we incorporate the techniques of survival analysis to analyze the longevity and potential acquisition of the IPO. Survival analysis aids our study by handling censored observations in an unbiased manner (Shumway, 2001). Generally, censored observations arise when the duration of a study is limited in time span. George, Spiceland, and George (1996) describe censored observations as those in which the terminal event (acquisition in our case) has not occurred by the time data are analyzed or the firm is withdrawn from the study. There are firms in our sample that never are acquired. There is also censoring of IPO firms that cease operations in their existing corporate form due to reasons other than acquisition, such as bankruptcy, inactivity, and stock exchange delisting, or for which data are no longer available. The techniques of survival analysis coupled with ex ante sample selection consider censored observations and thus avoid sampling bias. Generally, survival analysis provides more intuitive interpretations of the influence of explanatory variables (LeClere, 2000). We utilize Cox proportional hazards regression, a survival analysis technique, to examine the influence of accounting-based inefficiency measures on the likelihood of IPO acquisition. Principally, cash-flow-based proxies of inefficiency are observed; consequently, to further the contribution of our study, a comparison with the conventional accrual income-based and inventory-based inefficiency assessments is evaluated. In conjunction, we also consider the impact of other risk attributes on the likelihood of acquisition subsequent to going public.

Our findings document that increases in the operating inefficiency of an IPO, measured by one minus the ratio of cash flow from continuing operations to total assets, has a highly significant positive association with its potential acquisition over time. Moreover, operating inefficiency, measured by one minus the ratio of cash flow from continuing operations to sales, is likewise positively correlated with the likelihood of acquisition, subsequent to the IPO. These findings are robust throughout all our models, which control for industry effects, and sequentially incorporate IPO characteristics, firm-specific attributes, and market perceptions. Our findings are consistent with the "inefficient management rationale" for acquisition, where the inefficiently managed IPO, reflected by lower ratios of cash flow from continuing operations, over time, is a likelier acquisition target.

When we compare the cash-flow-based inefficiency measures to income-based and inventory-based accrual inefficiency measures, we find that the accrual measures are not significant, while the cash flow measures maintain their high level of significance. Especially, we comparatively test the inefficiency measures utilized by Palepu (1986) and Theodossiou et al. (1996); we likewise find these accrual-based measures to be insignificant, while the cash flow measures continue to be highly significant. Generally, we document that the cash-flow-based measures represent a more viable (based on significance) proxy of managerial inefficiency as a precursor of IPO acquisition. Overall, our study highlights the importance of the relative magnitudes of cash flow from continuing operations on the longevity of IPO firms.

With respect to IPO characteristics, we find that the venture capital-backed IPO and firms with a relatively higher price range of initial offers are more probable acquisition targets; alternatively, firms with higher post-IPO deviations of daily stock returns (volatility) are less likely to be acquired. Further, relative to firm-specific attributes, the IPO with higher relative sales levels and return on sales (ROS) is less likely to be acquired. Likewise, the interest coverage ratio marginally reduces the probability of acquisition. Alternatively, the IPO with higher ratios of book-to-market equity is a projected acquisition target. These findings confirm the usefulness of IPO characteristics, firm-specific attributes, and market perceptions in predicting the subsequent acquisition of an IPO.

The remainder of this paper is organized as follows. The next section discusses the background information from previous research efforts that develops our hypotheses. Following this, we describe the research design, reviewing our sample selection, survival analysis methodology, and model specifications along with definition of variables. The fourth section presents our results. Concluding remarks are contained in Section 5.

2. BACKGROUND

2.1. Longevity of the Initial Public Offering (IPO)

The evolution of the IPO initially received attention from the perspective of the investor (Ritter, 1991; Loughran & Ritter, 1995). Ritter, and Loughran and Ritter, show that buying-and-holding IPO stocks is a "negative" wealth strategy. Based on realized returns, the IPO significantly underperforms the market; after three years an investment in an IPO results in a wealth factor of 0.83 relative to an investment in a matching firm already listed on the American or New York stock exchanges (Ritter, 1991). Likewise, to accumulate the same wealth five years after the offering date, an investor would have had to increase their investment 44 percent, relative to an investment in a non-issuer of the same size (Loughran & Ritter, 1995).

A variation from the investor wealth perspective is to look at the longevity of the IPO and its ability to survive in the aftermarket. Hensler et al. (1997) study the effect of several firm characteristics on the survival time of IPOs issued during the period 1976–1984. Defining "failure" as delisting for negative reasons, they find that IPO survival time increases with increasing size, age of the firm at the offering, and its initial return at the IPO. Jain and Kini (1999) subsequently look at the determinants of transition, within a five-year time frame, to the three basic post-IPO states of independent survival, outright failure, or acquisition. Looking principally at the comparative relationship between the characteristics of the three states, they find that firms considered to have greater risk, as measured by the standard deviation of aftermarket returns, are more likely to fail outright. However, relative to acquisition, they do not find this risk measurement to be significant.

Our study extends this work by concentrating on the potential influence of operating inefficiency on IPO acquisition within a five-year aftermarket time period. We integrate the acquisition literature and consequently focus on the impact of accounting-based measures of management inefficiency on IPO acquisition, while controlling for IPO characteristics.

2.2. Acquisition

There are two broad classes of acquisition strategies (theories) (Peel & Wilson, 1989). One strategy for corporate acquisition is "synergistic," the opportunity to combine corporate resources and realize value through economies of scale and scope. Synergistic gains are achieved from the elimination of common functions, along with improved technologies, increased leverage potential, and greater market share. The other strategy (theory) is that firm value can be significantly improved by the replacement of incompetent management, referred to as the "disciplinary takeover" or "improved management hypothesis" (e.g. Copeland & Weston, 1983; Jensen, 1986). Palepu (1986) classifies this the "inefficient management hypothesis," based on the finance theory premise that acquisitions provide the vehicle by which managers who fail to maximize firm market value are replaced. As Shleifer, Vishny, and Morck (1987) note, disciplinary takeovers eliminate existing management's non-value maximizing practices of excessive growth, lavish consumption, and overpayments to employees and suppliers. Similarly, Theodossiou et al. (1996) refer to the latter acquisition strategy as the "inefficient management rationale." Despite lower comparable profitability and probable financially distressed condition, the inefficiently managed firm is a popular acquisition candidate; firms with "know how" recognize the opportunity to value-add through acquisition succeeded by the remediation of inefficiencies.

Our study incrementally contributes to both the IPO and acquisition literature by examining whether accounting-based measures of management inefficiency influence the likelihood of aftermarket IPO acquisition. Based on the literature, we especially examine whether inefficiently managed firms, gauged by the relative level of a firm's cash flow from continuing operations, are likelier acquisition targets. Secondarily, we compare the cash flow measures with the customary accrual (specifically income-based and inventory-based) assessments of inefficiency to assess the relative significance of cash-flow-based inefficiency proxies as precursors of IPO acquisition.

2.3. Operating Inefficiency

In his model for predicting business failures, Theodossiou (1993) finds that failed firms exhibit higher overall means of the ratio of inventory to sales. Ensuing, Theodossiou et al. (1996) utilize this ratio in a study of the factors that influence the acquisition of financially distressed firms. They posit that the inventory to sales ratio gauges management's ability to turn inventory into sales, with higher relative values indicative of excessive inventory and probable management inefficiency. Their findings support the "inefficient management rationale" acquisition strategy; an important factor toward acquiring a financially distressed firm is the presence of inefficient management, estimated by inventory to sales.

While we acknowledge that the relationship of inventory to sales is a measure of firm financial health (with higher ratios indicating likelier financial distress), the ratio is not the best representation of management inefficiency. Inventory to sales is a somewhat restricted measurement of accrual-based accounting, subject to inventory cost flow assumptions (e.g. FIFO, LIFO) and liquidation issues (e.g. LIFO reserves). Palepu (1986) tests the broader accrual-based profitability measure of return on equity (ROE) as a proxy for management performance (efficiency) and did not find it to be a significant predictor of acquisition targets.[6] While accrual-based accounting measures, either narrowly stipulated (e.g. inventory management) or more comprehensively defined profitability measures (e.g. ROE, ROS), likely capture aspects of efficiency, we believe that they are not the best indicators of operating inefficiency.

Rather, we argue that operating efficiency is better represented by cash-flow-based measures. Overall efficiency, and ultimately firm longevity, is reflected by the ability of management to generate and control cash flow. Control of firm assets, principally cash, is the critical dimension of an efficient firm's operations. For instance, operating efficiency encompasses not only inventory management, but the collection of the subsequent sales and the prudent disbursement of cash. This is consistent with *The Goal* of a company, as declared by Goldratt (1984) is to make money (cash). A company must increase *throughput* ("cash coming in") while simultaneously decreasing *inventory* ("cash stuck inside") and *operational expense* ("cash going out" to turn inventory into throughput). Moreover, Fera (1997) perceives that performance measurement can no longer be based on traditional accrual accounting calculations of ROE or EPS (earnings per share); instead, measurement techniques that incorporate cash flows are superior indicators of performance or future growth, as well as key determinants of shareholder value. Accordingly, we specifically consider a firm's cash flow from continuing operations as the relevant accounting measure of a firm's operating performance and ultimately the efficiency of its management.

Comiskey and Mulford (1992a, b) and subsequently Mulford and Comiskey (1996) specifically link operating cash flow with operating efficiency. They suggest that a firm's operating cash flow, substantially below its accrual-based operating profit, is indicative of substandard operating efficiency. Principally, they emphasize that a decline in management efficiency (operating inefficiency) is reflected by a decline in the rate of accounts receivable collection, an increase in the level of inventory carried, and an increase in the rate at which accounts payable are settled. Ultimately, these negative changes in efficiency (greater inefficiencies) are reflected by a reduction in cash flow from continuing operations.

Likewise, Giacomino and Mielke (1993) suggest that cash flow from operating activities should be a firm's primary focus, as well as the variable of interest in performance evaluation. Stating that cash-flow-based ratios provide additional information over traditional financial ratios, they utilize nine cash operation-based ratios categorized according to "sufficiency" and "efficiency" to study relative performance evaluation. Consequently, we explicitly employ the "converse" of two of their three "efficiency" ratios to gauge a firm's operating inefficiency over time.[7] Expressly, we measure a firm's operating inefficiency utilizing (1) one minus the ratio of cash flow from continuing operations[8] to total assets (labeled INEFFICIENCY1) and (2) one minus the ratio of cash flow from continuing operations to sales (labeled INEFFICIENCY2).

Our study accentuates the importance of cash flow from continuing operations, while incrementally contributing to the IPO, acquisition, and operating efficiency literature. Particularly, we examine whether the presence of "inefficient management" is a significant influence on the aftermarket acquisition of IPOs. We hypothesize that the inefficiently managed IPO, reflected by lower ratios of cash flow from continuing operations (higher inefficiency scores), over time, is a likelier acquisition target. Our directional hypothesis, based on two measurements for operating efficiency (stated in alternative form) is as follows:

H1 (a). The likelihood that an IPO will be acquired varies directly with operating inefficiency (INEFFICIENCY1) measured by one minus the ratio of cash flow from continuing operations to total assets.

H1 (b). The likelihood that an IPO will be acquired varies directly with operating inefficiency (INEFFICIENCY2) measured by one minus the ratio of cash flow from continuing operations to sales.

3. RESEARCH DESIGN

3.1. Sample Selection

We utilize an ex ante selection approach (absent knowledge of whether the IPO is subsequently acquired). Our sample comprises firms that went public (i.e. IPO) between 1/1/1990 and 12/31/2001. These firms are identified using the SEC Edgar and SDC Global Issues databases. From these databases, 6,201 IPO firms are initially documented. From this potential sample, we exclude non-U.S. companies (e.g. ADRs), utilities, real estate investment trusts, unit offerings, closed-end funds, and firms primarily engaged in financial services; this reduces the IPO sample to 4,490 firms. When these firms are subsequently "matched" with the Compustat database (utilized to gather quarterly data), 1,031 firms are not found, further reducing our sample to 3,459 firms. We then limit our sample to five consecutive years after the IPO; consequently, another 1,432 firms are omitted due to missing values as well as unreliable data in the Compustat database, within the five-year period subsequent to the IPO. Likewise, 59 firms are omitted due to missing stock returns in the Center for Research in Security Prices (CRSP) database. Afterward, to determine if the IPO is acquired or delisted for other reasons, we utilize the Compustat and CRSP databases to track each firm, on a quarterly basis for five years. As a result, we omit 146 IPO firms that are delisted due to reasons other than mergers and acquisitions.[9] This results in a final sample of 1,822 IPO firms. We find that of the 1,822 IPO firms, 554 were acquired and 1,268 continued in their existing corporate form. Table 1 summarizes the results of the sample selection process.[10]

3.2. Methodology

Palepu (1986) utilizes a logit model to estimate the likelihood of acquisition for a sample of random firms. Jain and Kini (1999) subsequently use a multinomial logistic model to examine the likelihood of acquisition relative to the probability of survival and delisting due to other reasons for a sample of IPO firms. The logit model is appropriate when the likelihood of acquisition is not time-dependent.

Our study additionally incorporates time into the model, estimating the probability that an IPO will be acquired at any instant during the five-year period subsequent to the IPO, conditional upon not observing the firm being acquired up to that point in time. The "point of origin" for this study is the date of IPO, and our "duration" is five years subsequent to the IPO. We choose five years as the duration since the majority of ensuing IPO delistings occur within five years from the IPO date.[11] Consistent with Hensler et al. (1997), the hazard function is appropriate for our five years discrete failure (censored) time model of acquisition.[12] Accordingly, we utilize the Cox proportional hazard (survival) model (Cox, 1972) to estimate the slope co-efficients of the regressors; the estimation is based on approximating the likelihood of acquisition by the length of time the IPO continues in its initial public form until acquisition.[13]

The data is cross-sectional and time series (panel), therefore our hazard function, $h_{ij}(t)$, can be written as the following:

$$h_{ij}(t) = h_{0j}(t) \exp(x_{ij'}\beta) \qquad (1)$$

Table 1. Sample Selection Process.

Items	Source of Data	Number of Firms
Initial public offerings (IPOs)	SEC Edgars/SDC	6,201
ADRs		180
Unit offerings		552
Closed end funds		392
Financial services, utilities and REITs		587
Final IPO sample		4,490
IPOs not found in Compustat	Compustat	1,031
Final IPO and Compustat sample		3,459
Missing values and unreliable data	Compustat	1,432[a]
Missing stock returns	CRSP	59
Delisted due to reasons other than mergers and acquisitions	Compustat	146[b]
Final sample:		1,822
Delisted due to mergers and acquisitions	Compustat and CRSP	554
Non-acquired firms	Compustat and CRSP	1,268

Note: This table provides the data sources and sample selection processes that are used in this study. This study examines the firms that went public between 1/1/1990 and 12/31/2001. It excludes foreign firms (American Depository Receipts or ADRs), unit offerings, closed end funds, financial services, utility and real estate investment trusts (REITs). The IPO sample firms are then matched with the financial data and stock prices from the Compustat and the Center for Research in Security Prices (CRSP) data.
[a]Although 3,459 of the IPO firms are matched in the Compustat database, 1,432 of these firms have missing essential financial statement information throughout the five-year period subsequent to their IPO and must be excluded from the sample. In particular, we exclude IPO firms that do not have essential financial information (e.g. cash flows from continuing operations, average inventories, total sales, and total assets).
[b]We exclude IPO firms that ceased operations in their existing corporate form due to reasons other than mergers and acquisitions, such as bankruptcy, inactivity, stock exchange delisting, etc.

where $h_{0j}(t)$ is the baseline of hazard function for time j, $X_{ij'}$ is a vector of explanatory variables for firm i across time j and β is a vector of slope coefficients to be estimated.[14] The hazard ratio (HR) can be defined as[15]

$$HR_{ij}(t, x_{ij}, x_{i0}) = \frac{\exp(x_{ij'}\beta)}{\exp(x_{i0'}\beta)} \qquad (2)$$

The conditional log likelihood function (also known as a partial log likelihood function) of the hazard function can be written as

$$L_p(\beta) = \sum_{i=1}^{n} \left\{ x_i'\beta - \ln\left[\sum_{j\in R(t_i)}^{t} \exp(x_{j'}\beta) \right] \right\} \tag{3}$$

where t_i is a particular failure time ($t_i = \{0,5\}$), conditional on the risk set $R(t_i)$. The first order condition of the maximum partial log likelihood estimator

$$\frac{\partial L_p(\beta)}{\partial \beta} = \sum_{i=1}^{n} x_i - \sum_{j\in R(t_i)} w_{ij}x_j(\hat{\beta}) = 0 \tag{4}$$

where

$$w_{ij}(\hat{\beta}) = \frac{\exp\{x_j(\hat{\beta})\}}{\sum_{j\in R(t_i)} \exp\{x_j(\hat{\beta})\}}$$

Eq. (4) implicitly defines the estimated vector of slope coefficients($\hat{\beta}$). The standard errors of the estimated slope coefficients can be calculated as

$$\mathrm{SE}(\hat{\beta}) = \sqrt{\frac{1}{-\{\partial^2 L_p/\partial \beta^2\}}} \tag{5}$$

The Wald statistics for slope coefficients are calculated from the ratio of estimated slope coefficients($\hat{\beta}$) and its standard errors ($\mathrm{SE}(\hat{\beta})$); and the Wald statistics follow the standard normal distribution (z-statistics).[16]

3.3. Model Specifications

This study examines the impact of operational inefficiency on the likelihood that IPO firms will be acquired. Initially, we test whether cash-flow-based inefficiency measures are significant precursors for the acquisition of the IPO; we utilize two cash-flow-based measures of operating inefficiency recognized by Giacomino and Mielke (1993): INEFFICIENCY1 and INEFFICIENCY2. However, due to the high correlation between INEFFICIENCY1 and INEFFICIENCY2 (correlation = 0.712), we alternately include only INEFFICIENCY1 or INEFFICIENCY2 in the regression models as a measure of operating inefficiency.

The hazard model of IPO firms to be acquired at any time during the five-year period subsequent to the IPO date is specified by the following models.

3.3.1. Simple Model

In the simple model, the hazard model is defined as a function of cash-flow-based operating inefficiency measures and we control for IPO characteristics: the dummy for Venture Capitalists backed IPO (labeled DVCBACK), the offer price range of the IPO (PRCRANGE), and the post-IPO deviation of daily stock returns (DEV.RETURNS). These IPO characteristics (variables) are consistent with Jain and Kini (1999).

3.3.2. Firm-Specific Attributes Measures

The second model incrementally controls for firm-specific attributes: logarithmic of total sales (labeled SALE), retained earnings divided by total assets (the plowback ratio) (AGE), earnings before interest and taxes divided by total sales (return on sales) (ROS), current assets divided by current liabilities (current ratio) (CR), the interest coverage ratio of earnings before interest and taxes to total interest (ICBTQ), and average total assets divided by total sales (operating leverage) (OPLEV), in addition to IPO characteristics.

3.3.3. Full Model

The full model incrementally controls for market perceptions: the absolute value of the book-to-market equity (labeled MKTPCPT),[17] the market value of equity per share divided by earnings per share (PESHARE), and the market value of equity per share divided by cash flow from continuing operations per share (MCF), in addition to IPO characteristics and firm-specific attributes. In addition, to control for industry effects, we include the industry dummy variables using the two-digit of Standard Industrial Code (SIC). Our full model is specified as

Model 1[18]

$$
\begin{aligned}
\text{Prob(acquisition)} = F(&\beta_1^*\text{INEFFICIENCY1} + \beta_2^*\text{DVCBACK} + \beta_3^*\text{PRCRANGE} \\
&+ \beta_4^*\text{DEV.RETURNS} + \beta_5^*\text{SALE} + \beta_6^*\text{AGE} \\
&+ \beta_7^*\text{ROS} + \beta_8^*\text{CR} + \beta_9^*\text{ICBTQ} + \beta_{10}^*\text{OPLEV} + \beta_{11}^*\text{MKTPCPT} \\
&+ \beta_{12}^*\text{PESHARE} + \beta_{13}^*\text{MCF} + \beta_i^*\text{Industry Dummy Variables})
\end{aligned}
$$

Incrementally, we compare our cash-flow-based measures to conventional accrual-based assessments of operating inefficiency. Initially, we include the "analogous" accrual-based measures to "inefficiency1" and "inefficiency2"; INBEXAST (one minus the ratio of income before discontinued operations and extraordinary items to total assets) is included along with "inefficiency1," while INBEXSALE (one minus the ratio of income before discontinued operations and extraordinary items to sales) is included along with "inefficiency2." Then, consistent with Palepu (1986), we add ROE (the ratio of income before discontinued operations and extraordinary items to total equity). Moreover, corresponding to Theodossiou et al. (1996), we successively include the ratio of inventory to assets (labeled INVEAST) and inventory to sales (INVESALE).[19] The full model, controlling for IPO characteristics, firm-specific attributes, market perceptions, and industry effects is used for the comparative analysis. Our model that comparatively tests "inefficiency1" is specified as[20]

Model 2

$$\text{Prob(acquisition)} = F(\beta_1^*\text{INEFFICIENCY1} + \beta_2^*\text{INBEXAST} + \beta_3^*\text{ROE} + \beta_4^*\text{INVEAST}$$
$$+ \beta_5^*\text{DVCBACK} + \beta_6^*\text{PRCRANGE} + \beta_7^*\text{DEV.RETURNS}$$
$$+ \beta_8^*\text{SALE} + \beta_9^*\text{AGE} + \beta_{10}^*\text{CR} + \beta_{11}^*\text{ICBTQ} + \beta_{12}^*\text{OPLEV} + \beta_{13}^*\text{MKTPCPT}$$
$$+ \beta_{14}^*\text{PESHARE} + \beta_{15}^*\text{MCF} + \beta_i^*\text{Industry Dummy Variables})$$

All the variables and predicted signs are as defined in Table 2.

If the explanatory variable is expected to have a positive association with the likelihood of acquisition, the predicted sign of the coefficient is + with a corresponding HR > 1.00. Consistent with the "inefficient management rationale" for acquisition, the proxies for operating inefficiency are predicted to have a positive relation with acquisition; note, however, that ROE, in agreement with Palepu (1986), represents efficiency and is thus projected to have a negative association. With respect to the IPO characteristics, a larger offer price range is associated with greater pre-IPO risk and more uncertainty for the firm's future, and thus an expected positive correlation with the likelihood of a subsequent acquisition. Relative to the firm-specific attributes, an expectation of greater profitability is associated firm stability and consequently a reduced likelihood of acquisition; thus the negative prediction for sales, ROS, and the interest coverage ratio. Likewise, an "older" age of the firm, measured by the ratio of retained earnings to assets, represents permanence, less risk and accordingly a lower expectation of acquisition. Higher operating leverage, gauged by the ratio of assets to sales, signifies increased risk. Similarly, larger values of a firm's market perception (book-to-market equity) indicate a negative market assessment of the firm's

Table 2. Predictions of Sign for Independent Variables.

Explanatory Variables	Predicted Sign	Predicted Hazard Ratio	Description
A. Operating inefficiency			
INEFFICIENCY1	+	> 1.00	One minus (cash flow from continuing operations divided by average total assets)
INEFFICIENCY2	+	> 1.00	One minus (cash flow from continuing operations divided by total sales)
INBEXAST	+	> 1.00	One minus (income before extraordinary items divided by average total assets)
INBEXSALE	+	> 1.00	One minus (income before extraordinary items divided by total sales)
ROE	−	< 1.00	Income before extraordinary items and discontinued operations divided by total equity
INVEAST	+	> 1.00	Total inventory divided by total assets
INVESALE	+	> 1.00	Average inventory divided by total sales
B. IPO characteristics			
DVCBACK	?	?	Dummy variable for VC (venture capital)-backed IPO
PRCRANGE	+	> 1.00	Offer price range of IPO
DEV. RETURNS	?	?	Post-IPO deviation of daily stock returns
C. Firm-specific attributes			
SALE	−	< 1.00	Log of total sales
AGE	−	< 1.00	Retained earnings divided by total assets
ROS	−	< 1.00	Earnings before interest and taxes divided by total sales
CR	?	?	Current assets divided by current liabilities
ICBTQ	−	< 1.00	Interest coverage ratio
OPLEV	+	> 1.00	Average total assets divided by total sales
D. Market perceptions			
MKTPCPT	+	> 1.00	Absolute value of book-to-market equity
PESHARE	?	?	Market value of equity per share divided by earnings per share
MCF	?	?	Market value of equity per share divided by cash flow from continuing operations per share

Note: This table provides the ex-ante predicted signs of the slope coefficients and predicted magnitudes of the HR. All variables are quarterly data.

prospects and greater risk. We predict that both these "risk" proxies will have a positive relation with the likelihood of acquisition.

4. RESULTS

4.1. Descriptive Statistics

Table 3 presents descriptive statistics for each subset of our sample of 1,822 firms (25,025 firms-quarters observations): acquired (554 firms) and non-acquired (1,268 firms). We specify the mean and standard deviation for our cash-flow-based and accrual-based measures of operating inefficiency, as well as our control variables of IPO characteristics, firm-specific attributes, market perceptions, and industry effects. Additionally, we exhibit the difference in the means for the two groupings of firms, as well as the *t*-statistic testing the difference for significance. Based on *t*-statistics, the cash flow inefficiency measures ("inefficiency1" and "inefficiency2") are not significantly different across the acquired and non-acquired subsamples. However, this "univariate" test is preliminary and descriptive in nature; the focus for testing our hypothesis is the comprehensive multivariate analysis using survival analysis, which is documented in Table 6.

For comparative purposes, we note the mean values of the IPO characteristics for the acquired and non-acquired ("survivor") firms, over the period 1977–1990, in the study by Jain and Kini (1999).[21] The acquired and non-acquired IPO firms in their study were respectively backed by venture capital an average of 40.3% and 42% of the time; this compares with the respective mean values of 38.5% and 31% in our study. Relative to the offer price range of the IPO firms, Jain and Kini found means for the acquired and non-acquired firms of $1.97 and 1.96, while the firms in this study have respective average offer price ranges of $1.99 and 1.85. Lastly, the IPO firms in the Jain and Kini study had mean after-market standard deviations of daily returns of 3.2% and 3.3%. In comparison, in our study, the average post-IPO standard deviations of daily stock returns are 4.1% and 5%, respectively for the acquired and non-acquired IPO firms.

Regarding industry effects, compared to Hensler et al. (1997), we find differences between the two samples. For instance, the distribution of our sample, based on SIC codes, includes computer manufacturing (5.9%), communications (5.2%), computer/data (1.9%), and retailers (11.4%).[22] In contrast, the industry profile of Hensler et al. consists of computer manufacturing (13.6%), communications (11.7%), computer/data (8%), and retailers (4.6%).

Table 3. Descriptive Statistics.

Variable	Non-acquired (1,268 firms)		Acquired (554 firms)		Mean Difference	t-Statistics	Unit of Variable
	Mean	Std. Dev	Mean	Std. Dev.			
INEFFICIENCY1	0.988	0.122	0.989	0.113	0.001	0.81	Ratio
INEFFICIENCY2	1.013	0.794	1.015	0.751	0.002	0.11	Ratio
INBEXAST	0.994	0.053	1.002	0.054	0.008	6.81**	Ratio
INBEXSALE	1.037	0.781	1.069	0.387	0.032	2.46*	Ratio
ROE	−13.747	246.437	−6.286	171.611	7.461	1.63	Percent
INVEAST	0.152	0.172	0.130	0.149	−0.022	−8.87**	Ratio
INVESALE	0.114	0.135	0.105	0.123	−0.009	−4.52**	Ratio
DVCBACK	0.310	0.462	0.385	0.486	0.075	10.97**	Binary
PRCRANGE	1.850	0.708	1.991	0.456	0.141	14.55**	Dollars/share
DEV. RET	0.05	0.036	0.041	0.023	−0.009	−18.10**	Percent
SALE	3.536	1.509	3.476	1.341	−0.060	−2.81**	Log(Sales)
AGE	−0.249	1.548	−0.130	0.807	0.119	5.81**	Ratio
ROS	−0.112	1.251	−0.056	1.519	0.056	2.86**	Ratio
CR	2.916	4.162	2.962	3.328	0.046	0.79	Percent
ICBTQ	−4.013	1119.38	15.442	1482.42	19.455	1.08	Ratio
OPLEV	1.347	1.691	1.332	1.495	-0.015	−0.623	Ratio
MKTPRCP	1.291	19.431	1.547	76.057	0.256	0.42	Ratio
PESHARE	60.806	332.846	64.589	274.208	3.783	0.81	Percent
MCF	31.114	1056.53	43.051	673.13	11.937	0.83	Percent
Agriculture	0.003	0.058	0.001	0.026	−0.003	−3.52**	Binary
Construction	0.009	0.096	0.009	0.094	−0.0005	−0.34	Binary
Computer Mfg	0.053	0.224	0.073	0.260	0.020	5.82**	Binary
Communications	0.047	0.212	0.064	0.245	0.017	5.16**	Binary
Oil and Gas	0.030	0.170	0.035	0.185	0.006	2.19*	Binary
Computer/Data	0.017	0.128	0.025	0.155	0.008	4.02**	Binary
Optical	0.054	0.227	0.084	0.278	0.030	8.45**	Binary
Retailers	0.126	0.331	0.086	0.281	−0.039	−8.37**	Binary
Wholesalers	0.016	0.124	0.016	0.126	0.001	0.33	Binary
Restaurants	0.022	0.145	0.025	0.155	0.003	1.31	Binary
Drugs	0.042	0.200	0.039	0.194	−0.003	−0.86	Binary
Healthcare	0.028	0.166	0.055	0.229	0.027	10.02**	Binary
Airlines	0.008	0.090	0.002	0.040	−0.007	−5.46**	Binary
Miscellaneous (Business Svc)	0.169	0.375	0.155	0.362	−0.014	−2.52*	Binary
Others	0.376	0.495	0.331	0.488	−0.045	−5.18**	Binary

Note: This table presents the means, medians, and the standard deviations of the variables used in the regression analyses. The variables are defined in the previous table and they are stated in their real values. The total number of firms in the sample (1,822) consists of 1,268 non-acquired firms and 554 acquired firms. All data are stated quarterly. There are a total of 25,025 observations (firms-quarters).
*Statistical significance at 0.05;
**Statistical significance at 0.01.

4.2. Survival-Time Data

Since we incorporate the techniques of survival analysis to analyze the longevity and potential acquisition of the IPO, Table 4 provides information regarding our survival-time data. Panel A describes the data, showing both aggregate and per firm statistics. The average entry time of 171 days (almost 1/2 year) for a firm to enter the sample is somewhat "delayed" due to "missing" data; similarly, missing data leads to an average exit time of 1,405 days (3.85 years). The entry and exit times are consistent with the mean time at risk of acquisition per firm, which is 1,233 days (3.378 years),[23] with a minimum of 17 days after the IPO and a maximum of 1,825 days (five years). Likewise, the mean survival-period of the IPO firm is 13.735 quarters (3.4 years) after the IPO (minimum of 1 quarter, maximum of 20 quarters). The 554 acquisitions represent 30.4% of the sample of 1,822 IPO firms.

Panel B presents, in life-table format, the estimation of the cumulative failure (acquisition) function for our sample of 1,822 IPO firms. For each quarterly time period (91.25 days), within the study's five-year (0 to 1,825 days) window, the life-table shows the beginning number of firms and subsequently the number of acquisitions and censorings leading to the number of firms surviving to the next quarterly period.[24] The "acquisition" function is then calculated as the cumulative conditional probability that a firm will be acquired during the time interval, based on the Kaplan–Meier (1958) estimator. The calculation is based on calculating the conditional probability of survival through the specified quarterly time interval; that is the probability that the firm will continue to "survive" (not be acquired), conditional upon it having survived up to that interval of time.[25] The cumulative "acquisition" function (conditional probability) is then calculated as one minus the conditional probability of survival. For example, the calculation of the cumulative probability of acquisition for the quarterly time interval, 821 through 913 days (10th quarter after the IPO), is calculated:

$$1 - [(1 - 0.1227) \times ((1528 - (34/2) - 26)/(1528 - (34/2)))]$$

Basically, the 0.8773 {i.e. 1−0.1227} conditional probability of survival through 821 days is multiplied by the 0.9828 {i.e. (1528−(34/2)−26)/ (1528−(34/2))} conditional probability of survival in the time interval 821 through 913 days. This results in a conditional probability of survival from time period 0 through 913 days of 0.8622, which subtracted from one yields a cumulative conditional probability of acquisition equal to 0.1378.

Table 4.   Survival-Time Data.

Panel A: Representation of the Survival-Time Data

	Total	Per Firm			
		Mean	Median	Min	Max
No. of firms	1,822				
No. of observations	25,025	13.735	15	1	20
(First) entry time (days)		170.795	0	0	1,733
(Final) exit time (days)		1,405.021	1,730	17	1,825
Time at risk (days)	2246847	1233.176	1,317	17	1,825
No. of Acquisitions	554	0.304	0	0	1

Panel B: Life-Table Estimator of the Cumulative Failure (i.e. Acquisition) Function

Interval (days)		Firms (no.)	Acquired (no.)	Censored (no.)	Cumulative Failure	Standard Error
0	91	1,822	9	0	0.0049	0.0016
91	183	1,813	6	0	0.0082	0.0021
183	274	1,807	12	1	0.0148	0.0028
274	365	1,794	23	1	0.0275	0.0038
365	456	1,770	27	7	0.0423	0.0047
456	548	1,736	35	18	0.0617	0.0057
548	639	1,683	33	12	0.0802	0.0064
639	730	1,638	36	10	0.1005	0.0071
730	821	1,592	39	25	0.1227	0.0078
821	913	1,528	26	34	0.1378	0.0082
913	1,004	1,468	36	32	0.1592	0.0087
1,004	1,095	1,400	40	34	0.1835	0.0093
1,095	1,186	1,326	35	40	0.2054	0.0097
1,186	1,278	1,251	30	33	0.2247	0.0101
1,278	1,369	1,188	23	28	0.2399	0.0104
1,369	1,460	1,137	35	18	0.2634	0.0108
1,460	1,551	1,084	26	18	0.2813	0.0111
1,551	1,643	1,040	32	32	0.3037	0.0114
1,643	1,734	976	23	43	0.3205	0.0117
1,734	1,825	910	28	882	0.3610	0.0133

Note: Panel A describes the survival-time data. It presents the total number of observations, firms, and acquisitions, as well as the total time at risk. Data is also presented on a per firm basis (e.g. the mean no. of observations and time at risk). The 554 acquisitions represent 30.4% of the total 1,822 firms at risk.

Panel B displays the cumulative "failure" function. A Kaplan–Meier product-limit estimator yields a non-parametric consistent estimator of the "failure" function on a continuous time-scale. Specifically, the cumulative conditional probability that a firm will be acquired (i.e. "failure") during the time-interval is estimated.

4.3. Correlation Coefficients

We also examine the relations among the variables. Table 5 reports Pearson correlations for these variables. A significant correlation exists between "inefficiency1" (one minus the ratio of cash flow from continuing operations to average total assets) and "inefficiency2" (one minus the ratio of cash flow from continuing operations to sales), correlated at 0.712.

To ensure that the correlation between "inefficiency1" and "inefficiency2" does not create a multicollinearity problem, we partition our regression analysis. Accordingly, the models that we estimate, utilizing survival analysis, individually comprise "inefficiency1" and "inefficiency2" (see Table 6).

Similarly, we find a high correlation between the average inventories to total sales (INVESALE) and inventory to total assets (INVEAST) (correlation coefficient = 0.780). Therefore, our regression models individually comprise "INVESALE" and "INVEAST" (see Table 7).

4.4. Regression Results

4.4.1. Cox Proportional Hazard Analysis on the Full Sample
In Table 6, we present the results from examining whether the inefficiently managed IPO, gauged by ratios of cash flow from continuing operations, is a likelier acquisition candidate. Utilizing Cox proportional hazard regression, a survival analysis technique, Table 6 provides empirical support as to the proportional effects of operating inefficiency on the potential subsequent acquisition of an IPO. As noted, due to collinearity, the models presented in columns (1) through (3) include "inefficiency1"; alternately, columns (4) through (6) include "inefficiency2." While testing whether operating inefficiency is a significant precursor for the acquisition of an IPO, our models initially control for IPO characteristics, and then firm-specific attributes and market perceptions are sequentially included. Additionally, as previously noted, we control for industry effects.[26]

For each independent (explanatory) variable in the models, we report the "hazard risk ratio" (HR) and z-statistic (shown in parenthesis). Cox proportional hazard models yield "hazard risk ratios," indicating the effect of a one-unit change in the explanatory variable on the likelihood (percentage change) of acquisition. When an explanatory variable has no effect, the hazard risk ratio will equal 1.00 and/or be statistically insignificant. If the explanatory variable has a positive association with the likelihood of acquisition, the hazard risk ratio will be greater than 1.00 and statistically

Table 5. Correlation Coefficients among Independent Variables.

	INEFF1	INEFF2	INBEX AST	INBEX SALE	ROE	INVE- AST	INVE- SALE	DVC BACK	PRC RANGE	DEV. RET	SALE	AGE	ROS	CR	ICBTQ	OPLEV	MKTPRCP	PESHARE	MCF
INEFF1	1																		
INEFF2	*0.712*	1																	
INBEXAST	0.394	0.338	1																
INBEXSALE	0.195	0.307	*0.625*	1															
ROE	-0.148	-0.104	-0.206	-0.085	1														
INVEAST	0.139	0.098	-0.086	-0.066	0.048	1													
INVESALE	0.182	0.150	-0.009	-0.025	0.024	*0.780*	1												
DVCBACK	0.074	0.088	0.107	0.082	-0.050	-0.146	-0.106	1											
PRCRANGE	-0.088	-0.065	-0.047	-0.016	0.012	-0.028	-0.008	0.008	1										
DEV. RET	0.186	0.173	0.260	0.121	-0.104	-0.046	0.002	0.107	-0.134	1									
SALE	-0.228	-0.240	-0.248	-0.176	0.027	0.130	-0.011	-0.208	0.343	-0.326	1								
AGE	-0.374	-0.330	-0.546	-0.283	0.215	0.122	0.058	-0.196	0.081	-0.332	0.342	1							
ROS	-0.195	-0.301	*-0.607*	*-0.970*	0.081	0.044	0.012	-0.086	0.020	-0.139	0.181	0.301	1						
CR	0.098	0.177	0.004	0.078	0.036	-0.023	0.050	0.145	-0.028	0.100	-0.297	-0.024	-0.081	1					
ICBTQ	-0.152	-0.103	-0.156	-0.091	0.024	-0.026	-0.047	0.003	0.011	-0.038	0.035	0.145	0.101	0.037	1				
OPLEV	0.127	0.173	0.214	0.301	-0.048	-0.322	-0.136	0.073	0.045	0.036	-0.271	-0.158	-0.250	0.241	-0.061	1			
MKTPRCP	0.011	-0.014	0.040	-0.004	0.020	0.131	0.141	-0.137	0.004	0.140	0.038	0.093	-0.001	-0.070	-0.057	0.012	1		
PESHARE	-0.057	-0.063	-0.082	-0.054	0.024	-0.014	-0.025	0.013	-0.0004	-0.003	0.045	0.062	0.051	0.022	0.025	-0.042	-0.071	1	
MCF	-0.017	-0.021	-0.032	-0.017	0.017	0.004	0.002	-0.010	-0.004	-0.016	0.017	0.042	0.018	0.011	0.017	-0.011	-0.018	0.138	1

Note: This table presents the Pearson correlation coefficients among the variables. INEFF1 represents the INEFFICIENCY1, INEFF2 represents INEFFICIENCY2. The correlation table indicates that there is a high correlation between INEFFICIENCY1 and INEFFICIENCY2, INVEAST and INVESALE, and INBEXAST and INBEXSALE with ROS that may create multicollinearity problems in the regression analyses (the correlation coefficients are statistically significant at the 0.01 level or less). The total number of observations is 10,590 firms-quarters.

Table 6. The Cox Proportional Hazard Analysis.

	(1)	(2)	(3)	(4)	(5)	(6)
INEFFICIENCY1	8.074	6.305	6.337			
	(7.36)**	(6.20)**	(6.21)**			
INEFFICIENCY2				1.342	1.236	1.234
				(4.33)**	(2.87)**	(2.84)**
DVCBACK	1.311	1.274	1.280	1.321	1.275	1.281
	(3.03)**	(2.66)**	(2.71)**	(3.10)**	(2.67)**	(2.72)**
PRCRANGE	1.223	1.314	1.313	1.184	1.295	1.294
	(3.12)**	(3.78)**	(3.76)**	(2.64)**	(3.59)**	(3.58)**
DEV. RETURN	1.21e-08	1.19e-09	1.24e-09	9.26e-08	2.97e-09	3.05e-09
	(4.53)**	(4.57)**	(4.58)**	(4.13)**	(4.41)**	(4.42)**
SALE		0.883	0.885		0.867	0.869
		(3.01)**	(2.98)**		(3.44)**	(3.40)**
AGE		1.021	1.023		0.978	0.980
		(0.67)	(0.72)		(0.89)	(0.83)
ROS		0.976	0.977		0.982	0.982
		(2.30)*	(2.29)*		(1.67)	(1.66)
CR		0.964	0.965		0.955	0.957
		(1.31)	(1.28)		(1.54)	(1.51)
ICBTQ		0.99998	0.99998		0.99998	0.99998
		(2.13)*	(2.13)*		(1.89)	(1.89)
OPLEV		1.035	1.033		1.030	1.028
		(1.10)	(1.03)		(0.92)	(0.84)
MKTPCPT			1.001			1.001
			(15.94)**			(15.86)**
PESHARE			0.9998			0.9998
			(0.99)			(1.06)
MCF			1.00002			1.00002
			(0.51)			(0.54)
Wald Chi-square	83.87**	150.58**	512.90**	63.04**	174.66**	554.97**
Likelihood ratio	147.72	167.68	175.04	120.55	145.70	153.25
Number of firms	1,822	1,822	1,822	1,822	1,822	1,822
Acquired firms	554	554	554	554	554	554
Observations	25,025	25,025	25,025	25,025	25,025	25,025

Note: The table presents the regression results from the Cox proportional hazard model with only cash flow measures. The reported coefficients are stated in the Hazard Ratio (HR). The z-statistics are reported in parentheses below the coefficients. The Wald chi-square and the Likelihood ratio (calculated as twice the absolute value of the difference between the maximum likelihood functions for the restricted model (all slopes = 0) and the unrestricted model) that measure the goodness of fit for each model are reported for each regression result. The two-digit SIC code dummy variables are used to control for industry effects in each regression (the slopes of industry dummies are not reported). The total number of observations is 25,025 firms-quarters.
*Statistical significance at 0.05;
**Statistical significance at 0.01.

significant. Correspondingly, if the explanatory variable has a negative association with the likelihood of acquisition, the hazard risk ratio will be statistically significant and less than 1.00. By subtracting one from the ratio and multiplying by 100, the reader is able to interpret the percentage change in the likelihood of acquisition given a one-unit change in the independent variable (i.e. the estimated β coefficient).[27] Significance is noted by "**" or "*," referring respectively to p-value levels of "0.01" or "0.05."

While controlling for IPO characteristics, "inefficiency1" (one minus the ratio of cash flow from continuing operations to total assets) and "inefficiency2" (one minus the ratio of cash flow from continuing operations to sales) are alternately significant at the 0.01 level (respectively, see columns (1) and (4) of Table 6). The likelihood of acquisition for the IPO is approximately 707.4% greater[28] when it is inefficiently managed (gauged by one minus the ratio of cash flow from continuing operations to total assets); likewise, an acquisition is approximately 34.2% more likely for the inefficiently managed IPO (gauged by one minus the ratio of cash flow from continuing operations to sales). These results support Hypothesis 1(a) and 1(b).

While our focus is the impact of cash-flow-based inefficiency measures on the probability of acquisition subsequent to the IPO, we incrementally examine IPO characteristics, firm-specific attributes, and market perceptions. Columns (1) and (4) of Table 6 specifically control for IPO characteristics. The result for the venture capital-backed IPO is significant (HRs 1.311 and 1.321 with p-value 0.01), as is the price range of initial offers (HRs 1.223 and 1.184 with p-value 0.01); suggesting that the venture capital-backed IPO and firms with a relatively higher price range of initial offers are more probable acquisition targets. Alternatively, firms with higher post-IPO deviations of daily stock returns (volatility) are less likely to be acquired.[29]

Incrementally, columns (2) and (5) include firm-specific attributes. "Inefficiency1" remains significant at the 0.01 level with a HR of 6.305, inferring that unit increases in this "operating inefficiency" metric increase the likelihood of acquisition by approximately 531%; likewise, "inefficiency2" is still significant (HR 1.236, p-value 0.01). Of the firm-specific attributes, sales is significant (HRs 0.883 and 0.867, with p-values of 0.01), suggesting that the IPO with relatively higher sales is less likely to be acquired. Likewise, as shown in column (2), one percent increase in ROS reduces the likelihood of acquisitions by 2.4%. Increases in the interest coverage ratio marginally reduce the probability of acquisition by 0.002%. Also, as shown by columns (2) and (5), the findings for the IPO characteristics of "venture capital-backed," "price range of initial offers," and "deviations of daily stock returns" remain robust in these models.

Then, the market perceptions of the IPO are sequentially added to our model (see columns (3) and (6) of Table 6). Both "inefficiency1" and "inefficiency2" remain significant (HRs 6.337 and 1.234, p-values 0.01).[30] Of the variables that proxy the market perception of the IPO, increases in the absolute value of the book-to-market equity marginally increase the likelihood of acquisition (HR 1.001, p-value 0.01). Also, as shown by columns (3) and (6), the findings for the IPO characteristics of "venture capital-backed," "price range of initial offers," and "deviations of daily stock returns," as well as for the firm-specific attributes of sales, ROS, and interest coverage remain robust in these models.

Overall the results shown in Table 6 support Hypothesis 1(a) and 1(b), the likelihood of acquisition for the IPO is greater when it is inefficiently managed, gauged by either one minus the ratio of cash flow from continuing operations to total assets ("inefficiency1") or one minus the ratio of cash flow from continuing operations to total sales ("inefficiency2"). There is empirical support for the "inefficient management rationale" for acquisition, based on ratios of cash flow from continuing operations.[31]

4.4.2. Cash-Flow-based versus Accrual-based Efficiency Measures

Incremental to testing whether "inefficiency1" and "inefficiency2" are significant precursors for the acquisition of the IPO, we alternatively compare these cash-flow-based measures to conventional accrual (specifically income-based and inventory-based) assessments of operating inefficiency. The full model, controlling for IPO characteristics, firm-specific attributes, market perceptions, and industry effects is used for the analysis. Table 7 presents the comparative regression results.[32]

Initially we include the "analogous" income-based measures to "inefficiency1" and "inefficiency2"; INBEXAST (one minus the ratio of income before discontinued operations and extraordinary items to total assets) is included along with "inefficiency1," while INBEXSALE (one minus the ratio of income before discontinued operations and extraordinary items to sales) is included along with "inefficiency2" (see columns (1) and (4), respectively of Table 7).

Our findings document that the cash-flow-based "inefficiency1" maintains its high level of significance (HR 6.914, p-value 0.01), whereas the corresponding income-based "inbexast" is not significant. While the cash-flow-based "inefficiency2" is not significant at the 0.05 level, it is significant at 0.06 (HR 1.197). Relative to our control variables, our results suggest that, similar to Table 6, the IPO with a higher price range of initial offers is a more probable acquisition target, and alternatively there is a reduced

Table 7. The Cash Flow versus Accrual Measures.

	(1)	(2)	(3)	(4)	(5)	(6)
INEFFICIENCY1	6.914 (3.98)**					
INBEXAST	3.205 (1.61)	1.067 (0.08)	1.045 (0.06)			
INEFFICIENCY2[a]		8.834 (4.48)**	9.131 (4.48)**			
INBEXSALE				1.197 (1.88)	1.186 (1.71)	1.177 (1.63)
ROE		1.00005 (0.28)	1.00006 (0.32)	0.988 (0.25)	0.906 (1.15)	0.904 (1.17)
INVEAST			0.647 (0.82)		0.99996 (0.23)	0.99997 (0.19)
INVESALE						1.104 (0.18)
DVCBACK	1.150 (1.18)	1.160 (1.21)	1.132 (1.00)	1.180 (1.39)	1.181 (1.35)	1.167 (1.24)
PRCRANGE	1.445 (3.65)**	1.459 (3.57)**	1.425 (3.29)**	1.449 (3.61)**	1.451 (3.47)**	1.416 (3.18)**
DEV. RETURN	3.09e-13 (4.65)**	6.47e-15 (4.90)**	5.76e-15 (4.89)**	3.96e-13 (4.44)**	4.76e-15 (4.73)**	6.09e-15 (4.72)**
SALE	0.832 (3.58)**	0.826 (3.58)**	0.832 (3.44)**	0.809 (4.08)**	0.816 (3.80)**	0.824 (3.57)**
AGE	0.899 (1.29)	0.723 (2.74)**	0.728 (2.62)**	0.786 (3.12)**	0.620 (4.58)**	0.621 (4.53)**
CR	0.975 (0.69)	0.982 (0.51)	0.983 (0.48)	0.966 (0.89)	0.977 (0.60)	0.979 (0.58)
ICBTQ	1.00002 (0.20)	1.00003 (0.44)	1.00004 (0.51)	0.99997 (0.30)	1.000002 (0.02)	1.00001 (0.12)

OPLEV	1.046	1.044	1.036	1.052	1.058	1.061
	(0.97)	(0.88)	(0.69)	(1.09)	(1.15)	(1.21)
MKTPCPT	1.088	1.146	1.145	1.081	1.151	1.137
	(0.93)	(1.41)	(1.39)	(0.81)	(1.44)	(1.29)
PESHARE	0.99992	0.99996	0.99997	0.99987	0.99993	0.99993
	(0.40)	(0.19)	(0.17)	(0.59)	(0.32)	(0.33)
MCF	1.00008	1.00009	1.00008	1.00008	1.00009	1.00009
	(1.19)	(1.26)	(1.28)	(1.17)	(1.21)	(1.24)
Wald Chi-square	135.28**	124.26**	122.23**	89.52**	86.39**	84.12**
Likelihood ratio	148.79	154.76	152.67	133.89	142.86	139.06
Number of firms	906	862	853	906	862	853
Acquired firms	357	331	329	357	331	330
Observations	11,820	10,740	10,586	11821	10741	10,590

Note: The table presents the regression results from the Cox proportional hazard model with cash flow measures (INEFF1 or INEFF2) compared directly with accrual measures (INBEXAST, INBEXSALE, ROE, INVEAST, INVESALE). The reported coefficients are stated in the HR. The z-statistics are reported in parentheses below the coefficients. The Wald chi-square and the Likelihood ratio (calculated as twice the absolute value of the difference between the maximum likelihood functions for the restricted model (all slopes = 0) and the unrestricted model) that measure the goodness of fit for each model are reported for each regression result. The two-digit SIC code dummy variables are used to control for industry effects in each regression (the slopes of industry dummies are not reported). The total number of observations varies from 11,821 to 10,586 firms-quarters.

** Statistical significance at 0.01.

[a] Note that "inefficiency2", although not significant at the 0.05 level, is significant at 0.10 in columns (3) through (6), with significance of 0.060, 0.088, and 0.103, respectively.

likelihood that the IPO with greater volatility of the post-IPO deviations of daily stock returns, as well as relatively higher sales will be acquired.[33]

Incrementally, columns (2) and (5) test ROE (the ratio of income before discontinued operations and extraordinary items to total equity), consistent with the proxy for "efficiency" considered by Palepu (1986).[34] As shown, neither of the accrual-based measures of ROE, "inbexast," and "inbexsale" is significant, while the cash-flow-based measure of "inefficiency1" maintains its high level of significance (HR 8.834, p-value 0.01) and "inefficiency2" while not significant at the 0.05 level, is marginally significant at 0.088 (HR 1.186).

Then, corresponding to Theodossiou et al. (1996), we sequentially include the ratio of inventory to assets (labeled INVEAST) and inventory to sales (INVESALE) in columns (3) and (6), respectively. Contrary to Theodossiou et al., we do not find either "inveast" or "invesale" to be significant,[35,36] whereas the cash-flow-based proxy for inefficiency, "inefficiency1," continues to be highly significant (HR 9.131, p-value 0.01); "inefficiency2," however, wanes in significance (HR 1.177, p-value 0.103).[37]

Additionally, we utilize the "log likelihood ratio statistics"[38] to examine the marginal contributions of the cash-flow-based inefficiency measures versus the accrual-based measures. We find that the marginal effect of adding either "inefficiency1" or "inefficiency2" to the model is always significant; in contrast, the consequence of including the accrual-based proxies of inefficiency is statistically insignificant.[39]

Overall, the results shown in Table 7 provide additional support as to the efficacy of cash-flow-based measures in predicting IPO acquisition. Compared with the conventional accrual-based assessments, cash-flow-based measures represent a more viable proxy of managerial inefficiency as a precursor of IPO acquisition. There is further empirical support of the "inefficient management rationale" for acquisition, rooted in cash flow from continuing operations.[40]

5. CONCLUSION

This study examines the influence of operating efficiency on the aftermarket acquisition of an IPO. Prior IPO studies have not incorporated efficiency measures. While, on the whole we consider whether accounting-based efficiency measures explain the acquisition of IPOs, our focus is whether cash-flow-based measures of operating inefficiency signify the "inefficient management rationale" for acquisition. We specifically hypothesize that the inefficiently managed IPO, reflected by lower ratios of cash flow from continuing operations is a likelier acquisition candidate. Further, we compare the cash-flow measures of managerial inefficiency with conventional accrual-based assessments of inefficiency.

Utilizing survival analysis techniques, expressly Cox proportional hazards, we observe that for our sample of IPO firms (selected ex ante), the likelihood of acquisition is greater when the IPO is inefficiently managed. In particular, we document that increases in the operating inefficiency of an IPO, gauged by either one minus the ratio of cash flow from continuing operations to total assets or one minus the ratio of cash flow from continuing operations to total sales, significantly increases the likelihood for a potential subsequent acquisition. Moreover, when we compare our cash-flow-based measures to conventional accrual-based inefficiency measures, we find that the income-based and inventory-based accrual measures are not significant, while the cash flow measures maintain their high level of significance. Based on the findings, we conjecture that the accrual-based measures just capture one-dimensional aspects of inefficiency, whereas cash flow from continuing operations tends to be more robust in nature.

While providing further evidence in support of the "inefficient management rationale," as gauged by cash-flow-based proxies, for the acquisition of an IPO, we also control for (incrementally observe) IPO characteristics, firm-specific attributes, and market perceptions. We find that the IPO with increases in book-to-market equity and a higher price range of initial offers, as well as venture capital-backed is a more probable acquisition target; alternatively, there is a reduced likelihood that the IPO with greater volatility of the post-IPO deviations of daily stock returns, as well as relatively higher sales, higher ROS, and interest coverage ratios will be acquired.

Overall, our study underscores the importance of the relative magnitudes of cash flow from continuing operations on the longevity of IPO firms. We re-affirm our posture that cash flow from continuing operations is a fundamental accounting measure of a firm's operating performance. Generally, we document that the cash-flow-based measures represent a more viable (based on significance) proxy of managerial inefficiency as a precursor of IPO acquisition.

NOTES

1. In a April 28, 2003 Business Week article by Mara Der Hovanesian, London's REL Consultancy Group Ltd. (a cash flow management adviser) refers to the ratio of cash from operations to sales as "Cash Efficiency."

2. We deviate from Giacomino and Mielke (1993) and do not include the ratio of cash flow from continuing operations to income from continuing operations, in our models, as a third efficiency measure. We believe that this ratio is not driven by cash

flows (which are the intent of our cash-flow-based ratios); additionally, there is a "false" signal when both the cash flow from continuing operations and income from continuing operations are negative. Also, our additional sensitivity tests do not show this ratio to have any marginal significance; and consequently to conserve space, we do not report that analysis.

3. We mathematically denote two "inefficiency" measures (the "converse" of the "efficiency" measures) as "one minus" the respective efficiency ratios (e.g. "one minus the ratio of cash flow from continuing operations to total assets"); lower efficiency ratios will thus yield higher inefficiency scores and vice versa.

4. This five-year window is consistent with Loughran and Ritter (1995), Mikkelson, Partch, and Shah (1997), and Jain and Kini (1999).

5. Traditional ex post matched-pairs research designs have been criticized for potentially leading to biased statistical results (Zmijewski, 1984; Palepu, 1986; Chen & Lee, 1993; Morris, 1998; Shumway, 2001).

6. Palepu (1986) does find the excess return on a firm's stock, an alternative market-based proxy for management efficiency, to be a significant predictor of likely acquisition targets.

7. As previously noted (see footnote 2), we deviate from Giacomino and Mielke (1993) and do not include the ratio of cash flow from continuing operations to income from continuing operations as a third efficiency measure.

8. Cash flow from continuing operations is calculated as operating cash flow less any amounts from discontinued operations and extraordinary items. This is consistent with Flagg, Giroux, and Wiggins (1991), who emphasize that nonrecurring items can give a false signal.

9. Delisting for other reasons (e.g. bankruptcy) is considered to result from different behavioral and financial characteristics than does an acquisition or merger. To avoid a potential bias we exclude these 146 "other" delistings from our regressions. However, to ensure unbiased results, we rerun our regressions inclusive of these 146 other delistings (i.e. allowing them to be censored randomly) and find the results to be both quantitatively and qualitatively similar to those presented.

10. Our ex ante sample selection process is in accordance with Palepu (1986), who emphasizes that the prediction test sample should resemble the population as closely as possible. By starting with all the IPOs during the time-period of our study, we avoid what Palepu refers to as a "state-based" sample composed of an equal number of acquisitions and non-acquisitions (i.e. "matched-pairs"), which leads to biased statistical results. Note that while Palepu's sample is representative of the population, it is ex post in that the sample selection is based on knowledge of the firm's state (acquired or non-acquired). Our approach is consistent with Jain and Kini (1999), who also track IPO firms, selected ex ante for evidence of subsequent acquisition, failure, or survival.

11. In our original data compilation of IPO firms between 1/1/1990 and 12/31/2001 (prior to delimiting our sample to a five-year window), we observe that 1,190 out of 3,199 IPO firms are acquired within the first five years after their IPO. We observe that only 209 additional firms are acquired during the sixth to twelfth years after their IPO date. The remaining 1,800 IPO firms are still listed (survived in their original public form) 12 years after the IPO. The five-year duration period is also consistent with Jain and Kini (1999).

12. In contrast to the Hensler et al. (1997) study, Palepu (1986) and Jain and Kini (1999) do not examine the *duration* of the firm's survival until the firm is acquired or delisted for other reasons.

13. Hensler et al. (1997) utilize the accelerated failure time (AFT) variation of the hazard model, which is a parametric model restricting the baseline hazard function to adhere to a certain density function based upon a priori expectations. In contrast the baseline hazard function in our model does not make any assumptions and is distribution free.

14. Technically, our hazard model is considered semi-parametric; while the baseline hazard function, $h_{0j}(t)$, is distribution free, $\exp(X_{ij}'\beta)$ contains parameters β with a certain distribution.

15. HR can be thus specified since the baseline hazard function ($h_{0j}(t)$) does not affect the HR; therefore, this approach differs from the Hensler et al. (1997) model.

16. We utilize the Stata 8© statistical software to estimate the HR (Eq. 2) and the Wald statistics (z-scores) of the HR. The HR indicates the effect of a one-unit change in the explanatory variable (x_j) on the probability of acquisition.

17. The intent is that a high book-to-market equity signals a negative market assessment of a firm's prospects, whereas a low ratio is indicative of a positive market perception; the "driver" of the ratio is thus the firm market value in the denominator. The absolute value precludes a "false reading" in the market's risk perception for firms where a low market value is concurrent with negative book equity.

18. In our models, testing whether cash-flow-based inefficiency measures are significant precursors for the acquisition of the IPO, we alternately replace INEFFICIENCY1 with INEFFICIENCY2 (see Table 6).

19. Theodossiou et al. (1996) use the ratio of inventory to sales as a proxy of management inefficiency. We extend their work and also test the ratio of inventory to assets, which is consistent with our models that alternately test "inefficiency1" and "inefficiency2" where the denominator varies from assets to sales.

20. In alternate model 2 (where the denominator changes from assets to sales), "inefficiency2" is comparatively tested; INBEXAST is replaced with the analogous INBEXSALE and likewise INVEAST with INVESALE (see Table 7). ROS, another possible accrual-based profitability "efficiency" measure, which parallels ROE, is not included in our model due to its high correlation (as noted in Table 5) with "inbexast" and "inbexsale" (respectively, -0.607 and -0.970).

21. Note that of the 877 firms in the Jain and Kini (1999) study, there were 603 "survivors" (non-acquired), 149 acquisitions, and 125 non-survivors (outright failures due to bankruptcy and other non-acquisition terminal events).

22. The industry distribution percents are based on a weighted average of the acquired and non-acquired firms.

23. While the study has a five-year window, the acquisition date (for the acquired firms) was normally less than five years subsequent to the IPO, reducing the average time at risk to approximately 3.4 years.

24. The censorings for quarters 1 through 19 (386 censorings in total) are due to "missing" data (i.e. these firms are included in the "starting" sample but are "censored" during the study. The last (20th) quarter considers 822 firms to be "censored" in the context that their potential acquisition, within the study's five-year window, can no longer be observed. The weighted averages of the elapsed time in our

study for the 386 censorings as well as the "remaining" 822 firms are incorporated into the derivation of hazard rates and slope coefficients for the regressors in an unbiased manner.

25. The Kaplan–Meier (1958) estimator assumes that censored observations are uniformly distributed over the time interval; thus the convention is to reduce the size of the risk set by one-half of the firms censored in the interval.

26. The estimated statistics for industry dummy variables are not reported on the tables to conserve space.

27. For a more detailed discussion of Cox proportional hazard regressions and survival analysis techniques the authors refer the reader to George et al. (1996), LeClere (2000), and Shumway (2001).

28. A "hazard ratio" of 8.074 suggests that a one-unit change in "inefficiency1" makes an acquisition 8.074 times more likely to occur; a corresponding interpretation is that the percentage increase in the likelihood of acquisition is 707.4% (i.e. $(8.074 - 1.0) \times 100\%$).

29. Jain and Kini (1999) do not find evidence that the IPO characteristics of "VC-backed" and "post-IPO deviations of daily stock returns" affect the probability of acquisition relative to survival. They do not specifically test the significance of the "offer price range."

30. Note that "inefficiency2" contains "outliers" causing a relatively large standard deviation. When we run the regressions with the observations truncated or winsorized at the 5% and 95% levels, we find that "inefficiency2" remains significant at 0.01 with a noticeably higher hazard ratio of over 2.0.

31. To ensure unbiased results, we rerun our Table 6 regressions inclusive of the 146 "other" delistings (see Table 1 as well as footnote 9). When these firms are included (i.e. allowed to be censored randomly), our findings are robust, remaining quantitatively and qualitatively similar to those presented.

32. Note that the sample sizes for the regressions in Table 7 are reduced from the number of firms specified in Tables 1, 3, 4, and 6; this is due to "missing" values of the additional accrual-based proxies for "inefficiency." We run tests to see whether the missing values (deletion of firms from the analysis) are due to inventory data restrictions; we find that only 430 observations are "deleted" due to the inclusion of the accrual inefficiency measure based on inventory, an additional 1,064 are deleted due to ROE, while the majority (12,945) become "missing" observations when the income-based INBEX is added to the model (note that the total $407 + 1,064 + 12,945 = 14,439$ accounts for the difference between the 25,025 observations in Table 6 and the 10,586 minimum number of observations in Table 7). Relative to the deletions due to the inventory-based measures, there are a reduced number of observations across each industry code, but no industries are eliminated.

33. Other control variables (e.g. venture capital-backed, book-to-market equity), significant in Table 6, are not significant in the reduced sample-size models; however, alternatively, the age of the firm proxied by the plowback ratio of retained earnings to total assets, not significant in Table 6 is significant in Table 7 columns (2) through (6) (the higher the plowback ratio, the less likely an acquisition).

34. We additionally test the excess return on a firm's stock, an alternative market-based proxy for management efficiency, and contrary to Palepu (1986) do not find it to be a significant predictor of likely acquisition targets.

35. We rerun the analysis, testing the interaction of the inventory-based variables with industry "dummies." When "inveast" is interacted with industry, we find construction, computer/data, wholesalers, healthcare, and miscellaneous business services to be significant at less than 0.05; alternately, when "invesale" is interacted, we find construction, oil and gas, wholesalers, healthcare, and airlines to be significant at less than 0.05.

36. Pursuing Mulford and Comiskey's (1996) position that operating efficiency is reflected in the three areas of inventory, accounts receivable, and accounts payable, which in turn affect operating cash flow, after testing the Theodossiou et al. (1996) "inventory" measure, we proceed to test accounts receivable and accounts payable. We, individually, test the ratios of accounts receivable to total assets and accounts payable to total assets and find that they do not significantly affect the likelihood of acquisition in the full sample of IPO firms. Inventory, accounts receivable, and accounts payable, while potential precursors of cash flow problems, do not adequately gauge operating inefficiency. We do not report these results to conserve space and they are available upon request.

37. As noted (see footnote 30), we find that "inefficiency2" contains "outliers" causing a relatively large standard deviation. When we estimate the regressions in Table 7 with the observations truncated or winsorized at the 5% and 95% levels, we find that "inefficiency2" becomes significant at 0.01 with respective (columns 4, 5, 6) hazard ratios of 2.328, 2.326, and 2.480.

38. Pursuant to Griffiths, Hill, and Judge (1993), the log likelihood ratio test statistic (λ_{lr}) is computed as twice the absolute value of the difference between the maximum value of the unrestricted likelihood function (Lu) and the maximum value of the restricted (slope = 0) likelihood function (Lr); $\lambda_{lr} = 2|(Lu-Lr)|$, which is asymptotic to a chi-square distribution with degrees of freedom equal to the number of parameters tested.

39. For example, the log likelihood ratio test statistic of our model inclusive of "inbexast" as the sole inefficiency measure is 135.475 compared with 148.79 (see column (1) of Table 7) when both "inefficiency1" and "inbexast" are included; the difference of 13.315 infers that the addition of the cash-flow-based "inefficiency1" is significant at the 0.01 level (6.64 is the critical chi-square score at the 0.01 level of significance). In contrast, the test statistic when "inefficiency1" is the sole inefficiency measure is 147.12 and the addition of "inbexast" (test statistic = 148.79) gives a marginal increase of 1.67 (3.84 is the critical chi-square score at the 0.05 level of significance), inferring that the addition of the accrual-based "inbexast" is not significant.

40. Like Table 6, to ensure unbiased results, we rerun our Table 7 regressions inclusive of the 146 "other" delistings (see Table 1 as well as footnote 9). However, due to "missing" values of the additional accrual-based proxies for "inefficiency" and the resulting reduced sample size, there are effectively only four additional firms and the results are totally robust.

ACKNOWLEDGEMENTS

The authors would like to thank the Associate Editor and two anonymous reviewers for their helpful comments and suggestions.

REFERENCES

Chen, K. C. W., & Lee, C. W. J. (1993). Financial ratios and corporate endurance: A case of the oil and gas industry. *Contemporary Accounting Research, 9*(2), 667–694.

Clayton, R. J., & Fields, M. A. (1991). Prediction of acquisition candidates: Methodological comparisons. *The Mid-Atlantic Journal of Business, 27*(3), 233–250.

Comiskey, E. E., & Mulford, C. W. (1992a). Finding the causes of changes in cash flow. *Commercial Lending Review, 7*(3), 21–40.

Comiskey, E. E., & Mulford, C. W. (1992b). Understand the reasons behind changes in cash flow. *Commercial Lending Review, 8*(1), 29–43.

Copeland, T. E., & Weston, J. F. (1983). *Financial theory and corporate policy.* Reading, MA: Addison-Wesley.

Cox, D. R. (1972). Regression models and life-tables. *Journal of the Royal Statistical Society, Series B, 34*(2), 187–220.

Fama, E. F., & French, K. R. (1992). The cross-section of expected stock returns. *The Journal of Finance, 47*(2), 427–465.

Fera, N. (1997). Using shareholders value to evaluate strategic choices. *Management Accounting, 79*(November), 47–51.

Flagg, J. C., Giroux, G. A., & Wiggins, C. E. (1991). Predicting corporate bankruptcy using failing firms. *Review of Financial Economics, 1*, 67–78.

George, C. R., Spiceland, J. D., & George, S. L. (1996). A longitudinal study of the going concern audit decision and survival time. *Advances in Quantitative Analysis of Finance and Accounting, 4*, 77–103.

Giacomino, D. E., & Mielke, D. E. (1993). Cash flows: Another approach to ratio analysis. *Journal of Accountancy, 175*(March), 55–58.

Goldratt, E. M. (1984). *The goal.* Great Barrington, MA: North River Press.

Griffiths, W. E., Hill, R. C., & Judge, G. G. (1993). *Learning and Practicing Econometrics.* New York: Wiley.

Hensler, D. A., Rutherford, R. C., & Springer, T. M. (1997). The survival of initial public offerings in the aftermarket. *Journal of Financial Research, 20*(Spring), 93–110.

Hovanesian, M. D. (2003). Cash: Burn, baby, burn. *Business Week,* April 28, pp. 82–83.

Jain, B. A., & Kini, O. (1999). The life cycle of initial public offering firms. *Journal of Business Finance & Accounting, 26*(9/10), 1281–1307.

Jensen, M. (1986). Agency costs of free cash flow, corporate finance and takeovers. *American Economic Review, 76*(2), 323–329.

Kaplan, E. L., & Meier, P. (1958). Nonparametric estimation from incomplete observations. *Journal of the American Statistical Association, 53*, 457–481.

LeClere, M. J. (2000). The occurrence and timing of events: Survival analysis applied to the study of financial distress. *Journal of Accounting Literature, 19*, 158–189.

Loughran, T., & Ritter, J. R. (1995). The new issues puzzle. *The Journal of Finance, 50*(1), 23–51.

Mikkelson, W. H., Partch, M. M., & Shah, K. (1997). Ownership and operating performance of firms that go public. *Journal of Financial Economics, 44*, 281–307.

Morris, R. (1998). *Early warning indicators of corporate failure: A critical review of previous research and further empirical evidence.* Brookfield, VT: Ashgate Publishing.

Mulford, C. W., & Comiskey, E. E. (1996). *Financial warnings.* New York: Wiley.

Palepu, K. G. (1986). Predicting takeover targets: A methodological and empirical analysis. *Journal of Accounting and Economics, 8*, 3–35.

Peel, M. J., & Wilson, N. (1989). The liquidation/merger alternative: Some results for the UK corporate sector. *Managerial and Decision Economics, 10,* 209–220.

Ritter, J. R. (1991). The long-run performance of initial public offerings. *The Journal of Finance, 46*(1), 3–27.

Shleifer, A., Vishny, R. W., & Morck, P. (1987). *Characteristics of hostile and friendly takeover targets. (WP 213).* Chicago: University of Chicago, Centre of Research in Security Prices.

Shumway, T. (2001). Forecasting bankruptcy more accurately: A simple hazard model. *Journal of Business, 1,* 101–124.

Theodossiou, P. (1993). Predicting shifts in the mean of a multivariate time series process: An application in predicting business failures. *Journal of the American Statistical Association, 88*(422), 441–449.

Theodossiou, P., Kahya, E., Saidi, R., & Philippatos, G. (1996). Financial distress and corporate acquisitions: Further empirical evidence. *Journal of Business Finance & Accounting, 23*(5/6), 699–719.

Zmijewski, M. E. (1984). Methodological issues related to the estimation of financial distress prediction models. *Journal of Accounting Research, 22*(Suppl.), 59–82.

YOU CAN TRUST YOUR CAR TO THE MAN WHO WEARS THE STAR: A LOOK AT DISCRETIONARY DISCLOSURE BY TEXACO

Sabam Hutajulu and Timothy J. Fogarty

ABSTRACT

The accounting literature has focused upon cross-sectional analyses of mandated disclosures. This study instead assesses discretionary disclosure over a long period of time. Rather than select a single element of disclosure for many companies, this study attempts to summarize and appreciate the entirety of discretionary disclosure for a single company. In 2001, the Texaco Corporation was merged with Chevron, ending a 98-year history as a reporting entity. A review of their discretionary disclosures over the years demonstrates both the strategic and the reflective nature of corporate communications in its correlations to several variables that are also tracked over the history of this company.

Most observers trace the emergence of the modern accounting profession back to the passage of the Securities Laws of 1933 and 1934. As regulation compelled the production of information, verification became necessary. Eventually, academic accountants began systematic inquiries into the

Advances in Accounting, Volume 22, 201–228
ISSN: 0882-6110/doi:10.1016/S0882-6110(06)22009-1

composition, and influence of the information set that regulation produced. While this work has been very insightful, it has also contributed to several lacunaes in our appreciation of corporate disclosure.

The tendency of the literature has been to select individual items of disclosure for incorporation in large sample cross-sectional analyses. Typically, these have been selected from the elements of disclosure that are required to be present in standardized form and therefore have prioritized the financial statements and its associated notes. Other aspects of corporate communications tend to be ignored because they are more idiosyncratic in appearance and qualitative in nature. Perhaps, even more consequential, the typical assessment of disclosure precludes an appreciation for disclosure as a whole. Only on a wider scale can the social and political context of disclosure be examined. Since cross-sectional analyses also isolate a singular year, one is also denied the ability to observe change in disclosure over time.

In his book *The Prize*, published simultaneously with the broadcast of a multipart series on Public Broadcasting Service, Daniel Yergin asserts that the history of the twentieth century is the history of the struggle to control petroleum resources. Accordingly, the fortunes and prospects of those companies that bring oil to market are of particular importance to the US society and its economy (Yergin, 1992).

This paper offers an analysis of a single company in a way that addresses some of the shortcomings of typical assessments of corporate communication. Using the Texaco company's annual reports from the first organization of the company in 1902 to its end as a separate corporation in 2000, total discretionary disclosure (TDD) is examined. Parallels are noted, linking this body of information to important developments in the history of the industry and the company. This case study illustrates the potential of a longitudinal, holistic assessment of corporate communication practices.

BACKGROUND

The discovery of oil in Titusville, Pennsylvania in 1859 initiated a long series of events that has changed the nature of business and society. The demand for oil shaped the development of great fortunes, called for important revisions in the organization of commercial affairs and altered the face of global politics. Oil production has been marked by high risk in exploration and extraction, significant price volatility and the need to commit large amounts of capital. These features combine to suggest a high degree of information asymmetry between corporate executives and those with a keen interest in the resolution of these matters, such as investors and regulators (Shuman, 1940; Williamson & Daum, 1959; Williamson et al., 1963; Knowles, 1983; Brock, Klingstedt, & Jones, 1988; Yergin, 1992; Peirce, 1996).

Texaco finds its roots in the era when US companies constituted the entirety of the oil industry. The development of the Spindletop field in Texas at the turn of the century marked the transition from the Pennsylvania origins of the industry to its modern roots in the Southwest. Texaco was on the scene for most of this, actively engaged in all phases of the industry through two World Wars and a decade long depression (Greene, 1985; Texaco Inc., 1991).

The 1950s were Texaco's golden age. Well-balanced operations resulted in high profitability and high visibility[1] during the era. Along with other oil companies, Texaco came under heightened public scrutiny in the last quarter of the century as a company that despoiled the environment and exploited customer's dependence on oil. In the 1980s, Texaco was found guilty of interfering in the proposed merger of Getty Oil into Pennzoil. Damages of 10.5 billion forced Texaco into a Chapter 11 bankruptcy and reorganization. Another corporate black-eye occurred in the mid-1990s when Texaco settled an employment discrimination case for $176 million. The Texaco story ended when, in a wave of industry consolidation, Texaco accepted Chevron's offer of $64.87 per share for the company and the deal was approved by the US Justice Department (Greene, 1985; Hast, 1988; Time, 1998).

The history of Texaco and its industry show the potential value of discretionary disclosure. As powerful and as valuable as the financial statements can be, they cannot provide interested parties with sufficient information to understand the ebbs and flows of Texaco's prospects. However, lacking a regulatory mandate, discretionary disclosure is predicated upon sufficient managerial incentives to provide such information. This behavior needs to overcome the competitive disadvantage that may result from the release of proprietary information.

During the course of Texaco's existence, much transpired in the industry. The discovery of oil reserves in other parts of the world created a global market that nations would seek to control. Increasingly, sophisticated technologies would be brought to bear upon the processes of finding oil, bringing it out of the ground and refining it into useable products. New uses for petroleum and its byproducts would be identified that furthered the demand for this natural resource. Governments would become increasingly involved in regulating all aspects of the industry including the prices that it could charge, the profits that it could make and the harm that it could inflict upon the environment. Considerable effort has been expended from many participants to force the industry to serve a wide variety of economic, social and political objectives (Yergin, 1992).

In this volatile environment, Texaco experienced perhaps more than its share of highs and lows. Founded as an integrated company, Texaco's focus over the years varied from aggressive marketing to efficient refining to far-flung exploration. Texaco often found itself second behind Standard Oil of New Jersey in terms of the size of some of these activities. Texaco was challenged at various points in its history by inadequate economics of scale, by insufficient product to justify its downstream operations and by autocratic management (Greene, 1985).

HYPOTHESES DEVELOPMENT

The explanation for discretionary disclosure by corporations is neither intuitive nor consensual. Exploiting the unique possibilities of longitudinal analysis, this paper posits several rationales.

The first possible explanation finds its origins apart from the oil industry and the Texaco Company. Discretionary disclosure may increase on its own without any reference to the specifics of the corporate environment. If constituents, lead by financial analysts, are sufficiently important and empowered, they may demand disclosures well beyond that which regulation requires. If these groups find such information to be helpful, they may need more of it over time. Accordingly, the amount of discretionary disclosure that Texaco produces may increase over time based on this demand. Such a trend is consistent with a heightened insistence on institutional accountability (Singhvi & Desai, 1971; Brief, 1986, 1987; Lev, 1992; Eccless & Mavrinac, 1995; Rappaport, 1998). A hypothesis that captures this possibility is

H_1. Discretionary disclosure by Texaco increased during its years of operation.

Discretionary disclosure may also reflect the nature of the entity providing this information. Rather than meeting a demand imposed by interested external parties or made appropriate by the tenor of the times, discretionary disclosure may be made necessary by certain attributes that the firm possesses.

Looking at this source of influence is consistent with agency theory. This perspective suggests that important informational asymmetries exist between managers and owners. In order to avoid the costs of distrust that might be imposed by owners on agent managers, those that control corporations have an incentive to disclose information. Since this incentive varies in magnitude, so could discretionary disclosure differ over time (Leftwich, Watts, & Zimmerman, 1981).

Agency theory often looks to firm size. Incentives within larger firms are deemed to be qualitatively different from smaller firms. Larger firms present managers with more opportunities to consume the prerequisites of their positions undetected by their owners. Accordingly, managers of large firms may be more inclined to use disclosure to convince owners that this is not the case. Even apart from the agency perspective, the complexity more likely to be present in larger firms provides managers with more about which to disclose. Ceteris paribus, more disclosure is needed to do justice to describe a large company. Larger companies also have a larger, and possibly more powerful, group of external parties that could demand more information (Watts & Zimmerman, 1978, 1986; Rappaport, 1998).

The evidence that exists on firm size is cross-sectional in nature as it compares firms of different sizes at one moment in time. No study could be found that has investigated whether a single firm's disclosure is sensitive to the variability through time in that firm's size. Over a long period of time, firm size reflects economic conditions, firms' strategies and competitive success. In other words, size is neither constant nor monotonic. The possible relationship to disclosure is expressed in this hypothesis:

H_{2a}. Discretionary disclosure by Texaco is higher in years when Texaco was larger.

Another firm attribute that could be related to discretionary disclosure is the magnitude of its earnings. High levels of profitability may predispose managers to more elaborate descriptions of their success than they would otherwise provide. This ample level of success in the market may dampen the tendency to equate disclosure with competitive disadvantage. Low levels of profit, or the experience of losses may make managers unnecessarily defensive. This may be translated into very terse descriptions of operations and activities (Singhvi & Desai, 1971; Malone, Fries, & Jones, 1993). Explanation of losses may also be vague and brief. Prior studies note that firms that do not make money have much different disclosure patterns (e.g., Grant, Fogarty, & Prevtis, 2000). However, whether such cross-sectional findings can be extended to a longitudinal basis is unclear. The examination of one firm over a period of time would seem to provide a clearer interpretation of the role of past earnings on disclosure. To wit:

H_{2b}. Discretionary disclosure by Texaco is higher in years when Texaco's profitability was higher.

A third firm attribute pertains to the unique relationship between a firm and its creditors. Whereas all large firms have an equity base made up of many investors who have chosen to "buy and hold," access to debt financing must be earned with greater and more specific managerial diligence. Unlike the dividends that are discretionary payments to shareholders, interest payments made by creditors will vary in amounts with their perceptions of short-run corporate prospects. Accordingly, managers may use discretionary disclosures to project confidence for the benefit of the creditor class. Since creditors take careful note of the debt levels that a company carries, their concerns about the ongoing creditworthiness of a company may vary. Therefore, the selective deployment of discretionary disclosure may be more often used when the degree of debt financing is high (Jensen & Meckling, 1976; Schipper, 1981).

Many studies have evaluated companies based upon their comparative debt positions. However, whether a similar disclosure relevance can be observed for one company as it changes the mix of its financing through time is an open question. Progress along this theme can be made with the following hypothesis:

H_{2c}. Discretionary disclosure by Texaco is higher in years when Texaco has a higher level of debt.

Another way of looking at a company is through its governance structures. Different compositions of people charged with establishing corporate direction and policy may shape the nature and amount of corporate disclosure. Rather than looking at the attributes of the business itself, this approach looks at the key people behind the company.

A classic means of distinguishing companies pertains to the membership of its board of directors. Board membership reflects a balancing of two quite distinct objectives. On the one hand, people with deep knowledge of the company are needed to understand its abilities and limitations. On the other, outsiders are sought who can connect the firm to critical constituents and important types of resources. The relative numerical strength of outsiders has been considered critical in producing a higher level of accountability by effectuating a more substantive check upon managerial discretion.[2] Outsiders on the board may also act as a voice in favor of higher levels of disclosure, and against secretiveness. In this way, outside directors enact their orientation toward external parties with an interest in corporate affairs (Leftwich et al., 1981; Malone et al., 1993).

Rather than comparing different companies on the governance dimension, an examination of different years within the history of a single company has the advantage of controlling for many sources of variation that would shape the numerical balance between the two types of directors. This is encapsulated by this expectation:

H_{3a}. Discretionary disclosure by Texaco is higher in years where more outside directors served on its board of directors.

A second governance concern pertains to the duality between the board and the key manager of the company. Whereas the board has the official legal duty to set corporate policy, their power is diminished by their infrequent gathering and their tendency to be dominated by a company's chief executive officer (CEO). The CEO is often able to dominate a board to the extent that the board feels that no choice exists but to "rubber stamp" the CEO decisions and to validate the CEO's policy preferences. Although this state of affairs is not consistent with the fiduciary duties established in the law for board members, nor does it allow for the "reality check" that the board should provide in theory, this situation may happen often without a purposeful intention.

Board domination by a CEO is easier to accomplish when the CEO also serves as the Chairperson of the Board. This duplication of offices is not expressly discouraged by corporation law or by business tradition. It allows the CEO higher levels of access to board deliberation and decreases the chance that a board might be truly independent from management.

Whether or not the separation of the offices of CEO and Chairperson of the Board has bearing upon the level of discretionary disclosure is an open question. When two distinct humans occupy these key offices, they may have different priorities for disclosure. The resolution of two perspectives may result in more total disclosure than when there is one person with one idea about disclosure. Again, a longitudinal plane for an examination of the questions provides an opportunity to mitigate against other influences. This is done with the following hypothesis

H_{3b}. Discretionary disclosure by Texaco will be higher in years when there was a separation between the incumbents of the offices of CEO and Chairperson of the Board.

The final set of hypothesis pertains to the role of internal and external agendas. Discretionary disclosure can be seen as an extension of a dialog between a corporation and its constituents. As such, this disclosure can be initiated by the company to inform the readership about its priorities. Disclosure could be a response by the company to the concerns that the company perceives its constituent possess.

Firms have choices with regard to the strategies that they operationalize. Different strategies create different degrees of possibilities for corporate disclosure. Part of this is related to the relationship between a strategy and the need to keep information away from company competitors. Another element pertains to the ability to describe how a strategy will affect the company. While it is apparent that strategy affects the content of disclosure, it may also have a bearing upon the quantity of disclosure about those topics. If corporate disclosure has meaning, both its content and magnitude should follow the priority objectives that managers have established. To find to the contrary would suggest a certain degree of disingenuity in corporate disclosures. Therefore,

H_{4a}. Discretionary disclosure by Texaco should be higher for topics prioritized by management at any particular period point in time.

Certain events thrust corporations into the public's attention in ways that are uncomfortable for managers. Often, the pursuit of profits interferes with a company's ability to consider public goods such as the environment. On other occasions, corporate practices may be in conflict with the sense of justice and proper behavior that exists in a society. These situations require companies to either establish or repair their reputations as good corporate citizens. In accord with the notion that such goodwill efforts are necessary for corporate success, discretionary disclosure pertaining to these sensitive topics becomes necessary. If disclosure does relate in its magnitude to these particular pressures, a certain strategic purposefulness is evinced. A hypothesis that captures this inquiry is

H_{4b}. Discretionary disclosures by Texaco about social matters will be higher in years when such matters are made highly visible by the media.

Summary

The overall objective of the hypotheses of this paper is to establish a basis for the appreciation of a company's disclosures over a lengthy period of time. These hypotheses posit some alternative and some complementary notions about discretionary information. Whereas, H_1 suggests that these disclosures have an increasing trajectory of their own, the three parts of H_2 offer the idea that disclosures reflect the changing contours of the company. Within H_2, alternative possibilities of corporation size, income and debt are offered. In the two hypotheses of H_3, corporate governance structures form another set of possible influences on disclosure. Both the composition of the

Board and its leadership are put into question in this effort. Hypothesis 4 adds a different dimension. Instead of TDD, these hypotheses look at the reasons why selective disclosures might be made by matching their timing to internal strategies and external issues.

METHODOLOGY

The large volume of discretionary disclosures in the 98-year history of Texaco precludes the manual assessment of the data. Therefore, NUD*IST 4.0 was employed for the management and quantification of the data.[3] Using a sample of eight annual Texaco reports chosen at random, the necessary coding trees were built so as to allow the software to recognize the classifications of disclosures that were needed for the testing of the hypotheses.

NUD*IST quantifies texts into standardized text line units that constitutes 72 characters. This serves as the unit of analysis for the paper, providing a compromise between smaller units (e.g., words) and larger ones (e.g., paragraphs).

For purposes of this paper, no part of the financial statements, including the associated notes, is considered a discretionary disclosure. The emergence of governmental concern with the Securities Acts of the 1930s, together with the progressive elaboration of accounting regulation by a series of semi-public bodies (e.g., APB, FASB), has certainly expanded the scope of required disclosure in these areas. Although some discretionary data may be contained therein, finding it would be very difficult. On the other hand, the entirety of narratives such as the President's Letter and Management Discussion and Analysis[4] are considered completely discretionary disclosures. Furthermore, other "free form" narratives such as Review of Operations are also considered discretionary. This attribute makes these sources ideal as the targets of the data analysis.

Texaco's annual reports from 1903 to 2000 were considered by this paper. A quick review of these documents, however, revealed that between 1903 and 1927, Texaco's annual report comprised nothing other than the financial statements. The absence of discretionary disclosure, as it has been defined, in those years eliminates them from consideration for the empirical work.[5] Nonetheless, the lack of these disclosures in the early years does not preclude this paper's claim to have covered all discretionary disclosures over the history of the firm.

Hypothesis 1 is tested using TDD and some subsets of that metric. Specifically, non-financial information and future-oriented/forward-looking

(FOFL) information are measured and extracted. These types of disclosures are particularly important because they have been historically neglected despite their relevance to many interested parties (AICPA, 1994). Nonfinancial information is defined as information that is not measured in dollars or the change in quantities that are themselves measured in dollars. FOFL information is typically denoted by future tense verbs or phrases (e.g., will, is likely to) and includes both quantitative and qualitative expressions. The use of these subsets in this context will be to demonstrate the robustness of the general findings.

For purposes of Hypothesis 2a, company size was measured with total assets. Other measures such as total sales and market capitalization were much more volatile in their dependence upon oil prices. In order to eliminate inflation effects, assets for each year were restated in 1999 dollars.[6] Among the many measures of profitability for Hypothesis 2b, return on net-worth and earnings margin were selected. The first puts income in the context of stockholder's equity. The second contextualizes income with sales. These numbers are needed to avoid scale effects. In order to measure debt for Hypothesis 2c, the debt to equity ratio was used. For these purposes, the numerator is restricted to long-term debt, since the proper focus is upon equity equivalents (Ross, Westerfeld, & Jordan, 1995). The debt to equity ratio is the most used standard for comparisons of this sort in the literature.

Hypothesis 3 requires a measure of the proportion of outside directors on the Texaco Board in each period. Since the Board varied in size over the years, a proportion of outside directors to total directors was constructed. This was done through a comparison of the names listed as officers of the corporation and those listed as board members. The second part of the third hypothesis also used such a check of officers and board members, this time restricted to the CEO and Chairperson roles. This was reduced to a binary coding (0, 1) that distinguished years of the dual leader structure from the single leader structure.

The final hypothesis set also requires specific measures. With regards to corporate strategies, one objective measure of importance or salience in a given year resides with the total capital expenditure that is reported. Since the two critical strategies for a diversified oil company like Texaco are exploration/production and refining, they are the ones for which data were collected from the income statement. Again, yearly expenditures were restated into 1999 dollars to control for inflation. The last hypothesis concerns the relationship of disclosure to important social events. Following Wiseman (1982) and Patten (1992), environmental events were singled out for specific analysis with the designation of the 1969 Santa Barbara and the 1989

Exxon Valdez oil spills. The other events of interest that were used for the purpose of the non-environmental dimensions of the hypothesis were the several wars fought by the US, the price fixing success of OPEC and major litigation against the company (including employment discrimination in 1996/1997 and Pennzoil in the early 1990s). Thus, an understanding of the more unusual and more traumatic external events that have affected Texaco produces an informed set of phenomena to which selected disclosure could have been addressed.

RESULTS

Descriptive Information

From 1928 to 1999, Texaco provided 78,048 standard lines of TDD or about an average of 1,095 lines per year. This ranged broadly from a low of 136 lines in 1931 to a high of 2,854 lines in 1992. Discretionary disclosure also fluctuated greatly from year to year. For example, from 1929 to 1930, this disclosure fell off by 41%, but from 1935 to 1936 it increased by 134%. Considerable change is also apparent over the last 20 years. For example, gains of over 350 lines occurred in 1980, 1990 and 1992, but steep declines also occurred recently (e.g., 1984, 1993, 1998). TDD, as well as year-to-year marginal disclosure, is depicted in Fig. 1. This figure demonstrates that even though a distinct increasing trend exists, the pattern is by no means uniform or continuous on a year-to-year basis.

A similar trend can be observed for non-financial discretionary disclosure (NFDD). Varying from a low of 16 lines in 1931 to a high of 1,581 lines in 1992, Fig. 2 shows that non-financial information tends to comprise 499 lines in the average report. In percentage terms, non-financial information averaged 43% of total discretionary information (minimum 12% in 1931, maximum 63% in 1988). Over the years, the trend in non-financial information is distinctly increasing, but with a slope less steep than the total (15.46 as opposed to 30.25). Even larger year-to-year changes can be observed for the non-financial information, such as the 487% increase in 1936 and the 59% decrease in 1931.

A similar, but more extreme, pattern can be observed for the FOFL information that constitutes, on average, 8% of total discretionary information. This type of information ranged from a low of four lines (1%) in 1937 to a high of 507 lines (25%) in 1997. FOFL information, negligible until the late 1940s, ratched up slowly before a one-time spike in 1980 and a

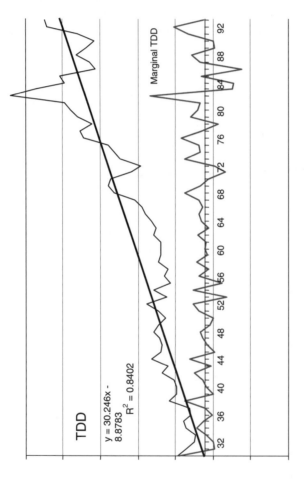

TDD

$y = 30.246x - 8.8783$
$R^2 = 0.8402$

Marginal TDD

Dimension	Min	Year	Max	Year	Average
Total lines in TDD	136	1931	2,854	1992	1095
Significant incremental lines between years	-763	1993	735	1980	
Percentage of incremental lines	-41%	1930	134%	1936	

TDD: total discretionary disclosure

Fig. 1. Total Discretionary Disclosure (TDD): Texaco 1928–1999.

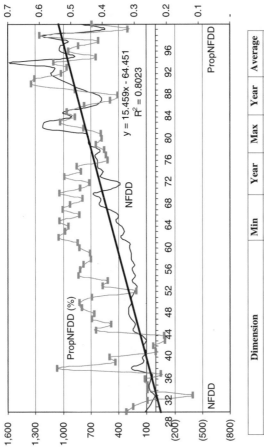

Dimension	Min	Year	Max	Year	Average
Total lines in NFDD	16	1931	1581	1992	499
NFPD as percentage of TDD (%)	12	1931	63	1988	43
Significant incremental lines between years	-698	1993	483	1992	
Percentage of incremental lines	-59%	1931	487%	1936	

NFDD: non-financial discretionary disclosure, PropNFDD: proportion of NFDD to TDD, TDD: total
discretionary disclosure

Fig. 2. Absolute and Proportional Non-Financial Discretionary Disclosure: Texaco 1928–1999.

more sustained period of highs in the mid-1990s. Fig. 3 shows the trend of FOFL since 1928.

Total assets possessed by Texaco rose gradually from $4.4 billion in the first year (1928) to a peak of $60.4 billion in 1984. Important international divestitures reduced asset size during the 1990s to a recent low that was only modestly above the average for the entire period of ($26.2 billion). Fig. 4 shows the trend of both total assets juxtaposed upon the trend of TDD.

The "Golden Era" for Texaco was also the period of its maximum sustained profitability. Between 1948 and 1970, the profit margin exceeded 10% each year. This contrasts with profit margins that only twice exceeded 5% from 1976 to 2000. Throughout the 72 years, Texaco was profitable in every year except two, 1932 and 1989, and had an average profit margin of 8%. Its best year was 1928, when its profit margin was 23%. Other profitability metrics reiterate these patterns. Fig. 5 shows the trend of both TDD and earnings/profit margin.

The debt to equity ratio of Texaco remained within a fairly tight band for most of the period under consideration. Specifically, this metric varied between 7% and 30% between 1928 and 1983. Thereafter, the debt to equity ratio normalized in the range of 40% and 60%, with severe spikes in 1984 (80%) and 1987 (104%). This ratio reflects Texaco's acquisition and divestiture activity of the last two decades, during which debt was first taken on and then shed. Fig. 6 shows the trend of TDD and the debt to equity ratio.

The proposition of Board members who were outsiders (OUTSIDER) ranged from slightly more than half (54%) in 1931, to much closer to all (93%) in both 1997 and 1998. On average, three-quarters of Texaco's Board tended to be outsiders. Most of the years under study saw Texaco led by the single office holder structure. In only nine years did a separate person hold the CEO title and the Chairman position. These years tend to occur in the later years (1964, 1970 and 1986–1992). The relatively few years in the dual structure may limit the ability to test its impact on discretionary disclosure. Fig. 7 shows the trend of TDD and the proportion of outside directors (OUTSIDER).

Other social disclosures (Social & Political or SP) show at least four peaks. The first occurred from the late 1930s to the early 1940s. The second came in the late 1960s to the early 1970s. The third and fourth appeared in the late 1980s to the mid-1990s. Although non-environmental social disclosures, in some years, nearly disappeared (two lines in 1947), they have also been quite salient (maximum of 462 lines in 1942). On average, Texaco devoted 97 lines to this type of information, or an average of 12% of TDD. Many of the early years were marked by a dearth of environmental issues (EI) content in the Texaco annual reports. This changed in the late 1960s

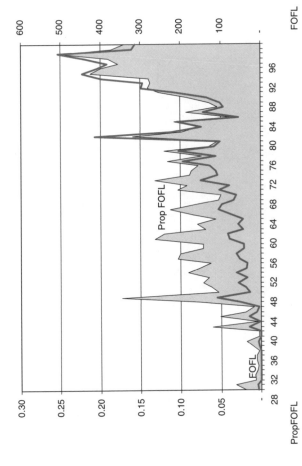

Dimension	Min	Year	Max	Year	Average
Total lines in FOFL	4	1937	507	1997	117
FOFL as % of TDD	1	1937	25	1997	8
Significant incremental lines between years	-192	1981	313	1980	
Percentage of incremental lines (%)	-90	1942	2,900	1941	

FOFL: future oriented – forward looking discretionary information, TDD: total discretionary disclosure,
PropFOFL: proportion of FOFL to TDD

Fig. 3. Trend of Absolute and Proportionate Future Oriented-Forwarding Looking Discretionary Information: Texaco 1928–1999.

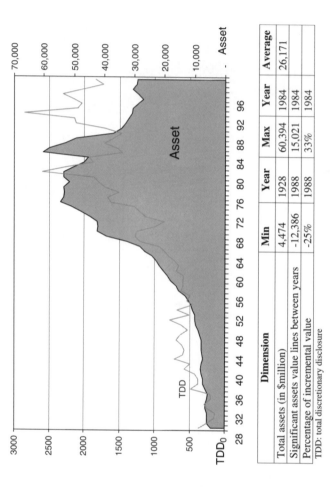

Dimension	Min	Year	Max	Year	Average
Total assets (in $million)	4,474	1928	60,394	1984	26,171
Significant assets value lines between years	-12,386	1988	15,021	1984	
Percentage of incremental value	-25%	1988	33%	1984	

TDD: total discretionary disclosure

Fig. 4. Trends of Total Assets and Total Discretionary Disclosure: Texaco 1928–1999.

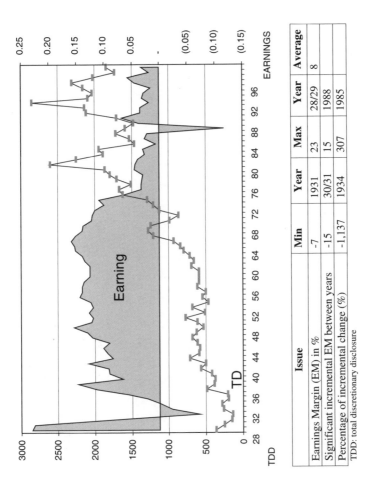

Issue	Min	Year	Max	Year	Average
Earnings Margin (EM) in %	-7	1931	23	28/29	8
Significant incremental EM between years	-15	30/31	15	1988	
Percentage of incremental change (%)	-1,137	1934	307	1985	

TDD: total discretionary disclosure

Fig. 5. Trends of Earnings Margin and Total Discretionary Disclosure: Texaco 1928–1999.

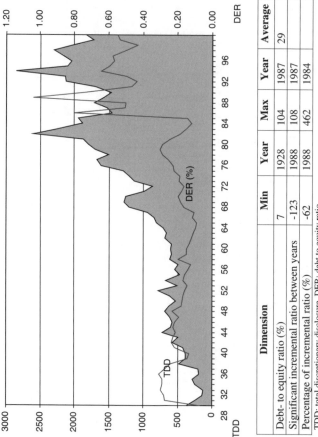

Dimension	Min	Year	Max	Year	Average
Debt- to equity ratio (%)	7	1928	104	1987	29
Significant incremental ratio between years	-123	1988	108	1987	
Percentage of incremental ratio (%)	-62	1988	462	1984	

TDD: total discretionary disclosure, DER: debt to equity ratio

Fig. 6. Trends of Leverage and Total Discretionary Disclosure: Texaco 1928–1999.

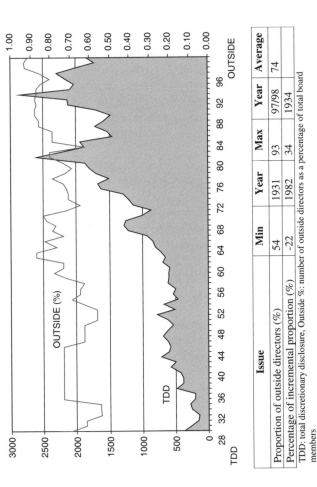

Issue	Min	Year	Max	Year	Average
Proportion of outside directors (%)	54	1931	93	97/98	74
Percentage of incremental proportion (%)	-22	1982	34	1934	

TDD: total discretionary disclosure, Outside %: number of outside directors as a percentage of total board members

Fig. 7. Trends of Board of Directors Composition and Total Discretionary Disclosure: Texaco 1928–1999.

and again in the late 1980s, although this was not sustained between those points. Fig. 8 shows the trend of non-environmental social/political disclosure (SP) and EI disclosure since 1928, in terms of the level of disclosure and their proportion to the TDD.

As expected, the salience of different strategies wax and wane in their appearance within discretionary disclosure. Both the exploration/production strategy and the refinery strategy hit a low mark in the 1934 report, with a scant ten and four lines, respectively.The former reaches an apex in 1980 with 543 lines of text, or 32% of all discretionary lines. The latter is most prominent in 1992 where 179 lines (14%) are devoted to this discussion. During the years, Texaco averaged an 809 million dollar expenditure on exploration/production and 170 million dollars on refining activities. Fig. 9 shows the trend of the exploration & production strategy and refinery strategy disclosures since 1928.

Hypothesis Tests

The first hypothesis stipulated an increase in discretionary disclosure over time. The Spearman Rho test was used to evaluate this relationship. It was found significant at $p < 0.001$ ($n = 0.94$). Hypothesis 1 was also evaluated using just the non-financial information and just the FOFL information. In both cases, the correlation was above 0.90, which was significant at $p < 0.001$. Texaco produced more discretionary disclosure as it proceeded through the twentieth century.

The idea of Hypothesis 2a is that there is a relationship between company size and disclosure degrees. The Spearman correlation between the two variables was 0.83, significant at the $p < 0.01$ level. This was also the conclusion of a Wilcoxon Rank Sum that organized the years according to relative degrees of disclosure and size.

Hypothesis 2b posits a positive relationship between profitability and the level of discretionary disclosure. The results of both the Spearman correlation test and the Wilcoxon Rank Sum test fail to confirm this hypothesis. The direction of the test coefficients is negative, rather than positive. Higher discretionary disclosure appears to occur in period of low corporate profits, not high corporate profits, although this is not a statistically significant relationship.

The final hypothesis pertaining to the attribute of the company relates the debt position of the firm to its disclosure levels. Hypothesis 2c, tested with both Spearman and Wilcoxon tests, proved significant and in the predicted direction at $p < 0.01$. This hypothesis is confirmed.

(A)

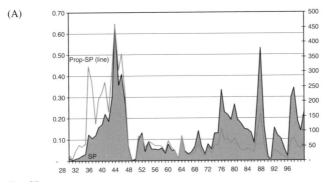

Prop-SP   SP

Issue	Min	Year	Max	Year	Average
Total lines in SP Disclosure	2	1947	462	1942	97
Significant incremental lines between years	-264	1987	248	1942	
Percentage of incremental lines (%)	-98	1947	1,100	1990	
SP as % of TDD	1	1989	64	1942	12
% Over TDD: Largest incr. between years	-24	1946	36	1934	
% TDD: Percentage of incremental lines	-98	1947	8,800	1990	

SP: social and political disclosure, Prop-SP: proportion of social and political disclosure to total discretionary disclosure, TDD: total discretionary disclosure

(B)

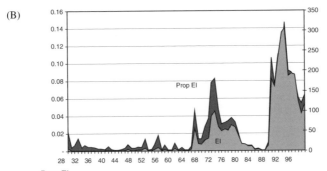

Prop EI   EI

Dimension	Min	Year	Max	Year	Average
Total lines of EI	2	1931	307	1993	41
Significant incremental lines between years	-120	1994	166	1989	
Percentage of incremental lines (%)	-89	1956	1300	1988	
EI as % of TDD	0.1	1942	14.7	1993	2.4
Percentage of Increment of EI over TDD	-91	1956	1402	1988	

EI: environmental information (absolute amount), PropEI: environmental information divided by TDD, TDD: total discretionary disclosure

Fig. 8. (A) Trends of Absolute and Proportional Social and Political Disclosure: Texaco 1928–1999. (B) Trend of Absolute and Proportionate Environmental Information: Texaco 1928–1999.

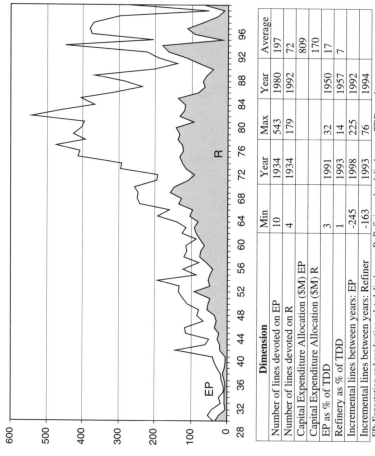

Dimension	Min	Year	Max	Year	Average
Number of lines devoted on EP	10	1934	543	1980	197
Number of lines devoted on R	4	1934	179	1992	72
Capital Expenditure Allocation ($M) EP					809
Capital Expenditure Allocation ($M) R					170
EP as % of TDD	3	1991	32	1950	17
Refinery as % of TDD	1	1993	14	1957	7
Incremental lines between years: EP	-245	1998	225	1992	
Incremental lines between years: Refiner	-163	1993	76	1994	

EP: Expectation and production related disclosures, R: Refining related disclosures, TDD: total discretionary disclosure

Fig. 9. Trend of Discretionary Disclosure Related to Dominant Corporate Strategy: Texaco 1928–1999.

Two hypothesis concerned governance structure. Hypothesis 3a, pertaining to the degree of outsider representation on the Board of Directors, is significantly related to discretionary disclosure at $p < 0.01$, using both tests. Hypothesis 3b, relating to the type of leadership structure (dual or singular) to disclosure, is also significant at the same $p < 0.01$ level. For this test, however, care is needed in its interpretation because of the disproportionality in the frequency of the two types of years that are being contrasted.

The final set of hypotheses pertains to uniquely important types of disclosure. A significant relationship exists between the levels of strategic disclosure and the degree of capital expenditure. This is true for both strategies considered, exploration/production and refining. In confirming Hypothesis 4a, this evidence suggests that Texaco tended to provide more description of the activities that the company spend more money on in any given year.

Hypothesis 4b related discretionary disclosure and a group of particularly important events that were selected due to the believed interest by important external constituencies on these occurrences. Using both absolute and proportionate measures, a significant association ($p < 0.01$) exists between the timing of major environmental oil-related calamities and disclosures related to environmental issues. A similar results exists around a set of social events. Disclosures increase markedly around the timing of World War II, the OPEC embargo, the Pennzoil fiasco and the discrimination litigation of the 1990s. Thus, Hypothesis 4b is confirmed.

DISCUSSION

Discretionary disclosure at Texaco has clearly increased over the years. For more than the first quarter of the company's existence (1902–1927), there was no such thing, at least as it has been operationalized in this paper. In contrast, the last fifth of the company's life (1980–2000) was marked by historically unprecedented levels of disclosure. The middle half-century (1928–1979) evinced a gradual transition from one extreme to the other.

The annual report of the more modern era not only contains much more discretionary information of a narrative form, but also contains types of information that were heretofore unrepresented in this media. Using Texaco, this paper documents the appreciable rise in non-financial information, and more recently FOFL data. If the AICPA's Jenkins Report (AICPA, 1994) is to be believed, these types of input are keenly and uniquely demanded by the users of annual reports. Even in the absence of regulation, a positive corporate communication response appears to have occurred.

Looking individually at the hypotheses, there seems to be no shortage of plausible explanations for the provision of discretionary disclosures. Beyond H_1, five relationships for TDD are posited. Four of these are solidly supported. In addition, discretionary disclosures were shown to be in keeping with the enactment of managerial focus on selected activities (strategy), as well as with the external events that are occasionally thrust upon the company, that are of a magnitude where a response is expected.

The paper provides information about several possible correlates of discretionary disclosure. Looked at in isolation, a case could be made that when firms have larger asset size, they will tend to disclose more discretionary information. The rise of Texaco as an important force in the oil industry was paralleled with its increase in willingness to disclose information. However, substantial questions about the relevance of asset size in this context might emerge from a closer assessment of the data. As asset size at Texaco diminished in the last decade, a corresponding decline in disclosure did not occur. Thus, the proposition that managers provide information as a natural response to increased complexity and volume may be true for increases only. Perhaps the stimulation of the demand for information, once responded to, creates a momentum of its own. In other words, disclosure levels may continue after the factors that called for them have changed or evaporated.

Disclosure seems to follow variations in the debt position of the firm more closely than it does in asset size. The statistically significant results of relating these two variables are reiterated by a visual observation that the high watermark of discretionary disclosure occurs at roughly the same time that Texaco elevated its use of debt financing. As Texaco transitioned from a company that used borrowed capital sparingly to one that had almost as much debt as equity, it also expanded its narrative treatments of its operations in its annual reports. The power of creditors vis-à-vis discretionary disclosure is difficult to gainsay.

The most surprising result was the negative relationship between profitability and disclosure. This hypothesis expected managers to be more forthcoming when they had excellent news to report. Instead, the opposite seems to be the case at Texaco. Apparently, the absence of favorable news creates an incentive to create more narratives. Perhaps, managers have an incentive to distract readers of their reports with information that points to other favorable features of past performance or future prospects. "Spin" might take more words and sections to accomplish than the simple and unvarnished relating of good news. In other words, success might speak for itself, whereas the lack of success might require carefully elaborated contextualizations.

This paper may be a product of the industry that it reports upon. That is, the relationships and regularities that it identifies may be limited to the oil industry.

As acknowledged, the oil industry is a very special one. That which motivates us to know more about it may also prevent us from generalizing beyond it. For example, oil and the other extractive industries are highly affected by global product prices that individual firms cannot effectively control. This may distort the impact of profitability. Furthermore, the astonishing capital intensity of this industry's operations may create a unique consequence of size. Nonetheless, in other important ways, the companies in the oil industry are obligated to behave in ways similar to all other large companies. Accordingly, a public that has heard quite a bit about environmental issues may demand disclosures that would calm its fears about the repeat of these problems. Only further research can disentangle the industry effects of corporate disclosure.

Several other potential limitations should be recognized. First, the use of a single company case study limits the generalization of the results of this study. Results from a single company study are very specific to the history and condition of that company. An application of the results, even to the companies within the same industry, should be limited and based on strict assumptions. Second, the use of annual reports as the only tool to study the discretionary disclosure policy may limit the explanation of agency theory in discretionary disclosures. Sufficient explanation of the agency theory perspective in discretionary disclosure has to include the entire dissemination of corporate communication such as annual reports, the SEC 10-K filing, proxy statements, web-site content, analyst meeting and other investor relation activities. However, since the annual report is issued by management at the end of every fiscal year, all material information in the other forms of disclosure, may have been incorporated in the annual report. Third, since the oil and gas industry is considered to be a high-risk endeavor that involves advanced technology, it is important to evaluate discretionary disclosure in relation to the proprietary theory of information. A proprietary theory of information may provide a better perspective on why management may withhold or delay disclosure of certain type of information. This theory may have to modify agency theory to provide a more precise basis on which management motivations for discretionary disclosure can be understood. Finally, the use of self-constructed coding tree and related definitions may limit the reliability of the disclosure counts in NUD*IST. This may be due to the fact that the construction of the coding tree and related definitions are data-driven instead of theory based. Therefore, different coders may produce different level of disclosure counts due to the ambiguity of language and the less than perfect conversion of it into the coding tree of this software.

The findings in this study indicate that over an extended period of time, the level of discretionary disclosure tended to increase. Except for earnings margin, all other variables such as size, debt, proportion of outside directors, leadership structure and investment opportunity set are associated with the level of discretionary disclosure. However, detailed analyses show that at several points in time, particularly during periods of lower earnings margins, management was not consistent in issuing discretionary disclosure. Some of the findings suggest that management used much discretion in the disclosure process in order to maintain their credibility. The inconsistent level of disclosure and the use of self-serving disclosures further reveal that management has not been completely forthright about the performance and the prospects of the company. In other words, there appears to be a tendency to use some degree of obfuscation in order to maintain credibility.

Future research will be needed if the goal is to shed light on the adequacy and quality of disclosure in the oil and gas industry. This paper is a first step in what could be a rich methodological vein that offers considerable insight.

NOTES

1. During the decade, Texaco became an early advertising sponsor for television. The Texaco Star Theatre featured commercials with memorable jingles such as the one that gave its name to this paper.

2. The belief in the value of external parties as independent board members has continued through the recently enacted Sarbanes-Oxley Act.

3. This software, formally titled Non-numerical Unstructured Data Indexing, Searching and Theorizing, provides a multi-functional way to conduct content analysis. An obvious advantage over manual methods is less propensity to err and the provision of an automatic indexing of the results. A full description of the processing of the data is beyond the scope of this paper.

4. A management discussion and analysis section is now required part of the annual reporting of publicly traded companies to the SEC. However, the contents of this section has not been stipulated by regulation.

5. The inclusion of these years would have the effect of strengthening the statistical evidence to accept the hypotheses.

6. This used conversion factors published by the American Institute for Economic Research.

REFERENCES

American Institute of Certified Public Accountants (AICPA). (1994). *Improving business reporting: A customer focus meeting the information needs of investors and creditors.* New York: AICPA.

Brief, R. (Ed.). (1986). Accounting thought and practice through the years. New York: Garland Publishing Inc.

Brief, R. (1987). Corporate financial reporting at the turn of the century. *Journal of Accountancy*, (May), 142–161.

Brock, H., Klingstedt, J., & Jones, D. (1988). *Oil and gas accounting*. Denton, TX: Professional Development Institute.

Eccles, R., & Mavrinac, S. (1995). Improving corporate disclosure process. *Sloan Management Review, 36*(4), 11–25.

Grant, J., Fogarty, T., Bricker, R., & Previts, G. (2000). *Corporate reporting of nonfinancial performance indicators and operating measures*. New York: Financial Executives Research Foundation, Inc.

Greene, W. (1985). *Strategies of the major oil companies*. Ann Arbor, MI: UMI Research Press-Research for Business Decisions.

Hast, A. (Ed.). (1988). *International directory of company histories* (Vol. IV). Chicago: St. James Press.

Jensen, M., & Meckling, W. (1976). Theory of the firm: Managerial behavior, agency costs and ownership structure. *Journal of Financial Economics, 3*, 305–360.

Knowles, R. (1983). *The first pictorial history of the American oil and gas industry 1859–1983*. Athens, Ohio: Ohio University Press.

Leftwich, R., Watts, R., & Zimmerman, J. (1981). Discretionary corporate disclosure: The case of interim reporting. *Journal of Accounting Research, 19*(Suppl.), 50–77.

Lev, B. (1992). Information disclosure strategy. *California Management Review, 34*, 202–230.

Malone, D., Fries, C., & Jones, T. (1993). An empirical investigation of the extent of corporate financial disclosure in the oil and gas industry. *Journal of Accounting, Auditing & Finance, 8*(3), 249–273.

Patten, D. (1992). Intra-industry environmental disclosures in response to the Alaskan oil spill: A note on legitimacy theory. *Accounting Organization and Society, 17*(5), 571–575.

Peirce, W. (1996). *Economics of the energy industries*. Westport, CN: Praeger. Qualitative Solutions and Research Ltd, 1997. *QSR NUD*IST 4 User Guide*, Sage Publications Software.

Rappaport, A. (1998). *Creating shareholder value, a guide for managers and investors*. New York: Free Press.

Ross, S., Westerfeld, R., & Jordan, B. (1995). *Fundamentals of corporate finance* (pp. 58–59, 65). Homewood, IL: Irwin Publishing Company.

Schipper, K. (1981). Discussion of voluntary corporate discretionary corporate disclosure: The case of interim reporting. *Journal of Accounting Research, 19*(Suppl.), 85–88.

Shuman, R. (1940). *The petroleum industry: An economic survey*. Norman, Oklahoma: University of Oklahoma Press.

Singhvi, S., & Desai, H. (1971). An empirical analysis of the quality of corporate financial disclosure. *The Accounting Review, 46*(1), 129–139.

Texaco, Inc. (1991). *A short history of Texaco, 1902–1991*. New York: Texaco, Inc.

Time. (1998). Texaco: A series of racial horror stories. *Time*, May 5, pp. 42–43.

Watts, R., & Zimmerman, J. (1978). Towards a positive theory of the determination of accounting standards. *The Accounting Review, 53*, 112–134.

Watts, R., & Zimmerman, J. (1986). *Positive accounting theory*. Englewood Cliffs, NJ: Prentice-Hall.

Williamson, H., Andreano, H., Klose, G., & Daum, A. (1963). *The American petroleum industry: 1899–1959. The age of energy*. Evanston: Northwest University Press.

Williamson, H., & Daum, A. (1959). *The American petroleum industry:1899–1959, the age of energy*. Evanston, IL: Northwestern University Press.

Wiseman, J. (1982). An evaluation of environmental disclosures made in corporate annual reports. *Accounting Organizations and Society, 7*(1), 53–63.

Yergin, D. (1992). *The prize: The epic quest for oil, money, and power*. New York: Simon and Schuster.

AN ALTERNATIVE ESTIMATION METHOD OF THE EQUITY RISK PREMIUM USING FINANCIAL STATEMENTS AND MARKET DATA

Martti Luoma, Petri Sahlström and Reijo Ruuhela

ABSTRACT

This paper develops a method to estimate the equity risk premium. The method exploits the Earn Back Period (EBP) formula presented by Luoma and Ruuhela (2001), which is a generalization of the P/E ratio. The EBP has a clear theoretical interpretation and can be used to compare stocks with different earnings growth rates, while the P/E ratio is not useful if stocks have substantially different growth rates. Since growth is taken into account, differences in EBPs are due to risk. Using this property, a stock's risk premium is derived from the stock's current P/E ratio and from its growth rate of earnings. For investors, this offers a practical method for evaluating stocks.

1. INTRODUCTION

The core of an investment decision is to assess whether a compensation, i.e. risk premium, is high enough to warrant accepting a particular risky investment project. Therefore, the estimation of the risk premium is one of the most

Advances in Accounting, Volume 22, 229–238
ISSN: 0882-6110/doi:10.1016/S0882-6110(06)22010-8

important tasks in an investment process. Because of the central role of the risk premium it is not surprising that much effort has been put into investigating it (see Kocherlakota (1996) for a review of market risk premium).

Asset risk premium estimation methods can be classified into two categories based on their theoretical framework. The first group is based on market equilibrium models, e.g. CAPM and APT. In this approach, a particular model is chosen and its parameters are estimated using market data and/or financial statement data. For example, in the CAPM framework we can estimate the market risk premium and the beta coefficient of a stock using market data to obtain an estimate of the risk premium of that stock. The main problems of this approach are the assumptions of the model and the estimation of the parameters. For example, in the CAPM framework it is assumed that the market is efficient. Furthermore, the assumptions of the model imply that the risk premium is always correct, i.e. the security lies in the security market line. Since it is assumed that the risk premium is correct, the estimation of it is probably not so interesting. Furthermore, recent evidence suggests that CAPM does not work well in practice.[1] Even though Fama and French (1993, 1996) suggest that the APT model describes expected returns better, Fama and French (1997) find that the estimates of the risk premium using CAPM and APT are both imprecise due to estimation problems.

Another way to tackle the question of the risk premium is to use some equity valuation method. The background of these methods lies in dividend discount models (see e.g. Okunev & Wilson, 1999). The main characteristic of these models is that they exploit both market and financial statement data by taking the market assessment of a company (price of an asset) and the company's accounting reports (financial statements) into account. Probably the most famous of these models is Gordon's model. It defines the price of a stock as a function of current dividend payment, constant dividend growth rate and required rate of return. Alternatively, the risk premium of a stock is obtained by plugging in the market price of a stock and solving the required rate of return. In addition to this rather simple model, different kinds of models that rely on the discounting of cash flows or earnings variables are proposed to value assets, e.g. EVA[2] and discounted free cash flows.

The purpose of this paper is to develop an alternative method to estimate the risk premium of a stock by exploiting the Earn Back Period (EBP) formula presented by Luoma and Ruuhela (2001). The method developed in this paper is based on the property that the differences in the EBPs of the stocks are due to risk even in the case of different growth rates. Using this property and the EBP formula a new method to measure the equity risk

premium using financial statements and market price of the equity is derived. Moreover, the strengths of the method are analyzed and possible
drawbacks discussed.

The rest of the paper is organized as follows. The EBP formula by Luoma
and Ruuhela (2001) is presented and its analog with P/E ratio illustrated in
the next section. The measure of the risk premium is then derived. In Section
3, the properties of the EBP and the new risk premium estimation method
are discussed. Section 4 provides a conclusion.

2. THEORETICAL FRAMEWORK

In spite of the fact that the P/E ratio is the most common stock valuation
measure, it is rather difficult to use in comparing different kinds of firms.
This stems from the fact that the P/E ratio is the number of years needed for
a firm to earn back its price, P, given its earnings, E. This interpretation of
the P/E ratio is feasible only if earnings have zero growth. Comparison
across firms is also possible but if firms have different growth rates it is not
reasonable. Some ad hoc methods, like PEG[3], have been proposed to take
growth into account but their problem is a lack of theoretical background
(see e.g. Peters, 1991). Stemming from that problem, Luoma and Ruuhela
(2001) present a new stock valuation measure, the EBP, which takes into
account different growth rates. The interpretation remains same as in the
case of P/E ratio with zero growth, i.e. the EBP is the number of years
needed for a firm to earn back its price. In that sense the EBP is a generalization of the P/E ratio. Because of this property, the properties of the
P/E ratio relevant to this study are introduced first.

2.1. Theory of the P/E Ratio

Let P_0 be the price of a stock in the beginning of a year 0, E_0 the (expected)
earnings of a stock in year 0, g the (expected) growth rate of earnings and r
the required rate of return $= r_f + \Delta r$, where Δr is risk premium and r_f is risk-
free rate of return.

To avoid the problem of the dividend policy, assume that E is earnings
available to shareholders, which could be paid out as dividends. Therefore,
the stock price is as follows:

$$P_0 = \sum_{t=1}^{\infty} \frac{E_t}{(1+r)^t} \tag{1}$$

It follows for non-growing earnings,

$$P_0 = \frac{E_0}{r} \qquad (2)$$

and for a constant growth rate in perpetuity,

$$P_0 = \frac{E_0(1 + g)}{r - g} \qquad (3)$$

This is the Gordon (1962) model with the above assumption of payable earnings. Using the Gordon (1962) model, the current P/E ratio for a stock is

$$\frac{P_0}{E_0} = \frac{1 + g}{r - g} \qquad (4)$$

Therefore, the P/E ratio is a function of the growth rate and the required rate of return. Since the required rate of return is a function of risk-free return and risk premium:

$$P/E = f(g, r_f, \Delta r) \qquad (5)$$

We can relax the constant growth assumption and define the price in terms of no-growth value from Eq. (2) plus the present value of growth opportunities ($PVGO$):

$$P_0 = \frac{E_0}{r} + PVGO = \frac{E_0}{r_f + \Delta r} + PVGO \qquad (6)$$

For this price, the P/E ratio is

$$\frac{P_0}{E_0} = \frac{1}{r_f + \Delta r} + \frac{PVGO}{E_0} \qquad (7)$$

Therefore, the P/E ratio depends on r_f, Δr and $PVGO$. From the practical point of view, the main problem of the P/E ratio is that both, risk and growth opportunities, affect the P/E ratio. Therefore, the P/E ratio is not a useful tool for the valuation of firms with different growth rates or for firms with different risk levels. For this reason, Luoma and Ruuhela (2001) present a generalized version of the P/E ratio, EBP, that takes into account different growth rates.

2.2. Theory of the EBP

To take growth into account, the EBP is defined to be the number of years that a firm with constant earnings growth rate needs to earn an amount equal to the price. Following Luoma and Ruuhela (2001), the EBP can be derived as follows:

Let P_0 be the price of a stock at the beginning of year 0, E_0 the (expected) earnings of a stock in year 0, g the (expected) growth rate of earnings and EBP = Earn Back Period.

It follows that (expected) earnings in year t are

$$E_t = E_0(1 + g)^t \tag{8}$$

According to the definition of the EBP

$$\sum_{t=0}^{EBP-1} E_0(1 + g)^t = P_0 \tag{9}$$

Using college algebra and leaving out zero subscripts for simplicity, the solution is

$$EBP = \frac{\ln(1 + g\frac{P}{E})}{\ln(1 + g)} \tag{10}$$

The main assumption of the model is that growth is constant. A theoretical advantage of EBP with respect to the P/E is that its scale is linear, meaning that a step anywhere on the scale has the same meaning. From a practical point of view, the advantage is that it clearly shows the time in years needed to earn back a price of the stock.

Next, two important special cases for the EBP are presented.

First, the EBP ratio for a non-growing but risky asset is

$$\lim_{g \to 0} EBP = \lim_{g \to 0} \frac{\ln(1 + g\frac{P}{E})}{\ln(1 + g)} = \frac{P}{E} \tag{11}$$

Therefore, for zero growth firms the EBP ratio is the same as the P/E ratio.

Second, the EBP for risk-free but growing asset is defined. Because the P/E for a risk-free asset[4] is $1/r_f$, it follows from Eq. (10) that the EBP for the risk-free asset is

$$EBP_{r_f} = \frac{\ln(1 + g\frac{1}{r_f})}{\ln(1 + g)} \tag{12}$$

Since interest payments are re-invested every year, $g = r_f$ for the risk-free asset[5] and Eq. (12) becomes

$$EBP_{r_f} = \frac{\ln 2}{\ln(1 + r_f)} \tag{13}$$

A stock's EBP is a function of the P/E ratio and growth rate (see Eq. 10). By assuming that stocks are correctly priced and that the growth rate is correctly estimated, the differences in EBPs are due to risk. This can be seen from Eq. (1) where the stock price depends on the discount rate that affects the risk premium, given risk-free rate of return and earnings expectations. As a consequence, stocks with the same risk premium, i.e. with same risk, have the same EBP. An analogy to the P/E ratio is that stocks with the same risk premium *and* with same growth have the same P/E ratio. Contrary to the P/E ratio, the EBP can be used to compare stock with different growth rates and the differences in the EBPs are due to differences in the risk premium.

2.3. Derivation of the Risk Premium using the EBP

By utilizing the above property of the EBP a stock's risk premium can be derived. To obtain a stock's risk premium we can solve the EBP for the stock and calculate, according to the definition of the risk premium (Δr), how much greater r_f must be in Eq. (13) so that $EBPr_f$ becomes equal to the EBP, i.e. we have to solve an equation with respect to Δr:

$$EBP = \frac{\ln 2}{\ln(1 + r_f + \Delta r)} \tag{14}$$

The solution for the risk premium is

$$\Delta r = \exp(\frac{\ln 2}{EBP}) - 1 - r_f \tag{15}$$

According to Eq. (15), the risk premium decreases steadily as the EBP increases, i.e. the risk premium is a monotonic transformation of the EBP and its value depends on the value of r_f.

In order to calculate the risk premium of a stock, we need the stock's EBP or we can use Eq. (10) to obtain an alternative form for Eq. (15)

$$\Delta r = \exp\left[\frac{\ln 2 \ln(1 + g)}{\ln(1 + g\frac{P}{E})}\right] - 1 - r_f \tag{16}$$

3. SOME PROPERTIES OF THE EBP AND THE RISK PREMIUM

As Eq. (16) shows, the Δr is a function of current P/E ratio and earnings growth. From a practical point of view, the current P/E ratio is quite easy to obtain. On the other hand, the needed estimate of the earnings growth may not be unambiguous. To investigate the sensitivity of EBP and the risk premium on growth rate and P/E ratio, we use a well-known approximate formula for an error of function with two variables, $z = f(x,y)$

$$\Delta z \approx \frac{\partial z}{\partial x}\Delta x + \frac{\partial z}{\partial y}\Delta y \tag{17}$$

where Δz, Δx and Δy are estimated errors of z, x and y, respectively and $\partial z/\partial x$ and $\partial z/\partial y$ are partial derivatives of a function z.

Applying Eq. (17) to Eq. (10) we have

$$\Delta EBP \approx \frac{\frac{P/E \ln(1+g)}{1+gP/E} - \frac{\ln(1+gP/E)}{1+g}}{(\ln(1+g))^2}\Delta g + \frac{g}{(1+gP/E)\ln(1+g)}\Delta\frac{P}{E} \tag{18}$$

To get some idea about the size of the error of the *EBP* we assume that the maximum errors of g and P/E are ± 20 percent. Assume further that the growth rate is 0.13 and the P/E ratio is 15. These are perhaps rather typical values in practice. In this case, the largest error of growth rate of 0.13 is ± 0.026 and for a P/E of 15 it is ± 3. Using Eq. (18) we obtain the errors for the *EBP*, which are presented in Table 1. The respective errors for the risk premium are also shown. According to Table 1, it is useful to have errors with the same sign since errors have opposite effects on the *EBP* in this example. Furthermore, errors in P/E ratios are more critical than errors in growth rates. This is a useful property since it can be expected that usually estimates of the P/E ratios are more accurate than estimates of the growth rates.

Table 1. Some Errors in the *EBP* and the Risk Premium for a Growth Rate of 13 Percent and a P/E Ratio of 15 where Errors are ± 20 percent.

Error of growth rate(%)	+20.0	−20.0	+20.0	−20.0
Error of P/E ratio(%)	+20.0	+20.0	−20.0	−20.0
Growth component of *EBP* error	−0.58	0.58	−0.58	0.58
P/E component of *EBP* error	1.08	1.08	−1.08	−1.08
Total error of *EBP* (years)	0.50	1.67	−1.67	−0.50
Total error of risk premium (in per cent units)	−0.4	−1.3	2.0	0.5

The *EBP* for the risk-free asset assuming, for example, a risk-free rate of 5.5 percent equals 13.1 according to Eq. (13). Therefore, it is not feasible for a risky asset to have $EBP > 13.1$ because in that case the risk premium would be negative according to Eq. (10). Hence nonfeasible combinations of growth rate and P/E ratio are those values, which fulfill an unequation

$$\frac{\ln(1 + g\frac{P}{E})}{\ln(1 + g)} > 13.1 \tag{19}$$

i.e. feasible values fulfill a condition

$$1 + g\frac{P}{E} \le (1 + g)^{13.1} \tag{20}$$

Feasible and nonfeasible areas for this example are depicted in Fig. 1. If a pair of growth rate and P/E ratio lies in the nonfeasible area, then the growth and/or the P/E ratio have been misestimated or the stock is over-priced.

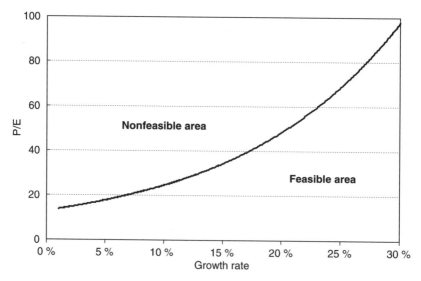

Fig. 1. Feasible and Nonfeasible Combination of P/E Ratio and Growth Rate Assuming a Risk-Free Rate of 5.5 Percent.

4. CONCLUSIONS

The advantages of the proposed risk-premium estimation approach are numerous. First, it is rather simple to use in practice. It uses only three variables, i.e. earnings, price and earnings growth, which can be obtained from financial statements and from a stock market. Furthermore, an investor can use the risk premium to assess whether stocks are mispriced and nonfeasible combinations of growth rates and P/E ratios can be detected. Second, it is not very sensitive to errors in growth estimate. This is important since it can be expected that in practice the growth estimate contains more or less estimation error. Third, compared to dividend discount models, the proposed method requires only the earnings growth estimate, while dividend discount models need estimates of the earnings growth and the payout ratio.[6] Fourth, the method does not have unrealistic assumptions and estimation problems for the equilibrium models. Fifth, the constant growth of earnings is needed only for years from the present time to EBP and the assumption of constant growth rate can be relaxed.

Possible errors in the method arise from two sources. First, the variables used contain estimation error. Second, the method does not take into account earnings growth after the EBP. However, this is probably not a serious problem since, it can be expected that firms usually do not have consistently high-earnings growth rates longer that their EBP. Furthermore, it is not realistic to predict growth rates beyond the EBP, which is usually 7–10 years. As a consequence, it can be assumed that growth rates after the stock's EBP have only a minimal impact on stock valuation.

NOTES

1. See, for instance, Banz (1981), Basu (1983), Fama and French (1992), and Lakonishok, Shleifer, and Vishny (1994).
2. See, for instance, Copeland, Koller, and Murrin (1994) and for evidence, Claus and Thomas (2001).
3. PEG is defined as P/E ratio divided by growth rate.
4. Let P be the price of a risk-free security and r_f its maturity yield. Therefore, the earnings for the risk-free security is $P \times r_f$ and the P/E ratio,

$$P/E = \frac{P}{P \times r_f} = \frac{1}{r_f}$$

5. Since interests are continuously compounded, the growth of the earnings (interest payments) of the risk-free security is the same as its maturity yield, i.e. $g = r_f$ in the case of a risk-free security. This holds under the assumption of constant interest rates. In practice, interest rates change over time. However, it can be assumed that interest rate changes are not predictable in the long run. As a consequence, the best prediction of the risk-free rate is the current risk-free rate.

6. The earnings growth rate is contingent on the payout ratio under the assumption of no external financing. In practice, however, external financing is possible. This means that dividend payments do not restrict earnings growth rates since a firm can raise new equity or debt to finance its growth and dividend payments. This means that the proposed model is better than models based on dividends since in the case of the proposed model we do not have to predict the payout ratio, which is contingent on earnings growth and the use of external financing. On the other hand, taxation affects this issue. However, the model can be adjusted to take into account taxation effects but since taxation systems vary across countries the simplifying assumption that taxation is not taken into account is made.

REFERENCES

Banz, R. W. (1981). The relationship between return and market value of common stocks. *Journal of Financial Economics, 9*, 3–18.

Basu, S. (1983). The relationship between earnings yield, market value, and return for NYSE common stocks: Further evidence. *Journal of Financial Economics, 12*, 129–156.

Claus, J., & Thomas, J. (2001). Equity premia as low as three percent? Evidence from analysts' earnings forecasts for domestic and international stock markets. *Journal of Finance, 56*, 1629–1666.

Copeland, T., Koller, T., & Murrin, J. (1994). *Valuation: Measuring and managing the value of companies*. New York, NY: Wiley.

Fama, E. F., & French, K. R. (1992). The cross-section of expected stock returns. *Journal of Finance, 47*, 427–465.

Fama, E. F., & French, K. R. (1993). Common risk factors in the returns on stocks and bonds. *Journal of Financial Economics, 33*, 3–56.

Fama, E. F., & French, K. R. (1996). Multifactor explanations of asset pricing anomalies. *Journal of Finance, 51*, 55–84.

Fama, E. F., & French, K. R. (1997). Industry cost of equity. *Journal of Financial Economics, 43*, 153–193.

Gordon, M. (1962). *The investment, financing and valuation of the corporation*. Homewood, IL: Irwin.

Kocherlakota, N. R. (1996). The equity premium: It's still a puzzle. *Journal of Economic Literature, 34*, 42–71.

Lakonishok, J., Shleifer, A., & Vishny, R. W. (1994). Contrarian investment, extrapolation, and risk. *Journal of Finance, 49*, 1541–1578.

Luoma, M., & Ruuhela, R. (2001). How to develop price per earnings ratio to a fair valuation measure of a stock? *Technical Analysis of Stocks & Commodities, 19*, 34–38.

Okunev, J., & Wilson, P. (1999). What is an appropriate value of the equity risk premium? *Journal of Investing, 8*, 74–79.

Peters, D. J. (1991). Valuing a growth stock. *Journal of Portfolio Management, 17*, 49–51.

PERSPECTIVES ON GLOBAL RESEARCH

PERFORMANCE REVIEWS, THE IMPACT OF ACCOUNTING RESEARCH, AND THE ROLE OF PUBLICATION FORMS

Salvador Carmona

ABSTRACT

Universities and national assessment bodies of higher learning perform research assessment exercises that constitute crucial events for the careers of scholars and for the funding of institutions. Nonetheless, there are debates about the weightings that should be assigned to different forms of research output such as books, research monographs, journal articles, or research projects. In this study, I draw on citation analysis to measure the impact of accounting research. The data shown in this paper indicate the superiority of generalist over specialist journals in the diffusion of accounting research; question the use of journal rankings, and suggest that books and research monographs exert a considerable impact on the diffusion of accounting research. Such findings have policy implications for national assessment bodies, universities, and the accounting academia.

INTRODUCTION

What counts as research in accounting? Universities, business schools, and national assessment bodies of higher learning evaluate research productivity

Advances in Accounting, Volume 22, 241–267
ISSN: 0882-6110/doi:10.1016/S0882-6110(06)22011-X

241

in order to make decisions on faculty tenure and promotion (Englebrecht, Iyer, & Patterson, 1994; Swanson, 2004), and, importantly, to allocate research funding among universities (e.g., the Research Assessment Exercise in the UK, see Whittington, 1997). Although these reviews have a long tradition and constitute crucial events in the success of an institution's mission (Johnson, Reckers, & Solomon, 2002), there is considerable debate about the weightings assigned to various forms of research output such as books, research monographs, journal articles, and research projects (Gray, Guthrie, & Parker, 2002). In the UK, for example, Humphrey, Moizer, and Owen (1995) found that only a small number of factors correlated significantly with departmental rankings: articles published in academic journals, total number of publications, and short research pieces.

The dissemination of knowledge constitutes a central aspect of the research process; the ultimate aim is to have research read and to influence ongoing and prospective investigations – not merely to achieve publication (Schneider, 1995). Drawing on the importance of research diffusion, review committees often rely upon certified measures of the dissemination of research (e.g., impact indexes of journal articles) to alleviate the considerable burden and cost that such assessments impose on institutions and panel members (Otley, 2002, p. 401). Although indicators of research diffusion accumulate considerable consensus (e.g., impact indexes of journal articles), their application to the accounting discipline needs to be qualified.

Few accounting journals are indexed in well-regarded databases. For example, the Accounting Research Directory (ARD) gathers data from *The Accounting Review; Accounting, Organizations and Society; Contemporary Accounting Research; Journal of Accounting, Auditing and Finance; Journal of Accounting and Economics;* and *Journal of Accounting Research.* Brown (1996) used the ARD in his investigation of the most influential authors, articles, PhD-granting institutions, and faculties. He admitted, nonetheless, that there were limitations to the database, saying "this is a small subset of journals."[1] Yet although it appears to be a contentious issue to draw upon databases containing only a small number of accounting periodicals and to use this limited information to assess such a crucial aspect of the research process as the diffusion of knowledge in the discipline, it is common practice. The Social Science Citation Index (SSCI) is another comprehensive database that collects data from all subjects in social sciences but indexes only the following accounting periodicals: *The Accounting Review; Auditing: A Journal of Theory and Practice; Accounting, Organizations and Society; Contemporary Accounting Research; Journal of Accounting and Economics;* and *Journal of Accounting Research.*[2] Overall, the sample of accounting journals indexed in databases is small, and this results in studies that are "limited in scope" (Hasselback, Reinstein, & Schwan, 2000).

In this study, I address the role that publication forms like journal articles and research monographs play in the process of dissemination of accounting research. In this manner, I examine the importance that such forms of publication may play in assessment exercises. In doing so, I also attempt to address the extent to which journal articles published in generalist, specialist, or related discipline journals may contribute to the diffusion of accounting research.

The remainder of this paper is organized as follows. The next section outlines the theoretical framework upon which the study is based. In particular, I address the role of publication forms like generalist and specialist journals, books, and research monographs in the dissemination of accounting research, followed by a description of the database used in this investigation. The results address an overview of the data included in the database, followed by a depiction of patterns of dissemination of research in generalist and specialist journals in accounting, as well as in related discipline outlets. The results section ends with an examination of books and research monographs in the diffusion of accounting knowledge. Finally, I discuss the results of this investigation and make some suggestions for future research in this area.

THEORETICAL FRAMEWORK

Journal Rankings, Generalist, and Specialist Outlets

Journal rankings are considered, at least implicitly, in reviews of research performance. The rationale rests on the belief that rankings provide objective data on diffusion for both periodicals and journal articles (e.g., impact indexes), and that the double-blind referee process used by journals serves as a good proxy for research quality. Drawing on these perspectives, review panels usually rate academic journals highly in the weightings of performance reviews (Brinn, Jones, & Pendlebury, 2001), which in turn signals to the academic community the research goals set by institutions of higher learning and policy makers. Investigations addressing journal rankings have relied upon either faculty surveys or citation analyses (Lowe & Locke, 2005).

A survey conducted by Ballas and Theoharakis (2003) on perceptions of quality and readability of journals, and completed by 1,230 accounting academics around the world, demonstrated the influence of three contextual factors: (1) researcher's geographic origin (e.g., North America, Europe, Asia, Australia, and New Zealand), (2) research orientation (e.g., financial accounting and capital markets, management accounting, auditing, accounting theory, taxation, and international), and (3) journal affiliation (e.g., authorship, membership on its editorial board).

There are a number of country-specific surveys examining perceptions of journal quality. Herron and Hall (2004) collected data from a sample of 616 tenure-track business school faculty members at AACSB-accredited[3] universities and colleges in the United States regarding their perceptions of 152 journals. Their results revealed significant differences in perceived quality across journals and scholarship areas, and the authors concluded that area-specific journal ratings (e.g., accounting information systems, audit, cost and managerial accounting, ethics, international accounting, financial accounting, history, and taxation), provide better information than does a single overall ranking list. Finally, in a web-based survey forwarded to all academics listed in the *British Accounting Review Research Register*, Lowe and Locke (2005) asked respondents to classify well-known accounting journals according to methodological perspectives. They found statistically significant ranking differences between researchers in the area of capital markets and finance versus academics from all other accounting areas.

As mentioned, there are few accounting journals in well-regarded databases, making it difficult to use *citation analysis* to produce journal rankings in this discipline.[4] Recently, however, Milne (2001) created a database that comprised citations from 27 academic journals in accounting to identify journal rankings according to the geographical bases of the outlet (e.g., UK, USA), and the authors (e.g., US, non-US). His findings revealed that, other than for a few journals, accounting periodicals have little general relevance to accounting academics as a whole. Furthermore, the diversity of citation behavior questions the theoretical validity of some attempts to generate universal journal rankings, even within a single country.

In sum, existing research from both the survey and the citation analysis persuasions cast doubts on the idea of universal journal rankings. Conversely, it is suggested that such categorizations should discriminate among geographical areas (Ballas & Theoharakis, 2003), methodological perspectives (Lowe & Locke, 2005), or the diverse areas of accounting research (Herron & Hall, 2004). Therefore, a study that adopts a standpoint of diffusion of knowledge to develop a ranking of academic journals for a specific accounting area seems in order, and may clarify the present debate in several respects.

First, such investigation would shed light on the rationale of performing area-wise journal rankings in exercises of research assessment, as suggested by the existing literature. Second, such study could contribute to the stream of research that examines the structure and diffusion of accounting knowledge within academic journals in accounting (Bricker, 1988). In particular, we still have much to learn about the extent to which the periodicals of a given area are interlocked. In this manner, such an investigation would enhance understanding about the patterns of dissemination in accounting research between generalist and specialist academic journals.

Arguably, there are three belief systems on the role of generalist and specialist journals in the diffusion of accounting research. On the one hand, some academics might predict that the exchange of knowledge between such groups of periodicals is non-existent or minimal. Under this belief system, the causes of such detachment would be attributable to the fact that the topics addressed and the theories advanced in specialist journals differ substantially from those of generalist outlets. On the other hand, those contending that such categorizations of journals are interlocked may argue for a different direction of the influence. Considering that the flow of knowledge goes from generalist to specialist journals, articles published in the latter would be those that set the research agenda by addressing innovative topics and methodological approaches. Consequently, the dominance of generalist over specialist journals is reflected in a tendency on the part of authors who publish in specialist periodicals to quote authors appearing in generalist outlets. The opposite line of reasoning is used by those arguing a pre-eminence of specialist over generalist periodicals in the diffusion of knowledge.

Journal Articles of Related Disciplines

University departments are often ranked according to the number of articles published in a list of journals. In economics, for example, Kalaitzidakis, Mamuneas, and Stengos (2003) used a listing of 30 academic journals in economics to rank departments in that area. The caveat of the resulting listing was that publications outside the Kalaitzidakis et al. sample did not count as research: journals in related disciplines such as psychology that exert an influence on economics research. This weakness was explored by García-Ferrer, Poncela, and Carmona (2004), who showed that two Nobel Laureates in Economics, Professors Granger and Engle, had only 20% and 35% of their publications included in the Kalaitzidakis et al. ranking. García-Ferrer and Poncela also found that apart from a reduced number of top academic journals, there is no significant difference among periodicals in the aggregate measures of impact indexes and citation life, a result that concurs with that reported by Milne (2001).

There are two belief systems concerning the importance of related discipline journals in assessments of research performance. On the one hand, some academics argue that research productivity in accounting should be measured by publications in a list that restricts its scope to accounting journals. Therefore, such a view conforms to the underlying assumption in the Kalaitzidakis et al.'s journal rankings; academics in a particular discipline, it is argued, make their reputations by publishing in the outlets most read by their peers – those that address disciplinary topics – whereas periodicals in related disciplines are seldom examined by the profession, and hence should not count as accounting research. On the other hand, others would assert that accounting is an interdisciplinary subject and, as such, benefits from insights and theories produced in related disciplines like economics, finance, management, marketing, operations, organization, and sociology. There is, therefore, a rationale for accounting academics to target publication in journals of related disciplines, and hence articles appearing in such journals should count as accounting research.

Books and Research Monographs

What is the role of books and research monographs in the dissemination of accounting research? Existing studies on the role of publication forms in accounting have focused on academic journals (Brown, 1996; Milne, 2001). Implicit in this approach is the idea that journal articles have higher quality and diffusion potentials than do publication forms such as books and research monographs. Nonetheless, existing research states that books and book chapters should be considered in measuring research productivity. In psychology, for example, Nederhof (1989) compared the impact of journal articles to that of monographs and book chapters from seven university departments in the Netherlands, and found that books and book chapters produced by a department had a larger impact than articles, where impact was measured in terms of citations received in the year of publication and the two subsequent years. Although the most influential works were published in book form, their average impact was somewhat lower than journal articles.

This debate is of interest for purposes of performance reviews. As noted by Otley (2002, p. 391), review panels spend considerable time assessing the contribution of publication forms without an "external 'imprimatur' of quality, such as books, research reports and working papers." Inasmuch as the evaluation of publication forms other than journal articles constitute a burden on review panels, it is relevant to explore the extent to which it is worth pursuing such task.

There are two-belief systems concerning the role of publication forms other than journal articles in performance reviews. On the one hand, some argue that journal articles represent the premier venue for the dissemination of accounting research. In the market of diffusion of research, readers tend to examine the outlets that publish the most relevant research, and top journals therefore signal the highest measure of quality. Compared to journal articles, other publication forms would play a subordinate role in the diffusion of accounting knowledge, which in turn lowers the weights given in performance reviews to books and research monographs. Conversely, others contend that publication forms other than journal articles play a definitive role in the process of dissemination of research, as attested by the influential number of works published by such highly regarded university presses as Cambridge University Press, Harvard University Press, Oxford University Press, University of Chicago Press, Yale University Press; as well as publishing companies like Blackwell, Elsevier, and Routledge; and institutions like the Institute of Management Accountants (US), the Certified Institute of Management Accountants (UK), and the Brookings Institution.

DATA

I have focused this analysis on accounting history because it exemplifies a dynamic area in accounting research (e.g., Herron & Hall, 2004). For example, Brown (1996) identified accounting history as one of the existing paradigms in accounting research. Arguably, such dynamism may explain the interest of generalist journals in launching special theme issues in this area: *Accounting, Organizations and Society* (1991); *Accounting, Auditing and Accountability Journal* (1996); *Critical Perspectives on Accounting* (1998); *Accounting and Business Research* (2002); *European Accounting Review* (2002); and the *Journal of Accounting and Public Policy* (2004). In addition, accounting history has three specialist academic journals: *The Accounting Historians Journal; Accounting, Business and Financial History;* and *Accounting History.*[5] This number of specialist journals may be regarded as relatively high if compared to other accounting areas. Management accounting, for example, has only two specialized research outlets: *Journal of Management Accounting Research* and *Management Accounting Research.*

Accounting history is one of the few accounting areas in which the profession is well organized around an international association: The Academy of Accounting Historians. Furthermore, this area of the profession holds world congresses (e.g., the 11th Edition of the World Congress of Accounting Historians will be held in Nantes in 2006), international conferences (e.g., the *Accounting, Business and Financial History* Conferences, which are held annually in Cardiff, UK; the 5th International *Accounting History* Conference will be held in Alberta, Canada, in August 2007), and specialized workshops and seminars (e.g., the European Institute of Advanced Studies in Management offers a series of workshops in accounting and management history).

Taken together, these data argue that accounting history can be regarded as an active research area, the study of which may help us gain a better understanding of the trajectory and patterns of diffusion of accounting research. Yet, the relatively small size of accounting history vis-à-vis other accounting areas makes it suitable for conducting a comprehensive citation analysis through a purpose-built database.

The supporting database of this study covers the period 1990–1999. During that decade, historical matters attracted considerable interest in the agenda of accounting research, as exemplified by debates such as the new accounting history (Miller, Hopper, & Armstrong, 1991; Miller & Napier, 1993), gender and accounting (Kirkham & Loft, 1993), the professionalization of accounting (Walker, 1991, 1995), and the underpinnings of the emergence of cost management practices in organizations (Fleischman & Parker, 1991; Carmona, Ezzamel, & Gutiérrez, 1997). Furthermore, bibliometric research considers that an observation period of 10 years provides a sound basis to unfold patterns of diffusion of research (Van Leeuwen, Visser, Moed, Nederhof, & Van Raan, 2003).

The database includes all accounting history papers published in generalist journals,[6] such as *Abacus; Accounting, Auditing and Accountability Journal; Accounting and Business Research; Accounting, Organizations and Society; The Accounting Review; Contemporary Accounting Research; Critical Perspectives in Accounting; The European Accounting Review; Journal of Management Accounting Research;* and *Management Accounting Research.* Additionally, I have included all papers published in the three specialist accounting history journals written in English: *The Accounting Historians Journal; Accounting, Business and Financial History;* and *Accounting History.* With data gathered from specialist and generalist journals, the database widens the scope of bibliometric studies in accounting that drew upon generalist journals (e.g., Brown, 1996; Reiter & Williams, 2002) or specialist outlets (e.g., Carnegie & Potter, 2000).

The nationality of the authors was measured by their academic affiliation. Co-authored papers were adjusted by the number of authors; for example, a co-authored paper by three individuals affiliated with universities established in three different countries counted 1/3 for each country. In order to simplify the procedures of citation analysis, the nationality of the author was measured by the academic affiliation of the first-named author of the paper.

For each paper, the following data were collected: authorship, academic affiliation of author(s), full reference of the paper (journal in which the paper was published, year, and issue), classification of the paper according to the taxonomy offered by Carnegie and Napier (1996): studies of surviving records of firms, using accounting records in business history, biography, prosopography, institutional history, public sector accounting, comparative international accounting history, and innovative research methods in accounting history. The articles were also cross-classified by the accounting field addressed in the investigation (e.g., financial accounting, managerial accounting, auditing, and behavioral accounting). Finally, for papers using primary sources, the extent to which the "nationality" of such evidence coincided with that of the first-named author was examined.

The database also comprised bibliography data. For each reference made in the text, the following aspects were considered: the language of the cited work; whether the quoted reference was a journal article or a different source (e.g., book and research monograph); whether the work cited aimed at addressing the wider contexts of the investigation by referring to general, non-accounting events (e.g., by outlining the economic situation of the country); and whether the work referenced aimed at embedding the findings of the paper in comparative analysis by referring to similar studies conducted in other countries.

Citations indexed in the database could also refer to articles published in generalist accounting journals different from those comprising the database (e.g., *Journal of Accounting Research*). To enhance the analysis, the set of generalist journals was split into two classes: Generalist A research outlets, which were used to build the database that supports this paper; and Generalist B journals, which comprised generalist accounting outlets not indexed in the database (e.g., *Journal of Accounting and Economics*). Furthermore, I coded references in either specialist or generalist journals to outlets of related fields (e.g., economics: *American Economic Review*; economics and business history: *Business History, Business History Review, Economic History Review*; finance: *Journal of Financial Economics*; management: *Academy of Management Journal*; organization: *Organizations*;

and sociology: *American Journal of Sociology*). All business and economic history journals were grouped under the heading of "History", whereas "Others" was used to code articles published in journals of related disciplines.

In calculating the number of citations to authors and journals, I have adjusted for self-citations. In the case of authors, I have eliminated author self-citations: references within Author A's work to Author A and Author A's co-authors. For journals, I have eliminated journal self-citations: references to Journal X articles within Journal X articles.

RESULTS

Overview of the Data Included in the Database

The database comprised 410 papers.[7] Scholars affiliated with Anglo-Saxon institutions of higher learning led the authorship of articles, which in turn showed UK scholars to be the most prolific (154.9 articles), followed by scholars from the USA (133.57 articles), Australia (59.06 articles), Canada (17.5 articles), and New Zealand (8.17 articles). On the other hand, non-Anglo-Saxon scholars authored 38.25 articles (9.32%). This group was led by France (14.33 articles) and followed by Spain (7.33 articles) (Table 1).

Over the ten-year period of this study, specialist academic journals published 266 articles, or 64.87% of the publications indexed in the database. *Accounting, Business and Financial History* published the largest number of articles (129 or 31.46%); followed by *The Accounting Historians Journal* (106 or 25.85%), and *Accounting History* (31 or 7.5%). The group of generalist journals accounted for 144 articles (35.85%); it was led by *Accounting, Organizations and Society* (37 or 9.02%); *Critical Perspectives on Accounting* (29 or 7.07%); *Accounting, Auditing and Accountability Journal* (25 or 6.09%); and *Accounting and Business Research* (22 or 5.36%).

The database indexed 17,709 citations. In concordance with results about authorship, a substantial portion of citations were made by authors affiliated with Anglo-Saxon academic institutions (16,280 citations or 91.93%), whereas scholars affiliated with non-Anglo-Saxon institutions of higher learning made 1,409 citations or 8.07%. US scholars were those that made the highest proportion of citations (6,723 or 37.96%), followed by UK academics (5,717 or 32.28%), and Australians (2,625 or 14.82%). In turn, the non-Anglo-Saxon group was led by Spain (395 or 2.23%) followed by France (375 or 2.11%).

Table 1. Authorship by Countries and Journals.

Journal	Australia	Belgium	Canada	Czech Republic	France	Germany	Greece	Italy	Japan	Malaysia	Netherlands	New Zealand	South Africa	Spain	Sweden	Trinidad and Tobago	Turkey	Uganda	UK	United States of America	Total of Country
Abacus	9.2										1								5	1.8	17
Accounting Business Research	1.5				1						1								15.7	2.8	22
Accounting History	10.5		3									1							13	3.5	31
Accounting, Auditing and Accountability Journal	5.5											1							8	10.5	25
Accounting, Business and Financial History	13.53	1	4		12	1	2		1	0.3	1	3.17	0.5	4		1		0.5	70	14	129
Accounting, Organizations and Society	2		2.5											0.67	1				17.53	13.3	37
Contemporary Accounting Research																				2	2
Critical Perspectives on Accounting	6.33	1		0.33								1							8.67	11.67	29
Journal of Management Accounting Research																				2	2
Management Accounting Research																			4	2	6
The Accounting Historians Journal	0.5																1			0.5	1
The Accounting Review	10		7		1	0.5						2		2.67					11.33	69.5	106
The European Accounting Review					0.33			1											1.67		3
	59.06	2	17.5	0.33	14.33	1.5	2	1	1	0.3	3	8.17	0.5	7.34	1	1	1	0.5	154.9	133.57	410

The Dissemination of Accounting Research across Academic Journals

The number of citations to journal articles was 3,724 or 21.02% of the 17,709 references (see Table 2), and were quite evenly split between generalist (1,786 or 47.59%) and specialist (1,938 or 52.04%) outlets. *The Accounting Historians Journal* was the specialist journal with the largest number of citations (985 or 26.45%), followed by *Accounting, Business and Financial History* (639 or 17.15%) and *Accounting History* (314 or 8.43%). On the other hand, citations made by generalist journals concentrated primarily on five periodicals: *Critical Perspectives on Accounting* (442 or 11.86%); *Accounting, Auditing and Accountability Journal* (402 or 10.79%); *Accounting, Organizations and Society* (394 or 10.58%); *Abacus* (205 or 5.50%); and *Accounting and Business Research* (178 or 4.77%). Overall, these five outlets accumulated 43.50% of the total citations made by generalist journals.

Table 3 shows citations to Generalist A and B and Specialist periodicals as well as those made to journals under the categories of "History" and "Others". As depicted in Table 3, Generalist A or B journals attracted a substantial portion of total references (2,851 or 76.55%), providing support for the belief that such periodicals play a key role in the generation and diffusion of accounting research.

Citations among generalist periodicals constitute a substantial proportion of the references received by this group of periodicals (1,441 or 50.54%). Although these data could provide reason to question the conclusion that research in this area is influenced by generalist journals, a similar flow toward generalist outlets exists from specialist journals. As shown in Table 3, references made by specialist journals largely targeted Generalist A or B periodicals: 1,410 or 72.75% of total references to journals of any class. In summary, the data in Table 3 indicate that the flow of citations within periodicals goes from specialist to generalist outlets, which in turn provides support for the belief that the latter represents an important source of knowledge in this area. In contrast to the influential role of articles published in generalist journals, studies appearing in specialist periodicals seemingly exert a lesser impact on research conducted in the discipline. For

Table 2.   Citations Made by Journals in the Database.

Journal	ABFH	AH	AHJ	AAAJ	AB	ABR	AOS	AR	CAR	CPA	EAR	JMAR	MAR	Total
Number of citations	639	314	985	402	205	178	394	6	18	442	65	34	42	3724
Percentage of total citations	17.15	8.43	26.45	10.79	5.50	4.77	10.58	0.16	0.48	11.86	1.74	0.91	1.12	100

Table 3. Citations made by Specialist and Generalist Journals (Adjusted for Journal Self-Citations).

	To Generalist A Journals	To Generalist B Journals	To Specialist Journals	To History Journals	To Other Journals	Total
References made by specialist journals	1,099 (56.71%)	311 (16.05%)	333 (17.18%)	140 (7.22%)	55 (2.84%)	1,786 citations (100%)
References made by generalist A journals	1,308 (73.24%)	133 (7.45%)	192 (10.75%)	120 (6.72%)	33 (1.85%)	1,938 citations (100%)
Total	2,407 citations (64.63%)	444 citations (11.92%)	525 citations (14.09%)	260 citations (6.98%)	88 citations (2.36%)	3,724 citations (100%)

example, journal self-citation in specialist journals accounts for 17.18% of total references and 10.75% of the citations made in generalist outlets. Overall, specialist journals received 525 citations (14.09%), a figure similar to that received by Generalist B outlets (444 or 11.92%).

Results shown in Table 3 reveal that History journals also influence research published in generalist or specialist outlets in accounting. Specialist journals had 140 citations (7.22%) to articles published in History journals, whereas articles in generalist journals cited works under the History heading 120 times (6.72%). Consequently, the influence of History articles on research performed in this accounting area is higher than that exerted by investigations in related fields (e.g., management, sociology, and economics). For example, articles published in journals of related disciplines received 55 citations (2.84%) from specialist journals and 33 references (1.85%) from generalist journals. In summary, journals of related disciplines accumulated 9.34% of total citations, which in turn provides some support for the notion that such journals exert an influence on accounting research.

In order to check for the consistency of these results, a journal ranking was constructed for this area. As a group, generalist journals not only accumulated the largest proportion of citations but, individually, they rated higher in the standings of most cited journals than did their specialist counterparts. The results shown in Table 4 indicate that three generalist journals lead in the ranking of the most influential outlets, with 1,532 citations or

Table 4.   Ranking of Journals in Accounting History
(Adjusted for Journal Self-Citations).

Journal	Published Since	Number of Citations Received	Adjustment Factor (Number of Years)	Citation Index
Accounting, Organizations and Society	1976	836	10	83.60
The Accounting Review	1926	433	10	43.30
Accounting and Business Research	1970	263	10	26.30
Accounting, Business and Financial History	1991	197	8	24.63
The Accounting Historians Journal	1974	224	10	22.40
Accounting, Auditing and Accountability Journal	1988	163	10	16.30
Journal of Accountancy	1905	163	10	16.30
Abacus	1962	151	10	15.10
Journal of Accounting Research	1963	127	10	12.70
Critical Perspectives on Accounting	1990	93	9	10.33
Economic History Review	1927	103	10	10.30
Business History	1958	90	10	9.00
Business History Review	1926	70	10	7.00
Accounting History	1996	20	3	6.67
Journal of Accounting and Public Policy	1982	29	10	2.90
Management Accounting Research	1989	28	10	2.80
European Accounting Review	1992	18	7	2.57
Administrative Science Quarterly	1956	24	10	2.40
Harvard Business Review	1922	20	10	2.00
Journal of Accounting and Economics	1979	20	10	2.00
Journal of Business Finance and Accounting	1974	20	10	2.00
Contemporary Accounting Research	1984	16	10	1.60

54.59% of total references made to journals listed in Table 4. *Accounting, Organizations and Society* achieved the top citation index (CI = 8.36), which is the result of dividing the number of citations by the number of years during which a journal could have obtained citations from articles indexed in the database. In addition, *Accounting, Organizations and Society* accumulated the largest number of citations – 836 – adjusted for journal self-citations. In the 1990s, for example, *Accounting, Organizations and Society*, a generalist journal, published the largest number of articles (37 pieces, see Table 1), which included a special issue on accounting history in 1991. The second position in the rankings is held by *The Accounting Review*, a journal that published only one accounting history paper during the 1990s. The data in the database indicate that the high standing of *The Accounting Review* is due to the considerable number of citations received from articles published in *The Accounting Historians Journal* (179 references or 41.33%), which regarded works published in *The Accounting Review* as a source of secondary materials, especially for events occurring during the first half of the 20th century. The third place in the standings is held by *Accounting and Business Research* (263 citations; CI = 26.30). In spite of being a mainstream accounting journal, the editorial policy of *Accounting and Business Research* has welcomed research in accounting history, and this has resulted in the publication of a number of influential articles (e.g., Ezzamel, Hoskin, & Macve, 1990, see below).

Accounting, Business and Financial History with a CI of 26.30 and *The Accounting Historians Journal* with a CI of 24.63 are the two most-cited specialist journals in the field. Although *Accounting, Business and Financial History* primarily publishes accounting history research based on UK settings, its editorial policy has encouraged studies on other countries' historiographies, resulting in the publication of country-focused special issues (e.g., France, in 1997) as well as commissioned papers on research published in languages different from English (e.g., in Spanish: Hernández Esteve, 1995). *The Accounting Historians Journal* also had broad aims and scope during the observation period of this study, although works published in this outlet usually addressed events in US settings.

Kendall's tau correlation coefficient was used to test for the consistency of the journal ranking. If the journal ranking was consistent for this area of accounting, the correlation coefficient for rankings calculated at two points in time would be positive and significant, either considering the entire journal ranking or after removing the most influential outlets from the ranking. Conversely, if the journal ranking lacked consistency, the removal of the most influential outlets from the standings would lead to a lack of significance in the Kendall's tau correlation for rankings of journals in different years.

Consequently, the correlation between the journal rankings were tested with and without the top three journals listed in Table 4 for the years 1992 and 1999. Data from 1992 were used because the sample of journals in the database was fairly complete in that year and periodicals were eligible to receive citations;[8] whereas 1999 constituted the last year of the period of study. The results from using the Kendall's tau coefficient show that there is no correlation between the journal rankings in 1992 and 1999 if the three top journals are removed from the standings. In contrast, there is a significant correlation ($tau = +0.41$; $p < 0.01$) when the three most cited journals are included in the rankings. Therefore, the findings of this study provide some support for the notion that a few journals constitute significant references for those working in the area, whereas accounting scholars do not discriminate among the other periodicals.

Taken together, results in Tables 3 and 4 provide support for the belief that generalist journals dominate their specialist counterparts with respect to the dissemination of accounting research. Furthermore, the data of this investigation suggest that there is no rationale for journal rankings in specific accounting areas.

Books and Research Monographs

The results of this study indicate that there are influential sources of accounting knowledge other than journal articles. Support for this contention stems from the frequency of citations referring to journal articles (3,724 or 21.02%) relative to works published in non-periodical sources, such as books and research monographs (13,985 or 78.98%).

Furthermore, Table 5 shows the most influential works in this area: those that obtained a CI higher than 2. The ranking is led by two pieces published in book form. Moreover, 11 out of the 27 most influential works were published as books: Edwards (1989), Johnson and Kaplan (1987), Chandler (1969), Chatfield (1977), Previts and Merino (1979), Brown (1905), Littleton (1933), Pollard (1965), Kedslie (1990), Larson (1977), and Garner (1954). Taken together, these results provide some support for the notion that books and research monographs constitute key venues for the dissemination of accounting knowledge.

The "Top 27" influential pieces in accounting history highlight some aspects of the diffusion of research in accounting history. A group of pieces address the debate on the emergence of cost accounting calculations (Johnson & Kaplan, 1987; Hoskin & Macve, 1986, 1988; Pollard, 1965; Hopper & Armstrong, 1991; Ezzamel et al., 1990). In the main, this debate examines the contention of the Neoclassical Economics School, which argues that increasing competition around the British Industrial Revolution and 19th century USA slashed the profit margins of firms. Consequently, firms implemented cost accounting calculations to improve organizational efficiency (Johnson & Kaplan, 1987). On the other hand, accounting historians of the Foucauldian persuasion contend that disciplinary and political motives lie at the heart of the implementation of early cost accounting systems (e.g., Hoskin & Macve, 1986, 1988; Loft, 1986; Miller & O'Leary, 1987). Furthermore, research under the labor-process school questions the

Table 5. The Most Influential Works
(Adjusted for Author Self-Citations).

Work	Number of Citations	Adjustment Factor (Number of Years)	Citation Index
Edwards (1989)	61	10	6.1
Johnson and Kaplan (1987)	54	10	5.4
Hopwood (1987)	52	10	5.2
Loft (1986)	52	10	5.2
Hoskin and Macve (1988)	51	10	5.1
Fleischman et al. (1996)	14	3	4.6
Miller and O'Leary (1987)	45	10	4.5
Hoskin and Macve (1986)	43	10	4.3
Carnegie and Napier (1996)	13	3	4.3
Funnell (1998)	4	1	4.0
Burchell, Clubb, Hopwood, Hughes, and Nahapiet (1980)	40	10	4.0
Chandler (1969)	38	10	3.8
Miller et al. (1991)	28	8	3.5
Hopper and Armstrong (1991)	28	8	3.5
Ezzamel et al. (1990)	32	9	3.5
Miller et al. (1991)	28	8	3.5
Chatfield (1977)	33	10	3.3
Parker (1990)	30	9	3.3
Previts and Merino (1979)	33	10	3.3
Brown (1905)	32	10	3.2
Littleton (1933)	31	10	3.1
Mepham (1988)	32	10	3.2
Pollard (1965)	30	10	3.0
Stewart (1992)	19	7	2.7
Kedslie (1990)	23	9	2.5
Larson (1977)	21	10	2.1
Garner (1954)	21	10	2.1

efficiency argument by contending that the deployment of management accounting techniques (e.g., budgets) was aimed at maximizing the efforts of workers without increasing their wages accordingly (e.g., Hopper & Armstrong, 1991). The labor-process school asserts that management accounting techniques played a significant role in the de-skilling of the labor process that occurred in Anglo-Saxon countries during late 19th and early 20th centuries.

Another group of pieces within the Top 27 most influential works represent comprehensive, secondary sources in accounting history research, which is the case of historiography studies such as those of Edwards (1989),

Previts and Merino (1979), Chatfield (1977), and Littleton (1933). Edwards (1989) drew on extensive analysis of secondary sources to address early practices of financial and management accounting in firms. Furthermore, he relied on primary sources to examine early practices of financial reporting by limited liability organizations. Previts and Merino (1979) provide a descriptive history of accounting history in the USA. The book constitutes a detailed and highly informative chronicle of American accounting from the colonial period to present. It traces the origins of the profession as well as the evolution of accounting in social, economic, and political terms and discusses the major figures that influenced accountancy and its practice. In contrast to Edwards (1989) and Previts and Merino's (1979) histories of accounting, the book of Chatfield (1977) addresses a history of ideas rather than presenting a chronicle of events or a factual summary. As noted by the author, relevance to contemporary problems was a primary test for inclusion of topics in the book. Lastly, Littleton (1933) offers a history of accounting to 1900 by examining the crucial events in each era. Unusual for a book written in 1933, it has an international focus, whereby it addresses the role of accounting in such important transformations as the shift from speculative ventures having terminable stocks in continuing businesses with permanently invested capital, as exemplified in the case of the East India Company (1600–1657).

A third group of works examines the accounting profession from either a sociological (Larson, 1977) or accounting standpoint (Kedslie, 1990), addressing aspects like closure of the profession to minority groups such as women.

In summary, the results indicate that articles published in generalist journals dominate specialist outlets in the diffusion of accounting research. Furthermore, the findings of this study provide support for the notion that other than for a few academic journals, accounting scholars do not discriminate among research outlets in an accounting area. Finally, the results suggest that publication forms like books and research monographs exert an enduring influence on the dissemination of accounting research.

GENERAL DISCUSSION

Universities and national assessment bodies of higher learning perform research evaluations that constitute crucial events for the careers of scholars and for the funding of institutions. Such reviews establish criteria of research quality to provide scholars with guidance, instil transparency in the process, and diminish the cost and burden that such evaluations exert on panel members (Otley, 2002). In the case of the Spanish research assessment exercise, for example, the norms enacted in the Official Gazette (*Boletín Oficial del Estado*) state the general pre-eminence of articles published in refereed journals over other publication forms, which in turn implies reliance on a journal ranking to discriminate among periodicals. In this study, the perspective of the dissemination of accounting research was adopted in order to address the rationale for using generalist, specialist, or related discipline outlets in journal rankings and to explore the perceived subordination of publication forms such as books and research monographs.

Citation analysis was used to examine patterns of dissemination of research in accounting. Given the small number of accounting journals indexed in databases such as the ARD and the SSCI, a purpose-built one that contained a wide array of generalist and specialist journals in the English language was created. The chosen area of study was accounting history, which may be regarded as a dynamic (Brown, 1996) and self-contained area (Lukka & Kasanen, 1996).

The results of this study indicate that Anglo-Saxon scholars dominate publications of journal articles in this accounting area. This finding does not seem to be influenced by the larger size of the Anglo-Saxon academic community vis-à-vis their non-Anglo-Saxon counterparts. For example, around the middle of the observation period of this investigation, the most prolific Anglo-Saxon country in the area of accounting history, the UK, registered 43 scholars with either research or teaching interests in accounting history (Gray & Helliar, 1994), whereas the *Società Italiana di Storia della Ragioneria* (Italian Society of Accounting History; Carmona, 2004) registered 155 members in the same year.

These findings are similar to those reported by Carmona and Gutiérrez (2003) in their analysis of accounting research. They gathered data from 13 top accounting journals and showed that 88.23% of the papers indexed in their database were authored by Anglo-Saxon scholars. In the case of accounting history, Carnegie and Potter (2000) found that 84.78% of articles published in specialist, accounting history journals were authored by Anglo-Saxon scholars. In short, these results indicate that the Anglo-centrism observed by Parker (1993) still persists and that research conducted by non-Anglo-Saxon scholars receives little visibility in international English-language journals.[9]

The finding that accounting research in international journals is dominated by Anglo-Saxon scholars has some policy implications. France, Italy, Spain, and the Germanic countries are deploying research assessment exercises.

Furthermore, policy makers in these countries establish criteria of publications in international journals in the English language as qualifying standards for positive assessments. In view of the small proportion of non-Anglo-Saxon scholars writing in international periodicals, such a policy has consequences for accounting research in those countries. Setting such criteria may signal goals of research visibility, but it ultimately involves the long-term endeavour of non-Anglo-Saxon scholars to publish regularly in international journals in the English language. Given the results of this study, a strict application of criteria of publication in international journals in the short term may imply a barely attainable goal leading to a considerable neglect of present research efforts in non-Anglo-Saxon countries. Therefore, the use of most highly ranked business journals in assessments of research performance is both discipline (Swanson, 2004) and country sensitive.

International journals have editorial policies that spell out visions of relevant research as well as notions of writing, structure, motivation, and focus. Scholars publishing in such outlets conform to the established understandings of relevance and academic etiquette which are imprinted in the culture of Anglo-Saxon institutions (Carmona, Gutiérrez, & Cámara, 1999; Brown, 2005). Thus, in the long term, for the policy makers of non-Anglo-Saxon countries to encourage scholars to publish in international journals may mean that Anglo-Saxon understandings of relevance and modes of writing become a substitute for national traditions of research. Paraphrasing Czarniawska (2006), the straight application of such policy could eventually result in accounting scholars doing anything but waiting for the next fashion coming from Anglo-Saxon institutions of higher learning.

Echoing concerns about universal journal rankings (Ballas & Theoharakis, 2003; Herron & Hall, 2004; Lowe & Locke, 2005), this investigation has produced a listing of journals for one area of accounting: accounting history. The results of this study demonstrate that a few journals play a significant role in the dissemination of accounting research. For the rest of the periodicals, there are no significant differences among their citation indexes. Therefore, these results are in-line with those reported by Milne (2001) for accounting and by García-Ferrer et al. (2004) for economics. The findings of both studies concur that, apart from a small number of periodicals, the academic community does not discriminate among academic journals.

These findings have clear policy implications. Review panels draw upon journal rankings to assess the quality of research and, similarly, a growing number of studies perform departmental rankings based on such listings (Kalaitzidakis et al., 2003). The data reported in this study suggest that a few outlets consistently rate high in these categorizations of periodicals, but that most of them have volatile standings. Furthermore, it is hard to find a breakpoint in the second group of journals that would lead to clear-cut distinctions between influential and less influential journals (see also Milne, 2001; García-Ferrer et al., 2004). Consequently, the results of this investigation advise review panels to exercise caution when using journal listings within specific areas of accounting. As far as departmental ranking is concerned, using such listings may result in departments not significantly different from many others and, eventually, in "a woeful lack of information in the ratings" (Thursby, 2000, p. 402).

Generalist accounting journals have a stronger impact on the diffusion of accounting research than do their specialist counterparts. As a group they receive substantially more citations than specialist periodicals do, and taken individually, they receive the highest ratings among the most influential periodicals in this area. These findings indicate that the flow of citations goes from specialist to generalist periodicals, suggesting that innovative, influential areas of research arise in the domain of generalist journals, and that articles published in specialist journals follow suit. For example, in the case of the debate on the emergence of cost accounting systems in organizations, articles were first published in generalist journals by Loft (1986) and Hoskin and Macve (1986, 1988) in *Accounting, Organizations and Society* and by Ezzamel et al. (1990) in *Accounting and Business Research*. Subsequently papers published in specialist periodicals deepened and extended the findings of these influential articles.

The number of specialist periodicals in accounting history during the observation period increased in 2004 from one to three, and then to four. Considering the subordinate role of specialist periodicals in the diffusion of knowledge in this area, it might be advisable to halt the process of establishing new outlets. In this way, articles published in specialist journals will not be dispersed. Arguably, efforts to improve the visibility of such outlets in the eyes of the academic community will result in more influential periodicals.

The results of this study (see Table 5) show that the ranking of the most influential articles is led by the works of Hopwood (1987), Loft (1986), Hoskin and Macve (1988), Fleischman, Mills, and Tyson (1996), and Miller and O'Leary (1987). This listing largely concurs with that of Brown (1996), who identified the works of Loft and of Hopwood, Miller, and O'Leary as some of the "classics" in accounting research. Therefore, the findings of this paper suggest the existence of paradigm stability in this accounting area.

In a related manner, the list of the Top 27 works contains only nine pieces published in the 1990s: Fleischman et al. (1996), Carnegie and Napier (1996), Funnell (1998), Miller et al. (1991), Hopper and Armstrong (1991),

Ezzamel et al. (1990), Parker (1990), Stewart (1992), and Kedslie (1990). Considering that the 1990s witnessed active debates in this accounting area, one could argue that it takes considerable time to disseminate research ideas. In order to examine this contention, the diffusion patterns of journals that were launched in or around the observation period (see Table 6) were examined by focusing on a specialist and a generalist outlet. Table 6 reveals that the diffusion of research published as articles follows a slow pattern in the case of new journals. Five years after publishing their first issues, the specialist journal shown in Table 6 had received only seven citations from journals included in the database, whereas the generalist journal had obtained 24 citations.

Technological improvements may enhance the low rates of diffusion of specialist journals in accounting history. Specialist periodicals in this area still do not fully benefit from indexing in electronic databases, not even by posting electronic versions of accepted papers in the journals' web page. These actions may improve the time-to-market of articles, and hence increase their relevance and visibility.

The findings of this study indicate that articles published in journals of related disciplines accumulate a considerable number of citations (9.34%), thereby influencing research in this area. Certainly, this result has implications for purposes of journal rankings. As shown in the case of Kalaitzidakis et al. (2003), it is tempting to use a restricted list of journals to assess the research productivity of departments and individuals. Nonetheless, such practices may be questionable (García-Ferrer et al., 2004). In the case of accounting, an interdisciplinary field that benefits from insights in related disciplines like economics, finance, management, marketing, operations, and sociology, the use of restricted journal listings would inevitably lead to a neglect in the attempts of accounting scholars to influence such disciplines reciprocally through articles adopting an accounting perspective.

The results of this study indicate that publication forms such as books and research monographs exert a decisive impact in accounting research, as shown by the fact that 11 of the 20 most influential works were published in

Table 6. Diffusion Patterns of Research Published in Recently Established Journals (Adjusted for Journal Self-Citation).

	Year of Foundation	1	2	3	4	5
Specialist journal	0		0	0	1	2	4
Generalist journal	0		0	3	8	3	10

book form. Although assessments of the quality of books and research monographs is time consuming (Otley, 2002), the results of this investigation advise that such publication forms cannot be neglected in performance reviews (Nederhof, 1989).

CONCLUDING REMARKS

Performance reviews in accounting grant considerable credit to journal articles. In this paper I adopt a perspective of dissemination of knowledge in order to examine the motivation of using a short or long list of accounting periodicals, vis-à-vis considering also other publication forms like books or research monographs, as well as journal of related disciplines. The results of this study have some policy implications. A number of non-Anglo-Saxon countries such as Spain and Italy are implementing, at the national level, policies of research assessment that place high value on publications in international journals. However, given the small number of journal articles published by scholars from such countries, caution is advised about the feasibility of such a policy in the short term and the consequences that it may have on some of the research traditions of those countries in the long term. The findings of this investigation also cast some doubt on the use of journal rankings by review panels; such listings include a small number of well-regarded outlets that rate consistently high; whereas the rest of the journals show high volatility in their standings. Furthermore, the data presented here indicate that journals in related disciplines and publication forms other than journal articles should be taken into consideration when assessing research in accounting.

NOTES

1. *The Journal of Accounting, Auditing and Finance* was not indexed in the ARD at the time of Brown's (1996) study.
2. *Review of Accounting Studies* and *Journal of Business, Finance and Accounting* have recently been accepted for indexing in the SSCI.
3. The Association to Advance Collegiate Schools of Business.
4. Studies in accounting using these databases have focused on the impact of specific journals (e.g., SSCI: *Journal of Accounting Research*, see Dyckman & Zeff, 1984; *Auditing: A Journal of Practice and Theory*, Smith & Krogstad, 1991), or, as noted above, on the identification of the "top 100" articles and the 123 most influential individuals in the discipline (ARD, see above Brown, 1996).

5. *De Computis*, a specialized, electronic journal in accounting history was launched in 2004.

6. I also checked all articles published in the *Journal of Accounting, Auditing and Finance; Journal of Accounting Research; Journal of Accounting and Economics;* and *Journal of Accounting and Public Policy* during the observation period. However, these outlets did not publish papers with a focus on accounting history.

7. Citations to archival sources were not included in the database.

8. *Accounting, Business and Financial History* was founded in 1990. Hence, articles published in such journals had the opportunity to be cited by 1992. On the other hand, *Accounting History* was not launched until 1996.

9. Hasselback and Reinstein (1994) found that 37% of US schools had no publications in any of the 40 journals considered in their investigation and that "the larger institutions granting accounting doctoral degrees tended to dominate the highest rankings" (p. 301).

ACKNOWLEDGEMENTS

This project is supported financially by the CICYT research grants # 01-0657 and SEJ-2004-08176-C02-01. I would like to thank Jose Carlos Molina for assisting with the management of the database. Previous versions of this paper were presented at the Annual Congress of the European Accounting Association (Seville, 2003); the Accounting, Business and Financial History Conference (Cardiff, 2003); and the World Congress of Accounting Historians (Oxford, Mississippi, 2004). I am grateful to the participants at these conferences and to Garry Carnegie, Dick Edwards, Mahmoud Ezzamel, Kari Lukka, and Steve Walker for their helpful suggestions.

REFERENCES

Ballas, A., & Theoharakis, V. (2003). Exploring diversity in accounting through faculty journal perceptions. *Contemporary Accounting Research, 20*, 619–644.

Bricker, R. J. (1988). Knowledge preservation in accounting: A citational study. *Abacus, 24*, 120–131.

Brinn, T., Jones, M. J., & Pendlebury, M. (2001). Why do UK accounting and finance academics not publish in top US journals? *British Accounting Review, 33*, 223–232.

Brown, L. D. (1996). Influential accounting articles, individuals, Ph.D. granting institutions and faculties: A citational analysis. *Accounting, Organizations and Society, 21*, 723–754.

Brown, L. D. (2005). The importance of circulating and presenting manuscripts: Evidence from the accounting literature. *The Accounting Review, 80*, 55–84.

Brown, R. (1905). *A history of accounting and accountants*. Edinburgh: Reprint Available from Beard Books (2003).

Burchell, S., Clubb, C., Hopwood, A., Hughes, J., & Nahapiet, J. (1980). The role of accounting in organizations and society. *Accounting, Organizations and Society, 22*, 5–27.

Carmona, S. (2004). Accounting History research and its diffusion in an international context. *Accounting History, 9*, 7–23.

Carmona, S., Ezzamel, M., & Gutiérrez, F. (1997). Control and cost accounting in the Spanish royal tobacco factory. *Accounting, Organizations and Society, 22*, 411–446.

Carmona, S., & Gutiérrez, I. (2003). Vogues in Management Accounting Research. *The Scandinavian Journal of Management, 19*, 213–231.

Carmona, S., Gutiérrez, I., & Cámara, M. (1999). A profile of European accounting research: Evidence from leading accounting journals. *The European Accounting Review, 8*, 463–480.

Carnegie, G., & Napier, C. (1996). Critical and interpretive histories: Insights into accounting's present and future through its past. *Accounting, Auditing and Accountability Journal, 9*, 7–33.

Carnegie, G., & Potter, B. (2000). Publishing patterns in specialist accounting History journals in the English language. *The Accounting Historians Journal, 27*, 177–198.

Chandler, A. D. (1969). *Strategy and structure: Chapters in the history of the industrial enterprise*. Cambridge: MIT Press.

Chatfield, M. (1977). *A history of accounting thought*. Huntington, NY: Krieger Publishing Company.

Czarniawska, B. (2006). The quiet European? *Journal of Management Inquiry* (forthcoming).

Dyckman, T. R., & Zeff, S. A. (1984). Two decades of the Journal of Accounting Research. *Journal of Accounting Research, 22*, 225–297.

Edwards, J. R. (1989). *A history of financial accounting*. London: Routledge, Chapman and Hall.

Englebrecht, T. D., Iyer, G. S., & Patterson, D. M. (1994). An empirical investigation of the publication productivity of promoted accounting faculty. *Accounting Horizons, 8*, 45–68.

Ezzamel, M., Hoskin, K., & Macve, R. (1990). Managing it all by numbers: A review of Johnson and Kaplan's relevance lost. *Accounting and Business Research, 20*, 153–166.

Fleischman, R. K., Mills, P. A., & Tyson, T. N. (1996). A theoretical primer for evaluating and conducting historical research in accounting. *Accounting History, 1*, 55–75.

Fleischman, R. K., & Parker, L. D. (1991). British entrepreneurs and pre-industrial revolution evidence of cost management. *The Accounting Review, 66*, 361–375.

Funnell, W. (1998). Accounting in the service of the holocaust. *Critical Perspectives on Accounting, 9*, 435–464.

García-Ferrer, A., Poncela, P., & Carmona, S. (2004). *From zero to infinity: The use of impact factors and journal rankings in the evaluation of academic economic research in Spain*. Mimeo, Universidad Autónoma de Madrid.

Garner, S. P. (1954). *Evolution of cost accounting to 1925*. Tuscaloosa, AL: University of Alabama Press.

Gray, R., Guthrie, J., & Parker, L. (2002). Rites of passage and self-immolation of academic accounting labour: An essay exploring exclusivity versus mutuality in accounting scholarship. *Accounting Forum, 26*, 1–30.

Gray, R. H., & Helliar, C. (1994). *The British accounting review research register*. London: Academic Press.

Hasselback, J. R., & Reinstein, A. (1994). A proposal for measuring scholarly productivity of accounting faculty. *Issues in Accounting Education, 10*, 269–301.

Hasselback, J. R., Reinstein, A., & Schwan, E. S. (2000). Benchmarks for evaluating research productivity of accounting faculty. *Journal of Accounting Education, 18*, 79–97.

Hernández Esteve, E. (1995). A review of recent Spanish publications in Accounting, Business and Financial History. *Accounting, Business and Financial History, 5*, 237–269.

Herron, T. L., & Hall, T. W. (2004). Faculty perceptions of journals: Quality and publishing feasibility. *Journal of Accounting Education, 22,* 175–210.

Hopper, T., & Armstrong, P. (1991). Cost accounting, controlling labor and the rise of conglomerates. *Accounting, Organizations and Society, 16,* 405–438.

Hopwood, A. G. (1987). The archaeology of accounting systems. *Accounting, Organizations and Society, 12*(3), 207–234.

Hoskin, K. W., & Macve, R. H. (1986). Accounting and the examination: A genealogy of disciplinary power. *Accounting, Organizations and Society, 11,* 105–136.

Hoskin, K. W., & Macve, R. H. (1988). The genesis of accountability: The west point connections. *Accounting, Organizations and Society, 13,* 37–73.

Humphrey, C., Moizer, P., & Owen, D. (1995). Questioning the value of the research selectivity process in British university accounting. *Accounting, Auditing and Accountability Journal, 8,* 141–164.

Kalaitzidakis, P., Mamuneas, P. T., & Stengos, T. (2003). Rankings of academic journals and institutions in economics. *Journal of the European Economic Association, 1,* 1346–1366.

Kedslie, M. J. (1990). *Firm foundations: The development of professional accounting in Scotland.* Hull: Hull University Press.

Kirkham, L. M., & Loft, A. (1993). Gender and the construction of the professional accountant. *Accounting, Organizations and Society, 18,* 507–558.

Johnson, H. T., & Kaplan, R. S. (1987). *Relevance lost: The rise and fall of management accounting.* Boston: Harvard Business School Press.

Johnson, P. M., Reckers, P. M. J., & Solomon, L. (2002). Evolving research benchmarks. *Advances in Accounting, 19,* 235–243.

Larson, M. S. (1977). *The rise of professionalism: A sociological analysis.* Berkeley: University of California Press.

Littleton, A. C. (1933). *Accounting evolution to 1900.* New York: American Institute Publishing Company.

Loft, A. (1986). Towards a critical understanding of cost accounting in the UK, 1914–1925. *Accounting, Organizations and Society, 11,* 137–169.

Lowe, A., & Locke, J. (2005). Perceptions of journal quality and research paradigm: Results of a web-based urvey of British Accounting Academics. *Accounting, Organizations and Society, 30,* 81–98.

Lukka, K., & Kasanen, E. (1996). Accounting a global or local discipline? Evidence from major research journals. *Accounting, Organizations and Society, 21,* 755–773.

Miller, P., Hopper, T., & Armstrong, P. (1991). The new accounting history: An introduction. *Accounting, Organizations and Society, 16,* 395–403.

Miller, P., & Napier, C. (1993). Genealogies of calculation. *Accounting, Organizations and Society, 18,* 631–647.

Miller, P., & O'Leary, T. (1987). Accounting and the construction of the governable person. *Accounting, Organizations and Society, 12,* 235–265.

Milne, M. (2001). *Debating accounting research journal rankings: Empirical issues from a citation-based analysis and theoretical dilemmas from economics.* University of Otago: Mimeo.

Nederhof, A. J. (1989). Books and chapters are not to be neglected in measuring research productivity. *American Psychologist, 44,* 734–735.

Otley, D. T. (2002). British research in accounting and finance (1996–2000): The 2001 research assessment exercise. *British Accounting Review, 34,* 387–417.

Parker, R. H. (1990). Regulating British corporate financial reporting in the late nineteenth century. *Accounting, Business and Financial History, 1*, 51–71.

Parker, R. H. (1993). The scope of accounting history: A note. *Abacus, 29*, 106–110.

Pollard, S. (1965). *The genesis of modern management: A study of the industry.* Cambridge: Harvard University Press.

Previts, G. J., & Merino, B. D. (1979). *A history of accounting in America.* New York: Wiley.

Reiter, S. A., & Williams, P. F. (2002). The structure and progressivity of accounting research: The crisis in the academy revisited. *Accounting, Organizations and Society, 27*, 575–607.

Schneider, B. (1995). Some propositions about getting research published. In: L. L. Cummings & P. J. Frost (Eds), *Publishing in the Organizational Sciences* (pp. 216–226). Thousand Oaks, CA: Sage.

Smith, G., & Krogstad, J. L. (1991). Sources and uses of Auditing: A Journal of Practice and Theory's literature: The first decade. *Auditing: A Journal of Practice and Theory, 10*, 84–97.

Stewart, R. (1992). Pluralizing our past: Foucault in accounting history. *Accounting Auditing & Accountability Journal, 5*, 57–73.

Swanson, E. P. (2004). Publishing in the majors: A comparison of accounting, finance, management, and marketing. *Contemporary Accounting Research, 21*, 223–255.

Thursby, J. G. (2000). What do we say about ourselves and what does it mean? Yet another look at economics department research. *Journal of Economic Literature, XXXVIII*, 383–404.

Van Leeuwen, T. N., Visser, M. S., Moed, H. F., Nederhof, T. J., & Van Raan, A. F. J. (2003). The holy grail of science policy: Exploring and combining bibliometric tools in search of scientific excellence. *Scientometrics, 57*, 257–280.

Walker, S. P. (1995). The genesis of professional organization in Scotland: A contextual analysis. *Accounting, Organizations and Society, 20*, 285–310.

Walker, S. P. (1991). The defence of professional monopoly: Scottish chartered accountants and satellites in the accountancy firmament (1854–1914). *Accounting, Organizations and Society, 16*, 257–283.

Whittington, G. (1997). The 1996 research assessment exercise. *British Accounting Review, 25*, 383–395.

SET UP A CONTINUATION ORDER TODAY!

Did you know that you can set up a continuation order on all Elsevier-JAI series and have each new volume sent directly to you upon publication? For details on how to set up a **continuation order**, contact your nearest regional sales office listed below.

To view related series in Business & Management, please visit:

www.elsevier.com/businessandmanagement

30% Discount for Authors on All Books!

A 30% discount is available to Elsevier book and journal contributors on all books *(except multi-volume reference works)*.

To claim your discount, full payment is required with your order, which must be sent directly to the publisher at the nearest regional sales office above.